Development, (Dual) Citizenship and Its Discontents in Africa

Drawing on rich oral histories from over two hundred in-depth interviews in West Africa, Europe, and North America, Robtel Neajai Pailey examines socio-economic change in Liberia, Africa's first black republic, through the prism of citizenship. Marking how historical policy changes on citizenship and contemporary public discourse on dual citizenship have impacted development policy and practice, she reveals that as Liberia transformed from a country of immigration to one of emigration, so too did the nature of citizenship, thus influencing claims for and against dual citizenship.

In this engaging contribution to scholarly and policy debates about citizenship as a continuum of inclusion and exclusion, and development as a process of both amelioration and degeneration, Pailey develops a new model for conceptualising citizenship within the context of crisis-affected states. In doing so, she offers a postcolonial critique of the neoliberal framing of diasporas and donors as *the* panacea to post-war reconstruction.

ROBTEL NEAJAI PAILEY is Assistant Professor in International Social and Public Policy at the London School of Economics and Political Science (LSE). A Liberian academic, activist, and author, she was previously Mo Ibrahim Foundation PhD Scholar at SOAS, University of London, and Leverhulme Early Career Fellow at the University of Oxford. Her core areas of research and policy expertise include the political economy of development, migration, race, citizenship, conflict, post-war recovery, and governance.

African Studies Series

The African Studies series, founded in 1968, is a prestigious series of monographs, general surveys, and textbooks on Africa covering history, political science, anthropology, economics, and ecological and environmental issues. The series seeks to publish work by senior scholars as well as the best new research.

Editorial Board

Other titles in the series are listed at the back of the book.

Development, (Dual) Citizenship and Its Discontents in Africa

The Political Economy of Belonging to Liberia

ROBTEL NEAJAI PAILEY
London School of Economics and Political Science

CAMBRIDGE
UNIVERSITY PRESS

CAMBRIDGE
UNIVERSITY PRESS

University Printing House, Cambridge CB2 8BS, United Kingdom

One Liberty Plaza, 20th Floor, New York, NY 10006, USA

477 Williamstown Road, Port Melbourne, VIC 3207, Australia

314–321, 3rd Floor, Plot 3, Splendor Forum, Jasola District Centre,
New Delhi – 110025, India

79 Anson Road, #06–04/06, Singapore 079906

Cambridge University Press is part of the University of Cambridge.

It furthers the University's mission by disseminating knowledge in the pursuit of
education, learning, and research at the highest international levels of excellence.

www.cambridge.org
Information on this title: www.cambridge.org/9781108836548
DOI: 10.1017/9781108873871

© Robtel Neajai Pailey 2021

First published 2021

A catalogue record for this publication is available from the British Library.

Library of Congress Cataloging-in-Publication Data
Names: Pailey, Robtel Neajai, author.
Title: Development, (dual) citizenship and its discontents in Africa : the political
economy of belonging to Liberia / Robtel Neajai Pailey.
Description: Cambridge, United Kingdom ; New York, NY : Cambridge University
Press, 2021. | Series: African studies series | Includes bibliographical references and
index.
Identifiers: LCCN 2020022762 | ISBN 9781108836548 (hardback) |
ISBN 9781108873871 (ebook)
Subjects: LCSH: Economic development – Liberia. | Citizenship – Liberia. |
Liberia – Economic conditions.
Classification: LCC HC1075 .P35 2021 | DDC 338.96662–dc23
LC record available at https://lccn.loc.gov/2020022762

ISBN 978-1-108-83654-8 Hardback

Contents

Figures and Tables

Figures

Tables

Acronyms

ABA	American Bar Association
ACDL	Association for Constitutional Democracy in Liberia
ACS	American Colonisation Society
AfCFTA	African Continental Free Trade Area
AFL	Armed Forces of Liberia
AfT	Agenda for Transformation
AU	African Union
BIN	Bureau of Immigration and Naturalisation
CBL	Central Bank of Liberia
CCL	Coalition of Concerned Liberians
CDFs	County Development Funds
CEDAW	Convention on the Elimination of All Forms of Discrimination against Women
CENTAL	Centre for Transparency and Accountability in Liberia
CIA	Central Intelligence Agency
CPA	Comprehensive Peace Agreement
CSA	Civil Service Agency
CWIQ	Core Welfare Indicators Questionnaire
DEA	Drug Enforcement Agency
DED	Deferred Enforced Departure
DV	Diversity Visa
ECOMOG	Economic Community of West African States Monitoring Group
ECOWAS	Economic Community of West African States
EFLA	European Federation of Liberian Associations
ERU	Emergency Response Unit
EU	European Union
GAC	General Auditing Commission
GC	Governance Commission
GDP	gross domestic product

GEMAP	Governance and Economic Management Assistance Programme
GSA	General Services Agency
HIPC	Heavily Indebted Poor Countries
ICERD	International Convention on the Elimination of All Forms of Racial Discrimination
IDPs	internally displaced persons
IGNU	Interim Government of National Unity
IMF	International Monetary Fund
INCHR	Independent National Commission on Human Rights
INPFL	Independent National Patriotic Front of Liberia
LAA	Liberia Airport Authority
LACC	Liberia Anti-Corruption Commission
LACOSC	Liberian American Community Organisation of Southern California
LAMCO	Liberian American Swedish Mining Company
LECBS	Liberia Emergency Capacity Building Support
LEITI	Liberia Extractive Industries Transparency Initiative
LFF	Liberian Frontier Force
LISGIS	Liberia Institute of Statistics and Geo-Information Services
LNP	Liberia National Police
LRA	Liberia Revenue Authority
LSA	Liberian Studies Association
LTA	Liberia Telecommunications Authority
LURD	Liberians United for Reconciliation and Democracy
MODEL	Movement for Democracy in Liberia
MOJA	Movement for Justice in Africa
MoS	Ministry of State for Presidential Affairs
MRU	Mano River Union
NEC	National Elections Commission
NGOs	non-governmental organisations
NPFL	National Patriotic Front of Liberia
NSA	National Security Agency
NTGL	National Transitional Government of Liberia
OAU	Organisation of African Unity
OTC	Oriental Timber Company
PAL	Progressive Alliance of Liberia
PAPD	Pro-poor Agenda for Prosperity and Development

PPCC	Public Procurement and Concessions Commission
PPP	Progressive People's Party
PRC	People's Redemption Council
PRS	Poverty Reduction Strategy
RFTF	Results-Focused Transitional Framework
RIA	Roberts International Airport
SES	Senior Executive Service
TOKTEN	Transfer of Knowledge through Expatriate Nationals
TPS	Temporary Protected Status
TRC	Truth and Reconciliation Commission
TWP	True Whig Party
UDHR	Universal Declaration of Human Rights
UK	United Kingdom
ULAA	Union of Liberian Associations in the Americas
ULAG	United Liberian Association in Ghana
ULO-UK	Union of Liberian Organisations in the United Kingdom
UN	United Nations
UNDP	United Nations Development Programme
UNHCR	United Nations High Commissioner for Refugees
UNIBOA	United Bassa Organisation in the Americas
UNMIL	United Nations Mission in Liberia
UNPOL	United Nations Police
UPP	United People's Party
US	United States
USD	United States Dollars
WHO	World Health Organization

Acknowledgements

Nearly a decade in the making, this book represents one of my most challenging professional endeavours to date. When I embarked on a doctorate at SOAS, University of London, in 2011, little did I know that what began as an overly ambitious PhD project would eventually morph into a monograph. For this, I thank my strong network across the globe, including God, family, funders, advisors, friends, and associates.

My mother and father, Ethel Neajai Johnson Pailey and Abraham Robert Pailey, gifted me with an insatiable love of knowledge and drive to succeed which anchored me in times of uncertainty. I am indebted to my mother in particular for her prayers, positive energy, and phone calls. Six weeks of hibernating in her house – where I was fed heaps of home-cooked Liberian food – fortified me with the energy and headspace to complete this manuscript.

Without the Mo Ibrahim Foundation's generous three-year PhD funding, this book would still be an idea in my head. While the SOAS Department of Development Studies provided partial funding for PhD fieldwork, the Leverhulme Trust and Oxford Department of International Development fully financed my postdoctoral data collection. Additionally, the International Development Research Centre (IDRC)-funded project 'Diasporas as Neglected Agents of Change' facilitated data collection and gave me access to researchers in Haiti, Liberia, Sri Lanka, the United Kingdom, and the United States.

My PhD supervisor, Laura Hammond, and external examiner, JoAnn McGregor, were steadfast in their guidance and support, often telling me what I needed rather than wanted to hear. Academic mentors George Klay Kieh Jr, D Elwood Dunn, and Carl Patrick Burrowes offered crucial direction on aspects of Liberian political, economic, and social history, while my cousin Edward Emmett Dillon helped me access and interpret Liberian historical and contemporary legal documents. Young professionals Kortu M Ndebe, Gerald Yeakula,

Mahmud Johnson, and Ciata Stevens were exceptional as transcribers, wading through hundreds of hours of audio recordings to capture the authenticity of my field-based interviews.

Bronwen Manby and Beth Elise Whitaker set the bar high with their groundbreaking research on citizenship and dual citizenship trends in Africa, respectively, and shared valuable suggestions of how I could carve out my own scholarly niche. Maria Marsh, Daniel Brown, Atifa Jiwa, Natasha Whelan, Richards Paul, Anitha Nadarajan, and the entire Cambridge University Press African Studies series team gave of their time generously, while three anonymous reviewers delivered incisive feedback on an early draft of the book. With patience and perseverance, visual storyteller Chase Walker worked hard to generate the beautifully rendered, final cover image. And my closest friends – especially Amy Niang, Bukola Kpotie, Courtney Mosby, Ella Mankon Pailey, Genevieve Woods, Simidele Dosekun, Yen Pham, and Yvonne Nsiah – remained cheerleaders every step of the way in matters of the head and heart.

Last, but certainly not least, 202 Liberian and 7 Sierra Leonean respondents – speaking in official and unofficial capacities – were the lifeblood of my empirical analysis. They welcomed me into their worlds and revealed some of their innermost thoughts about a topic that is both personal and political. I can only hope that I have done them justice, and remain convinced more than ever that a better Liberia is possible.

Introduction

The 'Love of Liberty' Divided Us Here?

Liberia's official seal[1] captures competing contexts colliding and co-mingling (Figure I.1). It consists of a shield with an idyllic image of a passenger ship seen from the shore approaching new territory. An invisible, straight line connects the ship with an inviting palm tree jutting out of the earth. Its beak carrying a scroll conveying peace and freedom, a white dove hovers on the horizon. Beaming rays from a half-exposed sun appear in the background to complete the allegory of newness and discovery. In the foreground of the shield, on lush, green grass, lie a shovel dug into the earth and a plough representing the dignity of hard labour primarily from subsistence agriculture. Above the shield is a scroll proudly proclaiming Liberia's national motto: *The Love of Liberty Brought Us Here*. This pictorial symbolises Africa meeting its diasporas, yet it depicts the exploits of only a small fraction of Liberia's population at independence in the mid-nineteenth century – black trans-atlantic migrants[2] who championed civilisation, Christianity, and commerce as their triple heritage – and even less so now, almost 200 years later in a twenty-first-century post-war period.

---

[1] Liberia's seal, motto, flag, anthem, awards, and Declaration of Independence were subjected to scrutiny during a National Symbols Review Project in 2014. Its purpose was to fashion an all-inclusive political identity by revamping elements of the national symbols in order to facilitate unity and reconciliation. Nevertheless, the exercise was futile as no recommended revisions were ever implemented.

[2] I refrain from using the misnomer 'Americo-Liberian' throughout this book because free blacks who migrated to Liberia from the United States prior to 1868 were denied American citizenship and, therefore, could have not been considered 'American'. 'Americo-Liberian' also erroneously conflates all settlers who migrated to Liberia so instead I employ 'black settlers' or 'black migrant settlers' interchangeably because they encompass the full range of settlers, including West Indian and Congo River basin migrants.

1

Figure I.1 Liberia's official seal
Source: Ministry of Foreign Affairs, Republic of Liberia

From its inception in 1847 as Africa's first black republic, Liberia became a prime location for the convergence of a multitude of disparate actors, including repatriates from the United States, recaptives from the Congo River basin in Central Africa, emigrants from the Caribbean, and sixteen ethno-linguistic groups[3] already occupying the territory. Currently, this fusion has metamorphosed to involve a wide spectrum of domestic and diasporic actors comprising homeland Liberians, returnees, and former refugees, amongst others. While the 'love of liberty' signalled varied encounters between settlers and indigenes and their negotiations over land ownership, political participation, identity, and belonging in the nineteenth century, twenty-first-century concerns about citizenship and all its trappings were made manifest in a contested dual citizenship bill which lingered in legislative limbo from 2008 to 2018. Given that dual citizenship was the first contemporary policy mechanism specifically introduced in Liberia to address diasporic claims, this book deploys it to evaluate the country's long-standing attempts at constructing a unique brand of citizenship that is totalising, tactical, and timeless. In confronting how multiple subjectivities intersect to make or mar citizenship, *Development, (Dual) Citizenship and Its Discontents in Africa* explores what I call the political economy of

---

[3] I refer to these groups subsequently as 'indigenous' or 'indigenes' because they inhabited the territory that is modern-day Liberia before nineteenth-century black migrant settlement.

belonging to Liberia. This is a transactional system in which socio-economic transformation invariably depends on the provision of privileges/protections in exchange for the fulfilment of duties/obligations, and vice versa.

Citizenship has been tangentially mentioned in the literature on Liberian state[4] consolidation, nevertheless this is the first study to examine domestic and diasporic constructions and practices of Liberian citizenship across space and time and their myriad implications for development. By 'development' I do not mean mainstream pursuits of free-market capitalism, a singular quest for economic growth, or the privileging of Western whiteness and modernity; rather, I am referring to an alternative, emancipatory process whereby people's experiences of poverty, power, privilege, and progress are constantly mediated to effect change (Pailey, 2020). In essence, this book examines how structural transformation is conceived and contested by local, national, and transnational actors from the so-called Global South, with an emphasis on the country (Liberia) and continent (Africa) of my birth. It blends analysis of historical policy changes on citizenship with that of contemporary public discourse on dual citizenship to investigate how struggles over Liberian citizenship, in particular, have impacted development policy and practice in the country.

In so doing, I make three major contributions to scholarly and policy debates about citizenship as a continuum of inclusion and exclusion, and development as a process of amelioration for some and degeneration for others. First, given that identities, practices, and relations between people transform in the aftermath of violent conflict, I draw on the rich oral histories of over 200 interviewees in the capital cities of Liberia (Monrovia), Sierra Leone (Freetown), Ghana (Accra), the United Kingdom (London), and the United States (Washington) to develop a new model for conceptualising citizenship in the context of post-war emigration states. Second, I use political economy analysis to frame contestations around citizenship as sites where state-building, nation-building, and peace-building processes converge. And lastly, by

---

[4] When I refer to the 'Liberian state' in this book, I specifically adopt Christian Lund's (2006) notion of the 'state' as an ensemble of individuals and institutions exercising public authority, that is, structural power that is validated and recognised at multiple levels (Pailey, 2017a). Thus, I do not conflate the 'state' with 'government' because I believe the 'state' entails more than government.

underscoring the citizenship practices of domestic development actors as central to socio-economic change, I offer a postcolonial critique of the neoliberal framing of diasporas and donors as *the* panacea to post-war reconstruction.

My study demonstrates that interpretations of Liberian citizenship differ according to the lived experiences and socio-economic positions of Liberians at home and abroad, and ultimately influence their development practices, or lack thereof, as well as their rejection or endorsement of dual citizenship. Using Norman Long's (2001) actor-oriented analysis framework – which argues that actors respond to development-oriented policy prescriptions and interventions based on their 'life-worlds' (lived experiences) and 'social locations' (socio-economic positions) – I illustrate how historical and contemporary factors such as conflict, migration, and post-war recovery have simultaneously configured and reconfigured Liberian citizenship across space and time thereby influencing the introduction and postponement in the passage of dual citizenship legislation. Throughout this book, I maintain that citizenship has always been contested in Liberia, from its establishment as an experiment in black diasporic solidarity and self-rule to its current status as a site of rival post-war agendas. Invoking the compelling analysis of Liberian historian Clarence E Zamba Liberty (1977: 101–202), who argued that the most accurate account of nineteenth- and twentieth-century national life in Liberia sits somewhere between lauding and lamenting black settler 'ethnic elitism' – what he calls 'righteousness' and 'deprivation' narratives, respectively – I contend that what lies beneath twenty-first-century claims for and against dual citizenship is an evolving political economy of belonging to Liberia over the *longue durée*.

From Settler State Formation to Post-war State-building

Liberia's history has been characterised by migration, conflict, exile, and return, thus facilitating new configurations of citizenship across space and time. The country was initially established in 1822 as an outpost for free blacks and the formerly enslaved primarily by the American Colonisation Society (ACS), an association of influential whites who espoused abolitionist and deportationist ideals; yet it predates black migrant settlement (Kieh, 2012a: 168; Burrowes, 2016a: 22, 24–27; Burrowes, 2016b). Seeking increased autonomy from the

ACS and fearing British and French territorial encroachment, Liberia declared itself independent in 1847 and was thus the first African state to devise legal norms around membership and belonging. Despite gradually representing an amalgam of black identities and cultures (West African, West Indian/Caribbean, Central African, and North American), it adopted a 'hegemonic' framework of citizenship with restrictive pre-requisites such as private property ownership (Liberty, 1977: 273–274; Burrowes, 2004: 69). Modelled after the United States' initial conferral of citizenship on white male landed gentry, citizenship in nineteenth-century Liberia reflected a settler male ethos which excluded most indigenes, non-Christians, and women of both indigenous and settler orientation. Fearing racial inequalities borne by slavery in the United States and Caribbean, settlers further embedded in Liberia's Constitution a 'Negro clause' barring all non-blacks from obtaining citizenship.[5] Not until a century after state formation would Liberians – defined as 'Negroes' or of 'Negro descent' – generally be considered citizens, further illustrating that citizenship in Liberia has historically been a tool of marginalisation in the same way that post-independence citizenship laws across Africa have been wielded to disenfranchise. The nature of Liberia's black settler state formation precluded nationalism and did not lend itself to national identity consolidation (Pailey, 2014c). Unlike African countries that underwent fierce nationalist struggles against colonial rule, Liberia was declared the first black African republic nearly a century before independence movements began in earnest in the continent.

It was ruled consecutively from 1878 to 1980 by the True Whig Party (TWP), an oligarchy of descendants of black settlers (Guannu, 1989; Dunn, 2017). Before President William VS Tubman, Liberia's longest serving head of state, introduced an Open Door Policy in 1947 to court foreign investors, there were demands to incorporate indigenous populations and women fully into the citizenship mainstream (Kieh, 1992: 39, 42). In an erosion of government–citizen relations, however, Open Door mortgaged Liberia's rubber, iron ore, and forest reserves without value addition to primarily large-scale Euro-American multinationals while transforming the country into 'an export enclave for raw

---

[5] Currently, Liberia and Sierra Leone are the only two countries in Africa that have 'Negro' clauses although Sierra Leone's 2006 Dual Citizenship Act enables non-'Negroes' to naturalise.

materials' and exploited labour (Kieh, 1992: 39, 42). Tubman introduced the Unification and Integration Policy in 1946, subsequently
universalising citizenship for people of 'Negro descent' for the first
time in a decidedly failed attempt to construct a nation within a state
(Dunn, Beyan & Burrowes, 2001: 341). Elite Liberians travelled
abroad for vacation, business ventures, and higher education during
this period, but rarely did they remain outside of the country for long
stints until Tubman's successor, William R Tolbert Jr, was assassinated
in a 1980 coup. Rumoured to have been an orchestrated plot by the US
Central Intelligence Agency (CIA) during the height of Cold War
rivalries, the coup was led by a twenty-five-year-old indigenous master
sergeant in the Armed Forces of Liberia (AFL), Samuel Kanyon Doe,
and it toppled TWP hegemony.

Doe's military regime lasted until elections in 1985 which were
largely viewed as fraudulent, entrenching his power in an arbitrary
institutional arrangement. For many, Doe signified the beginning of
an indigenous political renaissance because, among other reforms, he
abrogated a 'hut tax' that had effectively made indigenous hinterland
inhabitants subjects of the Liberian state without granting them full
citizenship rights (Dunn, Beyan & Burrowes, 2001: 170; Dunn, 2009:
173). Yet, his grip on power declined over time. When an attempted
coup in November 1985 was rumoured to have been supported by
Liberians abroad, a wave of emigration ensued with large numbers of
Liberians leaving the country fearing reprisals (Dunn, Beyan &
Burrowes, 2001: 275; Dunn, 2009: 146). This fundamentally reconfigured Liberian citizenship making it transnational for the first time in the
country's history.

Liberian exiles in the United States led by future head of state Ellen
Johnson Sirleaf as well as Amos Sawyer, who would later become
Interim Government of National Unity (IGNU) president and
Governance Commission (GC) chairperson, lobbied against Doe's
autocracy through the Association for Constitutional Democracy in
Liberia (ACDL) but their cries for regime change fell on deaf ears.
These political elites in large part would eventually support[6] Charles
Taylor, a counter-revolutionary with political ambitions who trained
in Libya and launched an armed rebellion in 1989 from neighbouring

---

[6] In 2009, Sirleaf testified before the Truth and Reconciliation Commission (TRC)
that the ACDL donated US$10,000 to support Taylor's insurgency against Doe.

Côte d'Ivoire, therefore, prompting another wave of emigration. From 1989 to 1997, more than 200,000 Liberians were killed and between 500,000 and 750,000 internally displaced; in the first year alone, as many as 700,000 fled the country primarily to Côte d'Ivoire, Ghana, Guinea, Nigeria, and Sierra Leone. It is not clear how many Liberians returned after elections in 1997 brought Taylor to power. From 1997 to 2003, he ruled with authoritarian flair, involving Liberia in Sierra Leone's armed conflict thereby provoking two militias to agitate between 1999 and 2003 for his ouster. Liberians once again fled the country for safety, followed by a Comprehensive Peace Agreement (CPA) in August 2003 in Accra, Ghana, with Taylor exiled at the invitation of the Nigerian government. On 26 April 2012, he was eventually convicted on eleven counts of war crimes and crimes against humanity for aiding and abetting rebels during Sierra Leone's war.[7]

From 2003 to 2005 an interim government was established to pave the way for elections in 2005 after which Liberia's and Africa's first female head of state, Ellen Johnson Sirleaf, assumed the presidency in 2006. From 2003 onwards waves of return migration to Liberia grew in magnitude with post-war reform efforts in security, economic revitalisation, governance and the rule of law, and infrastructure and basic services eliciting renewed hope in a country once considered the 'heart of darkness' (Williams, 2006; Government of Liberia, 2008a). Despite its multilayered post-war challenges, Liberia underwent significant transformation during Sirleaf's two successive terms from 2006 to 2018 which created an enabling environment for diasporic return and re-engagement. Nonetheless, her neoliberal economic model of development and overreliance on returnee experts deepened inequalities and fomented resentment (Pailey, 2017a; Pailey, 2017b). Coupled together, recovery and return migration complicated relations between Liberians of different lived experiences and socio-economic backgrounds hence replacing unresolved nineteenth-century fissures between settlers and indigenes with twenty-first-century rifts pitting returnees against their homeland counterparts (Pailey, 2007b). In post-war Liberia the amalgam of different identities has transformed with homeland Liberians, returnees, and diasporas all vying for a stake in development. At the centre of this convergence are questions about citizenship, essentially

---

[7] Taylor was given a fifty-year jail sentence on 30 May 2012 and after losing an appeal was transported to a British prison to serve his time.

who belongs to the nation-state and who can legitimately participate in its reconstruction.

Dual Citizenship and Attempts to Reconstruct Liberian Citizenship

Citizenship in Liberia remained contentious even as I finalised this book in late 2019. For instance, there was a noticeable contradiction[8] between Article 28 of the country's 1986 Constitution – which affirms the right of Liberians by birth to retain Liberian citizenship indefinitely and entitles Liberians by ancestry to Liberian citizenship on the condition that they renounce their birthplace nationality upon reaching adulthood – and Sections 22.1 and 22.2 of its 1973 Aliens and Nationality Law, which automatically revoked the legal citizenship status of Liberian-born nationals of 'Negro descent' who naturalised in, declared formal allegiance to, entered into the armed forces of, voted in the elections of, or formally renounced Liberian citizenship in a foreign state (Government of Liberia, 1973; Government of Liberia, 1986). Modelled after the 1952 US Immigration and Nationality Act, the Aliens and Nationality Law of Liberia was never amended up to mid-December 2019, with some arguing that it failed to contend with contemporary realities.

For example, Section 20.1 of the Law stated explicitly that only those of 'Negro descent' born in Liberia could be citizens and only those born abroad whose fathers were citizens of Liberia during the time of their birth and resided in Liberia before their birth could be granted citizenship at birth. It also maintained that children born abroad to Liberian citizen fathers would lose their Liberian citizenship unless they resided in Liberia before the age of majority (eighteen) or took an oath of allegiance to Liberia between the age of majority and twenty-three. Many protested

---

[8] Although Liberia's revised Constitution was adopted in a July 1984 referendum following a constitutional review process and officially came into effect in January 1986, the reviewers neglected to reconcile the apparent inconsistencies between the Constitution and Aliens and Nationality Law on matters of citizenship. In 2012, Sirleaf commissioned a Constitution Review Committee to review and make recommendations for amending the 1986 Constitution based on a series of national consultations with Liberian citizens. Three years earlier, in 2009, the president had established a Law Reform Commission through Executive Order No. 20, which appears to have had overlapping functions with the Constitution Review Committee.

that the Law was anachronistic and overtly exclusionary because it defined citizenship along racial and gender lines thereby explicitly discriminating against non-blacks and women. Others reasoned that annulling the citizenship of a natural-born Liberian without due process was unconstitutional, as evidenced by a 2010 lawsuit filed in Liberia's Supreme Court and won on 23 December 2019 by US-based legal expert Alvin Teage Jalloh.[9] Responding to increased pressure from what appeared to be a strong transnational tide, Liberian lawmakers introduced a dual citizenship bill in 2008 to reconstruct markers of citizenship.

In their Proposed Act to Establish Dual Citizenship for Liberians by Birth and Background, four senators from Liberia's fifty-second Legislature, namely Cletus Segbe Wotorson, Sumo G Kupee, Jewel Howard Taylor (the ex-wife of Charles Taylor subsequently elected vice president in 2017), and Abel Massalay, endorsed amendments of Sections 20.1 and 22.1 of the Aliens and Nationality Law not only to enable Liberian citizen women to pass on citizenship to children born abroad but also to grant dual citizenship to Liberians by birth who naturalised abroad (or had aspirations to naturalise) as well as to those born abroad of Liberian parentage, respectively (Government of Liberia, 2008c). Two questions ultimately underpinned the proposed legislation, and, by extension, this book: why was it introduced in 2008 and why was its passage suspended for a decade? It is worth noting here that although Liberia's fifty-fourth Legislature under President George Oppong Weah endorsed referendum Proposition #1 in October 2019 based on a Dual Citizen and Nationality Act of 2019,[10] which reflected the general principles of the 2008 bill while placing additional restrictions on the political participation of would-be dual citizens, analysis in this book focuses on the latter because it was the first of its kind and had

---

[9] Jalloh's case was not in pursuit of dual citizenship, per se, but rather a lawsuit interrogating Sections 22.1 and 22.2 of Liberia's 1973 Aliens and Nationality Law, which, he argued, violated Article 20(a) of the 1986 Constitution guaranteeing due process. The Supreme Court decided in December 2019 that only Section 22.2 of the Law contravened the Constitution.

[10] The proposed constitutional amendments based on this bill were summarised as Proposition #1 for consideration in a late 2020 national referendum (Government of Liberia, 2019b). Nevertheless, members of the House of Representatives swiftly rescinded in mid-October 2019 their prior approval, leaving the dual citizenship proposition in limbo.

a much longer lifespan of ten years (Government of Liberia, 2008c; Government of Liberia, 2019a; Government of Liberia, 2019b).

According to chief sponsor of the 2008 proposed legislation, then senator Wotorson, the premise of suggesting amendments to the 1973 Aliens and Nationality Law was to respond to the needs of Liberians who emigrated as a result of intermittent armed conflict:

[A] lot of them [Liberians abroad] had to change their lifestyle, accept the dictates from a strange country for survival. In some countries it meant you had to become [a] citizen of that country to enjoy the benefits . . . But in taking that involuntary stance it qualified them for disqualification of their citizenships in their own country [Liberia] which, I believe, is unfair.[11]

Though the 2008 bill recommended broad sweeping changes with major implications for reconfiguring the meaning and practice of Liberian citizenship, its first iterations were low on substance and did not explicitly define the privileges and obligations of would-be dual citizens. This opened it up to targeted attacks because by categorically extending rights without explicitly extracting responsibilities, the bill neither 'transnationalised citizenship' fully (Gamlen, 2006: 5–6) nor conformed entirely to Liberia's political economy of belonging. Despite unequivocal support from many Liberians abroad about the potential benefits of dual citizenship – with a number of outliers here and there – for the most part those at home remained less convinced, argued then senator Taylor:

Liberians here [in Liberia], a lot of them are not working. They're unemployed and they feel as if Liberians coming from the diaspora who have had all of these opportunities want to come and take their space.[12]

As acknowledged by Taylor, there were (and still are) concerns that dual citizenship would represent a zero-sum game for those based in Liberia, further impinging upon their already limited access to political, economic, and social opportunities. Given backlash against the postponed 2008 bill, a barrage of assertions followed about the potential positive outcomes of dual citizenship if adopted, chief among which

---

[11] Interview in Monrovia on 6 March 2013. I would later find out through two interviewees in Monrovia that Wotorson's alleged reason for sponsoring the proposed bill was to enable his US citizen children and American grandchildren to legally inherit his accumulated wealth and property in Liberia.

[12] Interview in Monrovia on 6 March 2013.

was the claim that Liberians who naturalised in other countries would be able to retain their legal status as citizens thus contributing substantially to post-war recovery. The assumption herein is that dual citizenship would facilitate political, economic, and social renewal by transnationals. The converse argument could be applied, however, that there is no direct correlation between increased economic contributions by a country's diasporas and the retention of non-resident citizenship (Whitaker, 2011; Spiro, 2012; Pailey, 2014c; Pailey, 2018). Furthermore, the supposition that transnationals are the antidote to reconstruction, as is apparent in the vast literature on diasporas and development, negates and obscures the lived experiences of homeland development actors. Therefore, the position of the Liberian government in reconciling transnational *commands* with homeland *demands* is a central feature of this book.

While the intention of *Development, (Dual) Citizenship and Its Discontents in Africa* is not to focus exclusively on the legal parameters of Liberia's 1973 Aliens and Nationality Law, 1986 Constitution, and 2008 dual citizenship bill, I underscore how a specific study on Liberian citizenship construction and practice contributes to the general literature on citizenship in Africa. Citizenship represents, for me, a more appropriate framework for explaining broader political, economic, and social transformations in the continent because it challenges primordial references to ethnicity, religion, and region, especially within the context of conflict.

Liberian Citizenship a Microcosm of African Citizenships

Although contemporary forms of citizenship originated in Europe, Africa is a fascinating region for exploring political subjectivities because the continent inherited colonial legal systems with multi-tiered citizenships based on indigeneity, race, and ethnicity that persist today. In fact, contemporary contestations in Africa, violent and otherwise, centre primarily on claims for territorial legitimacy with citizenship most contentious in countries that experienced the greatest colonial-era migration – particularly of black Africans from other parts of the continent, Southeast Asian and Middle Eastern indentured labourers, and European settlers (Mamdani, 1996; Adejumobi, 2005; Manby, 2009). Contemporarily, contested forms of exclusionary citizenship maintain salience in conflict-affected countries like Liberia, as evidenced by their centrality in peace agreements brokered for Côte d'Ivoire, the Democratic Republic of the Congo, South Sudan, Sudan, and Zimbabwe (Manby, 2020). Nevertheless, while Africanist scholarship focuses increasingly on the politics of belonging, Africa remains relatively underrepresented in the general citizenship studies literature. In this book, I fill empirical and theoretical gaps by interrogating the presumed symbiotic relationship between dual citizenship and development in an African post-war polity.

Since independence, large-scale emigration has compelled an over-whelming majority of African states to adopt constitutional reforms granting dual citizenship with some provisions more limited than others (Manby, 2016). Although, admittedly, struggles over dual citizenship are global in scale and scope and do not represent African exceptionalism, Africa is a particularly relevant region of analysis. While most of the continent's post-independence citizenship laws represented colonial arte-facts that excluded rather than embraced multiple forms of legal national identity, violent contemporary contestations over citizenship and belong-ing have been prevalent in contexts as diverse as Cameroon, Central African Republic, Côte d'Ivoire, Morocco, Nigeria, Rwanda, Senegal, Sierra Leone, South Africa, South Sudan, Sudan, and Uganda. Despite reputed gains, the enactment of dual citizenship across the continent has not happened at lightning speed, primarily because of concerns that increased claims for non-resident citizenship may be driven as much by selfish political interests as by concerns about national reconstruction, economic development, or security, especially with the advent of multi-party competition, the involvement of emigrants in homeland politics, and the need for African politicians to establish constituencies abroad for support and funding (Whitaker, 2011). Given Liberia's post-war promi-nence in the African Union (AU), Economic Community of West African States (ECOWAS), and Mano River Union (MRU), it remains an impor-tant case study on the challenges of consolidating transnational citizenship because of its history of migration and conflict and the mounting pressure on the country to harmonise its citizenship laws with regional institutions. For example, at the time of my finalising this monograph in mid-December 2019, Liberia was the only country in ECOWAS and one of only seven countries in the AU that had not formally adopted dual citizenship.

I suggest that while citizenship reconfiguration processes across the continent of Africa and elsewhere accelerated the introduction of Liberia's dual citizenship bill of 2008, domestic backlash against grant-ing non-resident citizenship subsequently decelerated its passage. Using the contested bill as an entry point and foregrounding the rise in anti-migrant sentiments worldwide, *Development, (Dual) Citizenship and Its Discontents in Africa* examines Liberian citizenship construction through a historical prism, arguing that as Liberia transformed from a country of relative immigration to one of emigration, so, too, did the nature of citizenship change thus influencing claims for and against dual citizenship. As evidenced by Liberia, support for dual citizenship is primarily diaspora-driven with some studies indicating how trans-national communities actively engage in revising the meaning of citizenship in their countries of origin (Baranbantseva & Sutherland, 2011: 1). Consequently, transnationalism offers an important grounding for my analysis because it is concerned with how emigrants link their countries of origin and settlement, simultaneously, through inter-woven activities and relationships (Glick Schiller, Basch & Blanc-Szanton, 1992). Yet, while some scholars have demanded new ways of thinking about citizenship in emigration contexts, they privilege the citizenship claims of emigrants primarily (FitzGerald, 2000; Brand, 2006). I respond to this omission by juxtaposing the viewpoints of Liberians resident in Liberia and their transnational counterparts.

Just as I fill gaps in the literatures on transnationalism and citizenship by chronicling the perspectives of domestic citizens within the context of a post-war emigration state, I also build upon scholarship that examines citizenship in Africa. Although different from my study in breadth and depth, the body of literature on African citizenship construction is expanding, including Peter P Ekeh's (1975) notion of the continent's inherited 'two publics' which likely inspired Mahmood Mamdani's seminal work – *Citizen and Subject: Contemporary Africa and the Legacy of Late Colonialism* (1996) – evaluating how post-independence governments in Africa failed to fully transform colonial subjects into 'post'-colonial citizens. While some scholars have subsequently interrogated autochthony within Africa as a function of competing claims for political inclusion and citizenship, others have evaluated citizenship through the lens of xenophobia and exclusion (Konneh, 1996b; Nyamnjoh, 2006; Dorman et al., 2007; Geschiere, 2009; Bøås & Dunn, 2013; Keller, 2014). In particular, Bronwen Manby's *Struggles for Citizenship in Africa* (2009) and *Citizenship in Africa: The Law of Belonging* (2018) are perhaps the most comprehensive in their exploration of citizenship construction processes across Africa. However, Manby examines citizenship as legal status principally, while in this book I argue, as other scholars have, that the narrow legal contours of citizenship do not adequately account for how citizens within a particular polity experience the institution differently (Sassen, 2005; O'Connell Davidson, 2013).

Development, (Dual) Citizenship and Its Discontents in Africa thus frames citizenship as a process wherein norms, meanings, and identities are constantly negotiated by individuals and social groups, placing equal emphasis on how it defines legal status with associated rights and responsibilities and on how it is conceived, embodied, experienced, and contested in practice. I maintain that Liberian citizenship, like other forms of socio-legal identity across the globe, is 'multilayered', differentiated by gender, age, class, race, ethnicity, and so on, and that 'those who enjoy citizenship in the formal sense do not always enjoy equal access to its privileges and protections' (Yuval-Davis, 2000: 172; O'Connell Davidson, 2013: 190). This discussion is particularly relevant for some Liberians in-country who, by virtue of their subordinate socio-economic positions, do not benefit concretely from the rights of official citizenship just as Liberian diasporas who naturalised abroad were not entitled to legal Liberian citizenship up to mid-December 2019 despite engaging in citizenship practices from afar, such as sending remittances, lobbying political actors, paying property taxes, transferring knowledge and skills, and investing in key development sectors including infrastructure and agriculture. Although focused primarily on Liberia, this book draws upon previously mentioned Africa-based studies on citizenship and further contributes to the scholarly and policy literature on rebuilding states whose conflicts/crises/wars were fuelled by the politicisation of identity (i.e., Bosnia and Herzegovina, Côte d'Ivoire, Rwanda, Sierra Leone, and Sri Lanka).

Evolution of Citizenship and Emergence of Dual Citizenship

Citizenship represents a space of contestation and convergence not only in Liberian historical and contemporary discourse but also more generally in theory and practice. It has been construed over time to inscribe an individual within a particular polity yet current forms of citizenship transcend the nation-state. What has been termed citizenship in modern times has its antecedents in the Greek city-state, which defined a citizen as a white male resident, ruling out foreigners, women, and the enslaved (Hoffman, 2004: 18). This definition further evolved from the era of feudalism to the emergence of the European nation-state dating back to the Treaty of Westphalia in 1648 'which launched the modern system of nation-states as the principal actors within the world system' (Kashyap, 1997: 4; Turner, 2000: 137). As modern nationality laws were formulated from the nineteenth and twentieth centuries, European countries adopted a *jus sanguinis* (ancestral lineage) and/or *jus soli* (birthplace) principle thereby defining which inhabitants of a nation were citizens and non-citizens (Koslowski, 2001: 206). States in formerly colonised spaces and places followed suit during independence by embracing similar ways of delineating who belonged and who did not.

Throughout the contemporary era, citizenship has been defined generally as legal status and lived experience (Isin & Turner, 2007: 16); a system of rights, political activity, community solidarity, individual and group engagement (Joppke, 1999: 632; Bosniak, 2000: 451; Barry, 2006: 20–21); and simultaneously as identity, practice, and a set of relations (Pailey, 2014c; Pailey, 2016). Citizenship, therefore, is the process by which identity becomes anchored in law with certain trends emerging out of an increased tendency towards more cosmopolitan forms of belonging, such as dual citizenship (Barry, 2006: 25). However, scholars often disagree about whether or not dual citizenship should be an extension of the modern form of legal, political, social, cultural, and economic engagement. European bilateral treaties regarding nationality during the latter half of the nineteenth century brought about norms against dual citizenship in customary law accumulated in the 1930 Hague Convention on Certain Questions Relating to the Conflict of Nationality Laws, which affirms that all persons should only have one citizenship (Koslowski, 2001: 206). Even though historical precedents once deterred nation-states from permitting dual citizenship, 75 per cent of governments worldwide now recognise it not because of increased internationalisation, per se, but due to a confluence of domestic and diasporic politics (Koslowski, 2001; Vink et al., 2019).

Citizenship as 'Bounded' or 'Unbounded'

Rapid international migration and mobility coupled with globalisation have ruptured state-centric conceptions of citizenship, identity, and belonging, with scholars asserting that dual citizenship or multiple citizenships are becoming the rule rather than the exception in the twenty-first century (Jacobson, 1996; Spiro, 1997; Rubenstein & Adler, 2000; Sassen, 2005). Rather than an indicator of the erosion of sovereignty, efforts by countries of emigration like Liberia, for instance, to institutionally embrace their citizens abroad highlight a reassertion of nation-state autonomy based on the Westphalian doctrine of territorial dominion in which a renegotiating of the terms of the social contract enables 'citizenship a la carte' (FitzGerald, 2012: 285–286). This involves 'voluntaristic ties rather than being coercively "ruled", a menu of options for expressing membership, an emphasis on rights over obligations, and the legitimacy of plural legal and affective national affiliations' (FitzGerald, 2012: 285–286). Using Mexico as a case study, FitzGerald (2012: 292) argues that transnational citizenship *is* being transformed but that this process is a result of the strengthening not the weakening of state sovereignty. In the twenty-first century, in fact, countries have enhanced mechanisms to control movement of people within their borders 'by deploying increasingly sophisticated technologies of identification and control including citizenship, passports, visas, surveillance, integrated databases and biometric devices' (Brubaker, 2005: 9). This is certainly the case in Liberia where, as of mid-December 2019, the 1973 Aliens and Nationality Law still prohibited dual citizenship.

While scholars wrestle with the tendency to dismiss the state as a site of national identity and citizenship formation altogether, conceptions of the traditional state as an 'administrative unit' and 'spatially discreet homogenous political identity' are being called into question by social and political theorising of diasporas who unsettle the very idea that 'state' and 'nation' are inevitably entangled (Adamson & Demetriou, 2007: 490). In using the term 'diasporas' throughout this book, I am referring to transnational actors who express identity through political, economic, and social practices linking homelands (origin countries) and hostlands (countries of diasporic settlement). Current debates about citizenship illustrate the processes by which diasporas affect the citizenship regimes in their host nations, yet there are emerging parallel discourses focused entirely on how diaspora communities influence citizenship regimes in their countries of origin (Baranbantseva & Sutherland, 2011: 1). This debate has situated claims for dual citizenship at the centre as in my case study of Liberia. Most legal means by which emigrants are incorporated by homeland governments maximise their individual liberties but their non-resident political participation may come at the cost of allowing members to influence policies to which they are not directly subject and tilts citizenship towards claiming rights rather than fulfilling obligations (FitzGerald, 2006). In this regard, my book demonstrates that diasporas are contested as are their citizenship and development claims and this contestation comes principally from homeland actors who are supposedly recipients of their largesse.

Contrary to claims by proponents of dual citizenship, transnational forms of citizenship may not necessarily evidence strong ties to the homeland state because in many cases little is required of non-resident citizens, neither paying taxes nor military service; essentially, there is no cost to maintaining one's original citizenship (Spiro, 2012: 311, 318). On average, non-resident citizens may have less of an interest in homeland governance than resident citizens, an argument often advanced by homeland Liberians who challenge the reputed merits of dual citizenship. There is no empirical basis, moreover, for claiming that dual citizenship necessarily enforces homeland–emigrant ties, rather dual citizenship simply enables 'external populations to secure citizenship in their places of external residence without relin-quishing the material and sentimental advantages of retained original citizenship' (Spiro, 2012: 319). This is why some states such as Ethiopia, India, and Turkey have opted for a compromise by granting quasi-citizenship to their non-resident nationals which enables certain privileges but stops short of authorising political rights (Joppke, 2005; Spiro, 2012: 324). For example, Ethiopia's Parliament passed a law in August 2019 allowing non-citizen diasporas to invest, buy shares, and set up lending businesses in the homeland thus serving as a concessionary model for the small number of countries in and outside Africa that still prohibit dual citizenship.

Some scholars position themselves in the middle of what appears to be a binary between state-centric ('bounded') and transnational ('unbounded') citizenship, maintaining that the two are not mutually exclusive. My arguments are closely aligned with this positioning because I consider Liberia's political economy of belonging to be a hybrid manifestation of both resident ('bounded') and non-resident ('unbounded') forms of identity and practice. This will become clear in Chapter 2 where I discuss the myriad ways in which Liberians in my study conceive and practise Liberian citizenship regardless of their residence or legal citizenship status. For the sake of simplicity, I use interchangeably the terms 'transnational' and 'non-resident' citizenship to demarcate what the vast literature describes as 'extraterritorial', 'deterritorial', 'unbounded', 'expatriate', or 'emigrant' forms of citizenship.

Liberian Citizenship as Identity, Practice, and a Set of Relations

Just as the meaning of citizenship across the globe is constantly shifting, I argue throughout this book that Liberian citizenship has been constructed and reconstructed because of historical and contemporary processes of conflict, migration, and post-war recovery. In my analysis, Liberian citizenship is simultaneously theorised in legal, political, and sociological terms. First, Liberian citizenship is passive, characterising an identity anchored in legal status, cultural and national affiliation. Second, Liberian citizenship is active, signifying a bundle of practices enacted by a multitude of actors. And third, Liberian citizenship is interactive, represented by a set of relations between the Liberian government and citizens in Liberia and abroad (government–citizen relations) and between Liberians across spatial landscapes (citizen–citizen relations) – similar to the manner in which Fierke (2007) frames security as a set of relations between the protector and protected, the threatener and threatened. Citizenship can be understood as active or passive depending on whether or not it was configured 'from below' or 'from above' (Kuisma, 2008: 616). For instance, whereas the French Revolution engendered citizenship 'from below', thus making citizenship active in France, the unification of Germany under the Treaty of Versailles produced citizenship 'from above', thereby making German citizenship more passive in orientation (Kuisma, 2008: 616). I assert that while mid- to late nineteenth- and early twentieth-century Liberian citizenship was passive and fixed 'from above' by a hegemonic state, late twentieth- and early twenty-first-century citizenship has been largely active and reconstructed 'from below' by citizens themselves, primarily through processes of protest. This level of meta-analysis will become clear in the next chapter explaining why I adopted actor-oriented analysis as my conceptual framework as well as in subsequent empirical chapters about Liberian state formation and citizenship construction.

In the section that follows, I present in summary form an overview of this book and its constituent chapters.

Contestation and Convergence over Citizenship in Eight Chapters

Development, (Dual) Citizenship and Its Discontents in Africa is divided into eight chapters beginning with this Introduction that contextualises the entire scope of my study. Chapter 1 explains why investigating Liberia's political economy of belonging required multi-sited fieldwork in three continents, a theoretical framework (actor-oriented analysis) which considers myriad responses to development interventions, and deep thinking about my positionality. In Chapter 2, I evaluate how Liberian citizenship is currently conceived and practised in Liberia and across transnational spaces within the context of post-war development. I argue that contemporary citizenship construction sits on a continuum between identity (passive citizenship) and practice (active citizenship). This chapter further establishes that the fluidity of conceptions of Liberian citizenship transcends the legal definition articulated, up to mid-December 2019, in the country's 1973 Aliens and Nationality Law thus subjecting the Law to critique. Chapter 3 demonstrates how the globalisation of liberal citizenship norms – including universalised notions of citizenship as a human right – and the diffusion of dual citizenship in Africa have stimulated claims for non-resident citizenship in Liberia. It also reveals that Liberians at home and abroad evaluate dual citizenship as a policy prescription and development intervention differently based on their unique life-worlds and social locations with homeland actors particularly resistant.

Chapter 4 is the first in a three-part series of chapters examining historical and contemporary factors that altered Liberian citizenship and influenced the introduction and suspension in passage of the 2008 dual citizenship bill. In it, I argue that four conflict interfaces in Liberia and across transnational spaces have fundamentally configured and reconfigured citizenship construction and practice. The chapter shows that conflict – manifested in physical and structural violence – simulta- neously ruptured and sealed government–citizen and citizen–citizen rela- tions thereby casting citizenship as a site of enduring struggle. Here, I review some of the conflict literature, exploring how the manipulation of citizenship was a catalyst for Liberia's armed conflicts and how it continues to propel tensions amongst homeland, diaspora, and returnee Liberians in the post-war era.

Chapter 5 indicates that migration to and from Liberia in the nine- teenth, twentieth, and twenty-first centuries profoundly modified the meaning and practice of citizenship by creating categories of Liberians that have defied the legal definition of citizen. While the introduction of the 2008 dual citizenship bill was an attempt to reconcile the (forced) migration of hundreds of thousands before, during, and after intermittent armed conflict, it was postponed because, for some, naturalisation abroad has signified a rejection of the fundamental tenets of Liberian citizenship as bounded by a single, geographical territory. Because of the dearth of quantitative data on Liberian pre- and post-war migration, I include in this chapter a qualitative mapping of the migration patterns of respondents in my five urban fieldwork locations to illustrate how experiences of migration definitively impacted citizenship status conditions and choices.

In Chapter 6, I interrogate the underlying assumption that Liberian diasporas and returnees are the remedy to reconstruction, donor-driven or otherwise. I maintain that a disproportionate number of diaspora recruits implicated in public sector graft cases justified restrictions on non-resident citizenship in the same way that a one-size-fits-all agenda for post-war recovery undermined government–citizen relations. This chapter further employs terms I coined, such as dichotomy of diasporic developmentalism, *diaspocracy*, and Taylor–Corkrum nexus, to demonstrate that although reconstruction may require the active citizenship of all Liberians, what Liberia needs is not 'all hands on deck' but rather only those hands that are truly committed to socio-economic transformation. My concluding chapter scrutinises how Liberian domestic and diasporic citizen interventions during the Ebola outbreak of 2014–2016 merged together state-, nation-, and peace-building objectives. It summarises key arguments and findings about Liberia's political economy of belonging and lists a set of policy recommendations and projections for future research, chief among which is the need to base legal citizenship reconfiguration on empirical analysis rather than on the whims of political entrepreneurs. This chapter also discusses the implications of my study for other post-war countries, in Africa and beyond, currently examining the tenets of citizenship.

Conclusion

In the same way that dual citizenship signifies a central topic of twenty-first-century public discourse, Liberia's official seal is subject to constant scrutiny because it reflects the exclusion that permeated the first one hundred years of the country's existence as a nation-state. Having never been formally colonised and more recently emerging from a protracted armed conflict, Liberia represents a stark case study in African citizenship construction because of its idiosyncratic history of black settler state formation and historical trajectory as a country of both immigration and emigration. In this chapter, I established how Liberian citizenship – and, by extension, the political economy of belonging to Liberia – has evolved since the founding of the nation-state in 1847 with proposed dual citizenship legislation serving as a contemporary manifestation of that reconfiguration across space and time. My Introduction outlines the book's rationale, unique contributions, scope, and organisation.

In the next chapter, I provide methodological, theoretical, and biographical contexts for evaluating the factors that influenced the introduction and postponement in the passage of Liberia's 2008 dual citizenship legislation.

1 | *Methodological, Theoretical, and Biographical Reflections*[*]

Introduction

In mid-May 2013 at the Buduburam Refugee Camp on the outskirts of Accra, Ghana's capital, a petite seamstress[1] hurtled out of a one-room house to fetch rainwater pouring endlessly from her corrugated rooftop. I paused my audio recorder nearly four times during an interview with this thirty-eight-year-old former refugee who had opted in 2012[2] for local integration in Ghana after living there for twenty-three years. Torrential showers splashed through her punctured window screens, exposing us to the elements. Dripping wet, the woman re-entered the house holding a bright-blue bucket on the crown of her head – filled with what I assumed was water for washing clothes and bathing – and placed it in a corner of the room. She sat down on a small wooden bench facing me and we continued the interview, shouting to hear each other above the loud clamour of rain.

Just one month earlier I had sat comfortably in the refurbished rooftop office of a forty-eight-year-old Liberian businessman and consultant[3] in downtown Freetown, Sierra Leone's capital. Exuding confidence and privilege, the man had lived and worked in similar settings across five different countries within sub-Saharan Africa for two decades. When he offered me a chilled orange Fanta in a sleek hourglass bottle, I could not help noticing his form-fitting tailor-made

---

[*] The last section of this chapter is derived in part from Pailey (2017c).
[1] [DL90] Interview in Accra on 11 May 2013.
[2] On 30 June 2012, the United Nations (UN) invoked a refugee cessation clause officially ending the refugee status of Liberian nationals across the globe, with some exemptions. Former refugees who had not successfully resettled in a third-party country were either locally integrated into their refugee hosting countries or repatriated back to Liberia.
[3] [DL79] Interview in Freetown on 19 April 2013.

suit. As the man walked to the single leather recliner facing me, his shiny shoes made a soft noise on the white porcelain tiles. I placed my recorder on his mahogany table and pressed play.

As indicated in the settings of vignettes earlier, the Liberian actors I interviewed for this book, as well as the spaces and places they occupy, are emblematic of distinct life-worlds (lived experiences) and social locations (socio-economic positions). Divided into three sections, this chapter outlines my rationale for selecting respondents with an overview of their demographic profiles (Section I); the conceptual framework, actor-oriented analysis, which inspired my multi-sited fieldwork (Section II); and insights about my own positionality (Section III). The methodological, theoretical, and biographical reflections that follow are intended to contextualise how I came to understand Liberia's political economy of belonging and its relationship to contestations over development and dual citizenship.

Section I: From One-Room Boxed Houses to Flawless Rooftop Offices

For fourteen months – between June 2012 and July 2013 – I travelled to five urban centres across three continents – namely, Monrovia, Liberia; Freetown, Sierra Leone; Accra, Ghana; London, United Kingdom; Washington, DC, United States – seeking out Liberians of different ages, genders, educational levels, incomes, birthplaces, countries of citizenship, and migration histories to examine how they conceived and practised Liberian citizenship in general, viewed dual citizenship in particular, and how their lived experiences and socio-economic positions influenced the introduction and postponement in the passage of dual citizenship legislation. The 202 Liberians I interviewed comprised 181 diasporas, homelanders, and returnees speaking unofficially, as well as 21 officials speaking in their capacities as government of Liberia representatives or regional diaspora heads of organisations. They were divided thus:

(1) three Liberian ambassadors, each in London, Freetown, and Accra;
(2) three additional embassy officials in Washington and Accra;
(3) three heads of Liberian diaspora organisations in London, Washington, and Accra;

(4) four Monrovia-based sponsors of the 2008 dual citizenship bill;

(5) eight Monrovia-based executive branch policymakers;

(6) ten permanent returnees in Monrovia;

(7) eleven circular returnees in Monrovia;

(8) fifty homeland Liberians in Monrovia;

(9) 110 Liberian diasporas residing in London, Washington, Freetown, and Accra.

I make no claims that these respondents represent Liberians world-wide, especially since statistics on emigrants are difficult to ascertain. However, my exploration of their life-worlds and social locations does reveal certain patterns in Liberia's contemporary political economy of belonging. To establish trends in the subregion, I also interviewed seven Sierra Leonean government officials in Freetown to assess how citizen-ship had been reconfigured in a neighbouring post-war country of emigration. The rationale here was to gauge the factors that influenced Sierra Leone's dual citizenship passage in 2006, its potential ramifica-tions, and the nodes of resistance to changes in the country's citizenship laws. While I was able to access two executive-level policymakers through my contacts in the Office of Diaspora Affairs, five parliamen-tarians were referred to me by the Liberian businessman profiled in the beginning of this chapter who was well connected to the upper echelons of Sierra Leone's political hierarchy.

Since the research methodologies employed in this study were meant to be exploratory in nature rather than representative, interviewees were selected through a snowball sampling method in which I contacted individuals I knew personally or professionally and asked them to recommend others who fit within my analytical categories. I spoke to respondents in public places, in work spaces, as well as in homes. Although our conversations were generally conducted in standard English, where necessary I used informal Liberian English to clarify terms and concepts.

Rationale for the Selection of Liberian Respondents

Of the seven categories of Liberian respondents – namely, legislative branch policymakers, executive branch policymakers, heads of dias-pora organisations, diasporas, homeland Liberians, permanent return-ees, and circular returnees – the first three spoke in their official capacities and are hereafter mentioned by name. I had access to these officials, some of whom were former colleagues, because I worked for the Liberian government as a mid-level aide to President Ellen Johnson Sirleaf from 2007 to 2011 and engaged with diasporas and returnees extensively as part of my portfolio.

Through interviews with the already-mentioned four sponsors of Liberia's 2008 dual citizenship legislation – namely then senators Wotorson, Kupee, Taylor, and Massalay – I was able to determine the range of individual and collective motivations for attempting to reconcile the legal definition of Liberian citizenship in the 1973 Aliens and Nationality Law and 1986 Constitution. Selected because their ministries/agencies were responsible for leading Liberia's post-war recovery agenda, cabinet-level policymakers were interviewed for an evaluation of development milestones and challenges, which I triangulated with documentary data from government and non-government sources. I was also able to gauge the perceived impacts of diaspora return migration and/or transnational activities on development, which influenced claims for and against dual citizenship. Those interviewed in 2013 held ministerial positions in foreign affairs (Augustine Ngafuan, who spoke in his capacity as immediate past minister of finance),[4] defence (Brownie Samukai),[5] lands, mines, and energy (Patrick Sendolo),[6] and justice (Christiana Tah).[7] Other respondents included the National Investment Commission chairperson (O Natty B Davis),[8] the Governance Commission chairperson (Amos Sawyer),[9] the former (and immediate past) minister of public works (Samuel Kofi Woods),[10] and the former (and immediate past) director-general of the Civil Service Agency, who had been appointed ambassador to France (C William Allen).[11] It is worth noting that of the eight executive-level policymakers I consulted, five were actively recruited from the United States – Samukai, Sendolo, Tah, Sawyer, and Allen – while three remained in Liberia for most of their

---

[4] Interview in Monrovia on 11 June 2013.
[5] Interview in Monrovia on 12 July 2013.
[6] Interview in Monrovia on 28 June 2013.
[7] Interview in Monrovia on 19 June 2013. Tah resigned in October 2014.
[8] Interview in Monrovia on 13 June 2013. Shortly after our interview, Davis was replaced by Michael Wotorson, a diaspora recruit who resigned in August 2014 and returned to the United States amidst the Ebola outbreak.
[9] Interview in Monrovia on 25 June 2013.   [10] Ibid.
[11] Interview in Monrovia on 4 June 2013.

professional lives – Ngafuan, Davis, and Woods. This information will crystallise later in Chapter 6 when I examine whether diasporas, and by extension returnees, have helped or hindered post-war recovery.

Foreign mission officials in London, Freetown, Accra, and Washington were pursued to clarify how the Liberian government's representation in these locales affects the practice of Liberian citizenship transnationally. Embassy respondents included then ambassadors to the United Kingdom (Wesley Momo Johnson),[12] Sierra Leone (Thomas Brima),[13] and Ghana (Rudolf Von Ballmoos).[14] Then ambassador to the United States Jeremiah Sulunteh was unavailable for an interview, so he instructed deputy chief of mission Jeff Dowana[15] as well as minister counsellor for public affairs Gabriel IH Williams[16] to converse with me. In Accra, Ambassador Von Ballmoos requested that second secretary Angela Lavela Von Ballmoos[17] explain the embassy's processes of engagement with Liberians in Ghana. Also speaking in official capacities were regional diaspora executives. In communicating with Prince Taylor[18] of the Union of Liberian Organisations in the United Kingdom (ULO-UK), Nee Allison[19] of the Liberian Community Association in the Washington Metropolitan Area, and Julia Richards[20] of the United Liberian Association in Ghana (ULAG), I considered how citizenship is manifested in the collective practices of Liberians residing in London, Washington, and Accra, respectively. The difficulty in locating a Liberian organisation in Freetown is indicative of the fact that Liberian and Sierra Leonean identities are fluid, as corroborated by Ambassador Brima, who said, 'The two countries [Liberia and Sierra Leone] are so interrelated that it's very difficult to actually differentiate a Liberian from a Sierra Leonean'.[21]

---

[12] Interview in London on 14 June 2012. Johnson, a former opposition party member of the Progressive People's Party (PPP) in the 1980s, was replaced in 2013 by Rudolf Von Ballmoos, a veteran Liberian diplomat who had most immediately served as Liberia's ambassador to Ghana.

[13] Interview in Freetown on 18 April 2013.

[14] Interview in Accra on 23 May 2013.

[15] Interview in Washington on 2 November 2012.   [16] Ibid.

[17] Interview in Accra on 23 May 2013.

[18] Interview in London on 16 June 2012.

[19] Interview in Washington on 2 November 2012.

[20] Interview in Accra on 18 May 2013.

[21] Interview in Freetown on 18 April 2013.

The basic criterion for the selection of interviewees speaking unofficially was their self-identification as Liberians regardless of their legal citizenship status. With demographic profiles captured in Tables 1.1, 1.2, and 1.3 hereafter, these respondents remain anonymous throughout the book and in instances where I use names they are actually pseudonyms. Beyond having psychological attachments to Liberia, informants were also either born in Liberia or born abroad to at least one parent who was a Liberian citizen at the time of their birth – representing the then legal definition of Liberian citizenship. The respondent pool did not include Lebanese residing in Liberia or those who would have been considered non-black because their 'Liberianness' was contested both constitutionally – based on the 'Negro clause' – and sociologically by Liberians at home and abroad, as will be discussed in subsequent chapters.

'Homeland' is the term I use to describe those who had spent most, if not all, of their lives in Liberia before the first war started in 1989, and most, if not all, of their lives in Liberia after the first 'post-war moment' in 1997. Exceptions were made for individuals who found short-term work and/or study opportunities outside of Liberia during these periods. Unlike other Monrovia-based respondents, such as permanent and circular returnees described later, homeland Liberians identified Liberia as the only 'home' they had ever claimed as their own. Individuals who considered post-war return to and residence in Liberia 'permanent' are classified as permanent returnees. What I gleaned from these respondents was their heightened level of engagement with Liberia while abroad, from participating in rallies for Temporary Protected Status (TPS) and Deferred Enforced Departure (DED)[22] extension in the United States to serving Liberia in the diplomatic corps, representing Liberia in the arts and humanities, and

---

[22] From 1991 onwards, thousands of Liberians relied on the renewal of TPS and DED by the White House to maintain a legal right to remain in the United States. These individuals, many of whom had been in America since fleeing Liberia's crises in the late 1980s and early 1990s, retained temporary legal status which allowed them to live, work, and pay taxes in the United States. However, the special TPS provision was terminated by the Trump administration in May 2017 for Guineans, Liberians, and Sierra Leoneans after the Ebola epidemic. DED for Liberians was scheduled to expire on 30 March 2020; however, the US president signed on 20 December 2019 a congressionally approved National Defence Authorisation Act, which provided DED holders and former TPS beneficiaries a pathway to permanent residency and US citizenship.

Table 1.1 *Gender and age distribution of 181 unofficial respondents*

Field site/gender and age	M	F	21–30 years	31–40 years	41–50 years	51–60 years	61–70 years	71–80 years	No age
London (30)	15	15	1	9	15	4	N/A	N/A	1
Washington (30)	14	16	9	4	4	6	5	2	N/A
Freetown (20)	14	6	3	7	3	4	2	1	N/A
Accra (30)	17	13	4	9	6	8	1	N/A	2
Monrovia (71)	36	35	26	20	15	5	4	N/A	1
Total absolute number/	96/	85/	43/	49/	43/	27/	12/	3/	4/
Percentage of total	53	47	24	27	24	15	7	1	2

Some respondents opted not to disclose their ages so they are designated as 'no age' in the last column of Table 1.1.

Table 1.2 *Highest education levels of 181 unofficial respondents*

Field site/ educational attainment	Below high school/ no school	High school diploma	Bachelor's degree	Master's degree	PhD or professional degree (i.e., law, medicine)
London (30)	N/A	8	11	10	1
Washington (30)	N/A	5	14	10	1
Freetown (20)	6	10	3	1	N/A
Accra (30)	3	14	6	6	1
Monrovia (71)	N/A	24	23	20	4
Total absolute number/	9/	61/	57/	47/	7/
Percentage of total	5	34	31	26	4

maintaining businesses and investments in Liberia. They are similar to homelanders in that they demonstrated an explicit commitment to remain in Liberia regardless of any adverse circumstances. Circular returnees, on the other hand, admitted that their return to Liberia was conditional and, therefore, temporary, based on a number of factors, including, but not limited to, peace and stability in Liberia, job security in the country, and familial obligations abroad. These respondents had relocated to Liberia for at least twelve consecutive calendar months – but less than six consecutive years – from 2003 to 2013. I regarded the one year minimum as an appropriate time frame for them to re-establish ties with Liberia while also leaving room for any periodic travel abroad.

I purposively sampled for a broad range of ages and deliberately sought to balance the number of men and women in my unofficial respondent pool. Whereas male and female informants in London, Washington, Accra, and Monrovia are equally or nearly equally distributed, as indicated in Table 1.1, the proportion of male interviewees is more than double that of females in Freetown. Many of the women I contacted in Freetown were either too shy to consent to being interviewed or lacked enough confidence in their abilities to engage despite my futile attempts to reassure them. I realised early on, however, that the low levels of formal education amongst the women I approached could be a primary reason for their reticence. As a case in point, I started interviewing a middle-aged woman with a sixth-grade education and had to stop because she could not understand concepts germane to my study, such as citizenship, or explain how she identified herself – as a Liberian, a Sierra Leonean, neither, or both. My inability to communicate fluidly with some respondents, particularly women, was due in large part to my very basic proficiency in Krio, Sierra Leone's de facto national language and a lingua franca developed by descendants of repatriated blacks from the West Indies, the United Kingdom, and the United States. In all five urban field sites I refrained from asking respondents about their ethnicity because it was politicised during Liberia's intermittent armed conflicts and remains a sensitive topic to broach. Moreover, the framework of this book, citizenship, is broader in scope although ethnic identity did come up indirectly as a criterion for national belonging with some respondents disclosing that it serves as an impediment to experiencing Liberian citizenship fully. This will be assessed more significantly in Chapter 2.

Predictably, respondents' educational attainments had a positive correlation with their employment status and income levels whereby some women were more marginalised than others. In cases where educational attainment was high, respondents reported higher levels of income, for those who opted to disclose this information. While twenty-seven of the thirty London-based respondents were employed with a median income of £35,000 per annum, twenty-six of the thirty Washington-based respondents were employed with a higher median income of US$71,000 per annum. Unlike in London and Washington, however, only five Freetown-based male respondents reported being employed with a wide variance in income levels. For instance, the businessman/consultant described earlier in the chapter reported an annual income of US$180,000 on the highest end of the spectrum, while a pastor reported an annual income of US$300 on the lowest end. A greater number of respondents in Accra (eighteen) disclosed being employed than those in Freetown. Similar to Freetown, however, Accra-based respondents reported a wide variance in income levels that exposed disparities in not only educational attainment but also gender. For instance, a male banker/economist and master's degree holder reported an annual income of US$170,000 on the highest end of the spectrum, while the seamstress profiled in the introduction of this chapter – one of the only eight female respondents employed in Accra – was a high school dropout who reported an annual income of US$600 on the lowest end. Although Chapters 2 and 6 provide a more nuanced analysis of the differentiated homeland engagement patterns of diasporas, it is important to state here that unlike for respondents in London and Washington, the limited employment prospects of interviewees in Freetown, generally, and Accra, to a certain degree, impeded their ability to formalise that engagement by actively practising Liberian citizenship from afar.

Wide income gaps within the Monrovia respondent pool also reveal divergent social locations. Although 30 per cent of homelanders reported being unemployed, the 70 per cent who were employed disclosed extensive variances in their income levels. For instance, a male development economist reported an annual income of US$91,000 on the highest end of the spectrum while two women – a programme assistant and an accountant, respectively – reported annual incomes of US$2,400 on the lowest end. Amongst permanent returnees, the highest income reported was US$200,000, the middle US$34,000, and the lowest US$4,200. Within the circular returnee respondent pool, five reported having an annual income of US$50,000 and above, while the lowest reported income earner received US$27,000 per annum. These discrepancies represent a microcosm of income inequalities within post-war Liberia which affects citizenship claims, and I discuss this in detail in Chapter 4 on how conflict configured and reconfigured Liberian citizenship.

Since the annual incomes, employment status, and education levels of actors profiled herein serve as the building blocks of a demographic profile, their citizenship status and migration patterns are equally important in developing a schema of their lived experiences and socio-economic positions. The citizenship status of respondents in particular is worth highlighting briefly because it signifies an important shift in Liberian citizenship configurations after 1989, which I examine more fully in Chapter 5. As Table 1.3 illustrates, most diasporas were born in Liberia yet London and Washington account for the majority of respondents who naturalised abroad and/or were born abroad. On

Table 1.3 *Place of birth/country of citizenship of 181 unofficial respondents*

Place of birth (PoB)/ Country of citizenship (CoC)	PoB Liberia	PoB Other	CoC Liberia	CoC Other
London (30)	28	2	6	24
Washington (30)	24	6	11	19
Freetown (20)	15	5	14	6
Accra (30)	30	N/A	29	1
Monrovia (71)	66	5	60	11
Total absolute number/ Percentage of total	163/ 90	18/ 10	120/ 66	61/ 34

average, respondents in London, Washington, Freetown, and Accra had spent approximately seventeen, twenty, seventeen, and fifteen years, respectively, in the countries in which they were interviewed. While all Monrovia-based homeland respondents had spent only short stints abroad and retained Liberian citizenship, their permanent and circular returnee counterparts had spent on average ten and twenty-two years abroad, respectively. That circular returnees resided outside of Liberia significantly longer than permanent returnees is not surprising since they represent the most transnational of all respondents captured in this book. It is also telling that Liberian-born circular returnees were more likely to naturalise abroad in contrast to all permanent returnees who had maintained their *jus soli* Liberian citizenship.

Rationale for the Selection of Five Urban Field Sites

Because this book investigates the meanings and practices of Liberian citizenship across space and time, I knew from the outset that my fieldwork would have to be multi-sited. I narrowed the spatial land-scape to capital cities given the growing body of scholarly literature on how certain urban centres, particularly global cities such as London, New York, and Tokyo, for instance, reproduce, refashion, and recon-figure identities, politico-economic engagement, and social practices (Sassen, 1991; Isin, 2000). I selected cities not only occupying different spheres of global influence, such as London and Washington, but also with sizeable Liberian populations, such as Monrovia, Freetown, and Accra. The latter three enabled me to produce subregional analyses while filling gaps in scholarship that focuses entirely too much on migrants in the so-called Global North – 'wider' diasporas – and not enough on the vast majority of so-called Global South migrants who travel exclusively within their subregions of origin – 'near' diasporas (Van Hear, 2009: 181). Moreover, I selected sites in Europe and North America to challenge normative assumptions that the 'field' only exists 'out there' in so-called hard-to-reach, poorly managed, otherworldly locales of the Global South. The four cities epitomising 'near' and 'wider' diasporas are in countries that permit dual citizenship, thus enabling me to determine whether this influenced endorsement or rejection of Liberia's proposed bill by transnational respondents. The cities also house Liberian embassies signifying that Liberia, with its meagre resources and inability to support foreign missions in every country, attaches a certain level of importance in implementing its foreign-policy agenda in these locales. Moreover, the selection of cities was my deliberate attempt to hone in on how access to urban spaces shapes citizenship construction and practices amongst a range of Liberian actors in Liberia and abroad.

Monrovia was my primary field site because it represents a locus of wide-ranging homeland identities. Importantly, rural to urban migration during/after armed conflicts and the limited opportunities available to rural dwellers have stretched the city's population beyond its capacity. Monrovia is neither a global city like London or Washington nor a West African hub like Accra. It is akin to Freetown in exemplifying a post-war capital struggling to reconstruct and reinvent itself. According to 2008 census figures[23] generated by the Liberia Institute for Statistics and Geo-Information Services (LISGIS), about one-third of Liberia's 3.4 million population at the time resided in Monrovia, a city that was constructed to only accommodate 500,000 people (Government of Liberia, 2009). Monrovia also enabled access to Liberian policymakers, foreign donors, multinationals, civil-society

---

[23] As the only post-war population register up to mid-December 2019, the 2008 census was the first of its kind to be conducted in Liberia in almost twenty-four years.

actors, and a growing repository of documentary data about Liberia's post-war development milestones and challenges.

Since West Africa hosts the largest number of Liberians outside of Liberia, I chose Accra and Freetown to explore how Liberian refugee diasporas in the subregion, for instance, compare with economic migrant diasporas who left Liberia for North America or Europe before armed conflict, and how the Liberian government engaged at that time with these disparate actors through embassies abroad. Conducting interviews in Accra allowed me to interact with Liberian migrants in the larger Economic Community of West African States (ECOWAS), a supranational entity which has a free movement of persons protocol. A growing body of published case-study analysis about Liberians in Ghana exists particularly because the Buduburam Refugee Camp at one point contained the majority of Liberian refugees in West Africa (UNHCR, 2004, 2007). Although most research has so far focused primarily on refugees in Buduburam, this book encompasses Liberian economic migrants in Accra and its environs as well as former refugees who locally integrated like the seamstress profiled earlier. As headquarters of the Mano River Union (MRU)[24] comprising Côte d'Ivoire, Guinea, Liberia, and Sierra Leone and founded on principles of economic cooperation, Freetown proved strategic because of its geographic proximity to Monrovia. Because of the shared border between Liberia and Sierra Leone, Liberians in Sierra Leone have managed to integrate seamlessly in a way that almost obliterates sharp markers of 'Liberianness'. As previously mentioned, the malleability of Liberian and Sierra Leonean identities prompted Sesay et al. (2009: 11) to call the two nationalities 'fraternal twins' and Edward Wilmot Blyden (1884: 15), a native of the Virgin Islands who naturalised in Liberia in the nineteenth century, to remark that they 'are one in origin and one in destiny'.

Washington and London were selected as hubs in the so-called Global North because they feature prominently in Liberian transnational politics. As headquarters of the World Bank, International Monetary Fund (IMF), and US Treasury, Washington is not only a centre of international development; it is also where Liberia was

---

[24] Co-founded by Liberia and Sierra Leone in 1973 and later joined by Guinea in 1980 and Côte d'Ivoire in 2008, respectively, the MRU predates the larger regional body ECOWAS which was founded in 1975.

first conceived by the American Colonisation Society (ACS) in 1816. As the United States is home to the bulk of Liberians outside of West Africa, in Washington Liberians have proven their mettle by assembling for mass rallies in front of the White House to bring about a cessation to protracted armed conflicts,[25] lobbying on Capitol Hill, and holding strategy meetings with members of Congress to regularise the status of compatriots on TPS and DED.[26] Washington and London also represent sites where diasporas have demonstrated that the personal is political. For instance, the United States and the United Kingdom provided the lobbying machinery for proposed dual citizenship legislation before and after 2008 under the auspices of the Coalition of Concerned Liberians (CCL), whose founder was based in Washington, and the European Federation of Liberian Associations (EFLA), whose then president was based just outside of London. I designated the European financial centre as a third node in the migration trajectory of Liberian actors beyond North America and Africa.

My multi-sited interviews helped me to discern systematic differences and/or similarities amongst actors in whether citizenship factored in how they conceived of themselves as Liberians (identities); how they contributed to post-war development (practices); how they engaged with the homeland and with other Liberians at home and abroad (sets of relations). While my positioning enabled access to different kinds of informants, I knew it would also influence the ways in which they responded to my questions. I addressed these limitations by deliberately selecting a combination of interviewees I knew and those I had never met. Where appropriate, I gently challenged respondents I knew personally to provide justifications for their beliefs rather than accepting them at face value. For instance, during an interview with a fifty-nine-year-old male permanent returnee entrepreneur[27] who had worked in diaspora engagement, I countered his assertions about the merits of dual citizenship by showcasing the academic literature which posits that non-resident citizenship does not necessarily evidence strong ties to the homeland state. Where possible, I also tempered interjections during interviews with Liberians whom I did not know to carve out

---

[25] [DL34] Interview in Washington on 17 October 2012.
[26] [PR3] Interview in Monrovia on 11 June 2013.
[27] [PR1] Interview in Monrovia on 7 June 2013.

a safe space for them to air grievances against seemingly privileged transnationals like myself. As a case in point, I refrained from rebutting a twenty-five-year-old female homeland administrator[28] who praised Charles Taylor for curbing capital flight that she believed was endemic in Sirleaf's government populated by returnees even though Taylor's regime was notorious for brute force and public sector graft. Although far from representative, these interviews reflect domestic and diasporic public discourse on dual citizenship and are further corroborated by Afrobarometer (2012, 2015, 2018) survey data on domestic citizens' perceptions of Liberian citizenship which will be explored in other chapters.

In the next section of this chapter, I provide a detailed summary of actor-oriented analysis as my theoretical foundation.

Section II: Development and Its Discontents

Actor-oriented types of analysis were popular in anthropology and sociology in the 1960s and 1970s, ranging from transactional and decision-making models to symbolic interventionist and phenomeno-logical analyses. Some studies fell short by reverting to a kind of methodological individualism 'that sought to explain social behaviour primarily in terms of individual motivations, intentions, and interests' without considering larger structural forces (Long, 2001: 14). Nevertheless, Long's brand of actor-oriented analysis, which this book adopts, considers the interplay between agency and structure and is concerned with 'actors' lived experiences, desires, understand-ings, and self-defined problematic situations' amidst broader processes of political, economic, and social change (Long, 2001: 27–28). In particular, it frames planned development interventions – such as dual citizenship in my study – as sites where the life-worlds (lived experiences) and social locations (socio-economic positions) of a range of actors converge and diverge. Borrowing from theories of practice, which will be discussed subsequently, the actor-oriented para-digm is steeped in social constructionist modes of analysis that place an emphasis on the agency of individual and collective actors as they navigate and negotiate structural impediments such as poverty.

---

[28] [HL11] Interview in Monrovia on 10 June 2013.

Actor-oriented analysis does not suggest that actors have a clear understanding 'of why they do things, in the first place, or of how their doing of things affects outcomes', rather it acknowledges that actors have the knowledgeability and capability to act in the first place regardless of their circumstances (Long, 2001: 3). It is concerned with how actors who are both local and external to particular venues – that is, homelanders and diasporas – engage in 'a series of inter-twined battles over resources, meanings and institutional legitimacy and control' (Long, 2001: 1). With its constituent elements of human agency, life-worlds, and interfaces, actor-oriented analysis represents the conceptual grounding for this book because in it I examine how Liberian actors across diverse spatial landscapes conceptualise and practise citizenship in a multitude of ways thereby impacting their disparate responses to homeland government policy prescriptions on transnational citizenship.

At the centre of actor-oriented analysis is the premise that all actors exhibit varying levels of human agency, or a combination of knowledgeability and capability, to cope 'even under the most extreme forms of coercion' (Giddens 1984; Long, 2001: 15). This approach requires distinguishing and codifying the strategies employed by actors, their rationales, and structural outcomes, with the understanding that these same individuals may intentionally devise tactics for solving problems 'even if this means being "active accomplices" to their own subordination' (Long, 1990: 10, 14). Thus, agency is not universal because it is constructed differently based on cultural and worldview interpretations. Like that of Liberians who live within and outside the territorial confines of the Liberian nation-state, agency further represents the application and management of relationships and networks across spatial landscapes (Long, 2001: 17). Expanding the knowledgeability and capability framework adopted by Giddens (1984), Long (2001: 18) maintains that agency surpasses intentional action to encompass emotions and perceptions of reality. This point is particularly relevant for my study because I contend that claims for and against dual citizenship are not only rational based on Liberian actors' socio-economic positions, but also emotive based on their lived experiences of conflict, migration, and post-war recovery. Each category of actors in my study displays different levels of power as evidenced by the impasse on dual citizenship. For instance, I show that the relatively elevated social locations of diasporas and returnees do not negate the agency of other actors such as domestic policymakers and homeland Liberians.

Furthermore, not all diasporas occupy positions of privilege as exhibited by the status of locally integrated/former refugees in Freetown and Accra.

Just as the notion of agency is appropriated in actor-oriented analysis, so, too, is the term 'life-world' borrowed from Schultz and Luckmann (1973) who define it as 'a lived-in and largely taken for granted world' that, according to Long (2001: 189), 'is *actor* rather than *observer* defined'. As such, everyday life is experienced as an 'ordered reality' shared with others in which actors negotiate relationships and navigate circumstances in the face of planned development interventions (Long, 2001: 189). Although my study is not an ethnography, I argue that what Long and others refer to as 'life-worlds' can be observed through oral histories captured in one-off interviews rather than those observed over the *longue durée*. During fieldwork in five urban centres across Europe, North America, and West Africa, for instance, I relied on respondents' verbal utterances to construct schemas of their life-worlds and social locations.

Actor-oriented analysis places a premium on the interactions amongst different sets of actors at the 'interface', and does not assume top-down imposition (Long, 2001: 27). It is at the site of interface where the different life-worlds and social locations of actors 'interact and interpenetrate' that change occurs (Long, 1992: 6; Arce & Long, 2000: 3, 8–9, 19–20):

Interface analysis concentrates upon analysing critical junctures entailing differences of normative value and social interest. It aims to depict not only the struggles and power differentials that emerge but also seeks to understand the cultural meanings, accommodations and compromises that underpin the interactions and transactions that evolve. Even those interfaces characterised by strong hegemonic tendencies – and therefore symbolically and organisationally geared to the enforcement and reaffirmation of authoritative knowledge and forms of domination – show evidence of countertendencies and 'counterwork' which exploit the inherent ambiguities and partial connections of interface phenomena.

Through this lens of analysis, one is able to glean how actors encounter and experience each other without assuming that one group dominates the other because:

[T]here are myriad ways in which so-called 'subordinate' or 'weaker' actors can create space for themselves, defend their own worldviews and standpoints, and subvert the best-laid plans and discourses of 'dominant' actors, while at the same time continuing to live in a world full of inequalities and vulnerabilities.

Here, Long (2001: 72, 238) echoes African American feminist scholar bell hooks (1989: 20–21) who frames marginality as not only 'a site of deprivation' or repression but also one of 'radical possibility, a space of resistance'. In my study, interface does not signify a physical encounter, per se, rather it is characterised by discourses on the tenets of Liberian citizenship in which diasporas influenced the introduction of dual citizenship legislation in 2008 as much as their homeland counterparts affected the bill's suspension. This underpins the construction of Liberian citizenship as a set of relations between homeland Liberians and diasporas, homeland Liberians and the Liberian government, as well as diasporas and the Liberian government.

Actor-oriented analysis further enables my examination of how diasporas and homeland Liberians, for instance, represent varying nodes of knowledge and power that are just as likely to contribute to conflict as they are to lead to compromise at the interface. Within interface certain boundaries come to be demarcated by various actors: between themselves and other actors, between themselves and institutions, and between themselves and development plans and activities (Villarreal, 1992: 254). While the researcher cannot affix arbitrary boundaries, he or she can identify the boundaries actors set and examine what kinds of changes these boundaries undergo during processes of interface (Villarreal, 1992: 254). Throughout this book, I illustrate how visible and invisible boundaries came to separate Liberian actors who devised caricatured stereotypes of one another emphasising differences to justify discordant views about dual citizenship. Yet, interface embodies not only spaces of disagreement, divergence, opposition, or circumvention, but also intervals of consent, convergence, accommodation, and re-appropriation. For example, while a small minority of respondents captured in this book expressed extreme opinions about the merits or demerits of dual citizenship, the vast majority of actors I interviewed were moderate and accommodating in their perspectives. Chapter 3 on dual citizenship and its discontents presents these viewpoints in detail.

Although Long (1992: 5) examines how individual actors – poor peasants, entrepreneurs, government bureaucrats, or researchers –

respond to development projects in localised, non-urban settings in the so-
called developing world, thereby revealing their different social locations
and life-worlds, I assess how Liberian actors in cities regard a proposed
policy intervention – dual citizenship – with its presumed development
outcomes, and what this reveals about their disparate experiences of being
Liberian and of practising Liberian citizenship at home and abroad.
Therefore, my macro-level study spanning urban centres in three continents and Long's micro-level studies in rural locales cohere in attempting
to understand the '"social life" of development projects – from conception
to realisation – as well as the responses and lived experiences of the
variously located and affected social actors' (Long, 2001: 15). In this
framing, development interventions such as dual citizenship are not
taken for granted methods of amelioration but rather objects of contestation and accommodation, simultaneously (Long, 1992: 9). Rather than
viewing intervention as a plan to be implemented 'from above', it should
be regarded instead as an ongoing process of transformation in which
different actors' pursuits are negotiated (Long, 1992: 9). What is particularly important in interpreting development as political, economic, and
social change is identifying the tactics employed by actors for confronting
'intervenors' in an attempt to circumvent or re-appropriate their inputs
(Long, 2001: 233).

Actor-Oriented Analysis Embedded in Social Constructionism

Long's actor-oriented analysis builds on other theoretical models that
attempt to reconcile structure and actor paradigms, such as theories of
practice. Similar to the 'actor' in actor-oriented analysis, practice theory adopts the term 'agent' to describe an individual actor where
individual actors/agents are the carriers of practice and neither completely autonomous nor completely controlled by externalities
(Reckwitz, 2002: 256). While practices can be theoretically dichoto-
mised between 'bodily and mental routines', practice theorists are
concerned with the 'interconnectedness of bodily routines of behaviour, mental routines of understanding and knowing, and the use of
objects (Reckwitz, 2002: 257–258). Similarly, I am preoccupied in this
book with how citizenship is construed as both a form of 'being' – identity,
or mental routines – and a form of 'doing' – practice, or bodily routines.
Scholars who have advanced theories of practice have been primarily
interested in the everyday lived experiences of particular agents or actors

although there is no grand, overarching theory (Bourdieu, 1977, 1990; Giddens, 1979, 1984; Foucault, 1984; Reckwitz, 2002: 244, 257). Bourdieu (1990) and Giddens (1984) were pioneers of theories of practice, where the former coined the term *habitus*, or embodied histories, while the latter devised concepts such as rules and resources, or *structures* (Everts et al., 2011: 324). As the bedrock of practice theory, and by extension, actor-oriented analysis, Bourdieu's conceptualisation of *habitus* does not imply that actors are mechanically controlled by their embodied histories. Rather, it illustrates how they develop and deploy tactics that are adapted to their individual and collective life-worlds and social locations in spite of internal strictures and external structures.

There is a fundamental difference between structuralist and phenomenological theories, where the former looks at macro-level aggregate structures and trends (i.e., Marxist/structuralist approaches), while the latter looks at micro-level changes affecting operational or acting units (i.e., actor-oriented approaches) (Long, 1990: 4). While phenomenological approaches may also examine macro-level change they are primarily concerned with granular accounts of actors' disparate responses to structural forces (Long, 1990: 4). Macro-level development theories of modernisation, dependency, and structural Marxism, for instance, centre external forces represented by powerful individuals, institutions, and enterprises while often ignoring 'local or endogenous forms of cooperation and solidarity' (Long, 2001: 11). Like Giddens' (1984: 25) theory of structuration, in which structures are neither completely constraining nor enabling, Long's brand of actor-oriented analysis does not negate structural forces, rather it accounts for them by emphasising encounters and exchanges which bring about confrontation and compromise between particular kinds of individuals and groups during development interventions (Long, 1990: 18). Whereas structuralist analysis may view transformation as linear or predestined, actor-oriented analysis interprets actors as both influenced by and influencing structural outcomes (Long, 2001: 11).

An actor-oriented paradigm serves as an alternative to structuralist analysis wherein external forms of intervention not only permeate the life-worlds of actors but also become transformed by them (Long, 1990: 6). This requires a more nuanced analysis of socio-economic change because it stresses the dynamic 'interplay and mutual determination of "internal" and "external" factors and relationships' thereby acknowledging the centrality of 'human action and consciousness' (Long, 1990: 6). For instance, this book demonstrates that both external and internal forms of development intervention – by donors, Liberian diasporas, the Liberian government, and homeland Liberians, for instance – have had a profound impact on Liberian citizenship construction and practice across space and time. One of the advantages of employing an actor-oriented theory of analysis is that one can begin to explain different responses to the same structural condition or planned intervention such as contemporary claims for and against dual citizenship by a multitude of Liberian actors. Therefore, the outcomes that arise – that is, a deadlock on the 2008 dual citizenship bill – are in part created by the very individuals and collectivities implicated. Neither 'disembodied ... [n]or passive recipients of intervention', these actors represent dynamic agents who 'process information and strategise in their dealings' with a range of internal and external individuals and institutions (Long, 1990: 7). As such, my study frames Liberians as possessing multiple levels of agency in the midst of structural change.

In the section that follows, I explore how one group of respondents captured in this book, diasporas, fits within actor-oriented analysis as both social actors and categories of practice.

Diasporas as Social Actors and Categories of Practice

There is a range of competing theoretical frameworks for diasporas. One school of thought conceptualises diasporas as *passive* and fixed, representing a state of being or an identity, while another defines diasporas as *active* and constructed (Safran, 1991; Sheffer, 1996; Brubaker, 2005). This book situates Liberia's diasporas in the 'interstices' (Bhabha, 1994) of the conceptual debate because for Liberians abroad being 'of' and 'within' the diaspora is not only an expression of identity, but it is also a category of practice just as Liberian citizenship is regarded as both identity and practice. With the proliferation of the meanings of diasporas, three core elements remain widely agreed about the term: (1) dispersion; (2) homeland orientation; and (3) boundary maintenance (Armstrong, 1976: 394–397; Safran, 1991: 84). In other words, diasporas can be characterised as dispersed collectivities residing outside their countries of origin who 'maintain regular or occasional contacts with what they regard as their homeland and with individuals and groups of the same background residing in other host countries' thereby underscoring their distinctness and unity abroad (Sheffer, 2003: 10–11). Therefore, when I refer to Liberia's diasporas in this book, I mean Liberians born in Liberia (or born to Liberian parents) who live outside the territorial boundaries of the Liberian nation-state; claim Liberia as their homeland; and engage at different levels with the homeland while maintaining a definitive Liberian identity in their host countries regardless of their citizenship statuses. I further illustrate Liberia's diasporas as actors whose life-worlds have shaped how they conceive and practise Liberian citizenship transnationally, how they engage with the homeland state, and how they interact with other Liberians, both at home and abroad, in interface situations. Of particular concern is how particular diaspora agents employ their knowledgeability and capability to influence specific policy outcomes in Liberia, such as dual citizenship, while others engage transnationally in other development interventions. Diasporas, in this sense, are not homogeneous actors but rather heterogeneous in their motivations and aims and represent a multitude of lived experiences and socio-economic positions.

The growing body of literature that frames diasporas as categories of practice is diametrically opposed to essentialist notions of diasporas as fixed identities. For example, Brubaker (2005) counters Tololyan (1991, 1996), Sheffer (2003), and others for perceiving diasporas as being a singular entity, preceded by a definite article 'the', who function as unitary actors possessing quantifiable memberships without any consideration of whether or not individuals within the groups being counted actually self-identify as members of diasporas at all. Rather than thinking of diasporas as bounded identities, it is more useful to think of how they are instead 'used to make claims, to articulate projects, to formulate expectations, to mobilise energies, to appeal to loyalties' (Brubaker, 2005: 12). Those who formulate loyalties and identities can be from the population in question or may be speaking on behalf of the homeland state but not all those who are claimed as belonging to a diaspora take on a diasporic stance (Brubaker, 2005: 12). Indeed, it is sometimes only a minority of the population who consistently adopts a diasporic ethos thereby constituting diasporas themselves (Brubaker, 2005: 12). The delineation of a diasporic stance is particularly relevant for my analysis as I show how specific groups of Liberians in the United States, for instance, would emerge from the woodwork yearly to campaign for the extension of TPS or DED until a pathway to permanent residency was authorised in December 2019. Similarly, Liberian diasporas in West Africa have been at the forefront of periodically lobbying on behalf of refugees in Ghana, Sierra Leone, and Nigeria. Thus, my study compares myriad diasporic political stances in different spheres of influence.

With the publication of the 2012 book *Politics from Afar: Transnational Diasporas and Networks*, diasporas have been increasingly designated as categories of practice. Just as civil society, interest groups, and parties participate in politics in order to influence outcomes, so, too, do diasporas although they bring a diverse set of resources, claims, and agendas to political life thereby challenging how it should be organised (Lyons & Mandaville, 2012: 7). For instance, diaspora political and social mobilisations in host countries are often a function of why and how they left their homelands in the first place (Adamson, 2002). Drawing on various case studies, for example, Østergaard-Nielsen (2001: 10) illustrates that refugees who leave their nations of origin on a collective basis tend to take on a more political stance towards their homelands than economic migrants who leave through individualised means. Diasporas from conflict-affected regions such as Liberia often become politically charged in order to transform what they perceive to be repressive tactics in their countries of origin and attempt to transform home by campaigning in the host nation, raising international attention about their countries of origin, and, in some instances, funding insurgent groups to topple unfavourable regimes (Appadurai, 1995; Danforth, 1995; Adamson, 2002). This is certainly evidenced by Liberia in which diaspora organisations have ranged from politically explosive and fixated entirely on deposing a head of state – like the United States-based Association for Constitutional Democracy in Liberia (ACDL) – to apolitical and solely focused on homeland humanitarian relief and development – like the United Kingdom-based ULO-UK. Triangulation of diasporic practices is crucial to understanding their wide-ranging roles in the conflict-peace-development nexus, including constructive contributions to international advocacy and mobilisations against war, remittances, philanthropy, knowledge transfer, foreign direct investment, and transnational entrepreneurship.

Diasporas' different modes of engagement may endow them with power 'above' and beyond the homeland state thereby disproportionately privileging their social locations at the interface. For instance, Shain and Barth (2003: 451) argue that while diasporas are geographically 'outside the state' they remain 'inside the people' by virtue of their claims to the homeland and how they employ national identity markers to influence homeland foreign-policy decision-making. Moreover, diasporas can be seen to wield authority over the homeland because of their power in the hostland (Shain & Barth, 2003: 461). Shain and Barth (2003: 466) posit that if the 'balance of power' between diasporas and the homeland state favours the former, then diasporas will be more equipped to shape the homeland's foreign policy. I expand their theory to include a discussion of how Liberian diasporas have actively shaped domestic homeland development policy by bringing into focus dual citizenship legislation as one iteration of that influence. However flawed Shain's and Barth's theory appears – in it they only employ Armenia and Israel as case studies for hypothesis-testing – their framework is still relevant for my analysis of how diaspora actors have reconfigured Liberian citizenship across space and time thereby impacting contemporary claims for and against dual citizenship.

According to Shain and Barth (2003: 462–465), the factors which determine the effectiveness of diasporic influences on homeland foreign policies – or homeland domestic policy, as I argue in this book – include: (1) the scale of diasporic motivations; (2) the politico-socio-economic positioning of the homeland and hostland (i.e., if the homeland is 'weaker' than the hostland and open to diasporic input then the capacity of diasporas to influence homeland foreign policies is heightened); and (3) power relations between the homeland and its diasporas (i.e., if the homeland is in need of diasporic assistance – financial and otherwise – and diasporas agree on the homeland's foreign-policy agenda, then diasporas' ability to influence said agenda is improved). Since Liberia remains a post-war state at the mercy of external financial and human capital, I argue in this book that the 'balance of power' between Liberia's diasporas and the Liberian state in many ways favours the former. It is precisely because of this disparity that dual citizenship legislation was introduced in 2008.

Notwithstanding power differentials between Liberians abroad and the homeland state, it would be misleading to assume that diasporas are the panacea to origin country development. As indicated previously, diaspora engagement with the homeland can have overwhelmingly negative consequences, manifested in money laundering, drug trafficking, arms smuggling, scams, or terrorist activities (de Montclos, 2005). Kapur (2007), in what he terms 'the Janus-face of diasporas', cautions that ideologically extreme nationals abroad can negatively impact democratic consolidation at home and in host countries. In practising 'long distance nationalism', some diasporas can be more politically extreme than their origin country compatriots and at odds with the homeland political machinery which explains why some of them may be in exile in the first place (Anderson, 1992; Kapur, 2007: 97). Because they reside outside of the homeland, some diasporas may take a hard-line stance politically since they do not have to contend with the consequences of their ideological leanings. Furthermore, empirical evidence has shown that diasporas' policy inputs and development interventions may pose critical challenges, especially in post-war settings. Given Liberia's migratory history and its struggles to reconcile political and socio-economic inequities that fomented armed conflicts, evaluating how historical and contemporary factors have influenced the introduction and postponement in the passage of dual citizenship legislation requires evaluating the multiple roles diasporas have played in fuelling conflict, facilitating peace, fast-tracking development, none, or all. This is particularly central to contestations around granting citizenship to non-resident Liberian transnationals who are perceived as representing an already-privileged category of practice. In subsequent chapters of this book, I provide in-depth analysis of how interface encounters between returnees and homeland Liberians, amongst other actors, have created polarised discourses on resident and non-resident forms of Liberian citizenship.

Besides examining interfaces between disparate individuals and institutions, actor-oriented analysis also acknowledges the researcher as an actor with his or her own life-world, social location, and agency. While some theories may obscure the role of the researcher, relegating him or her to a mere observer, chronicler, and interpreter of political, economic, and social phenomena, actor-oriented analysis views the researcher as part and parcel of these processes. This is particularly relevant for me, a Liberian researching the political economy of belonging to Liberia.

Section III: Navigating between 'Insider' and 'Outsider' Access

At the age of eighteen in 2000, I watched my mother raise her right hand and pledge allegiance to the so-called 'leader of the free world'. In the small room in downtown Washington with official-looking, mahogany furniture, I felt a sinking regret in the pit of my gut. Yet, all around me there was pomp and pageantry during the naturalisation proceedings. A six-foot US flag billowed in the background. As keynote speaker, the president of Howard University (where I was then a freshman undergraduate) regaled the newly minted citizens with clichés about what a wonderful place America was. However, my mother naturalised on that eventful day not because of some deep, abiding love for America, but because she needed US citizenship to regularise my status. Her revocation of legal Liberian citizenship represented, for me, the pinnacle of parental sacrifice.

Born in Monrovia, I immigrated to the United States in 1988 on a visitor visa, overstayed, and lived in undocumented limbo from the age of six until I was twenty. Those fourteen years of legal invisibility fundamentally shaped my consciousness as a Liberian citizen (Pailey, 2017c). I have come to define citizenship generally and Liberian citizenship specifically as a political construct, as much about 'doing' as it is about 'being'. I grew up in Washington, studied in Ghana, South Africa, Egypt, the United States, and the United Kingdom; nevertheless, I have maintained a metaphysical connection to Liberia that some would argue defies logic. I taught primary school English grammar at the Buduburam Refugee Camp when I was a twenty-year-old study abroad student at the University of Ghana. My undergraduate honours thesis, master's dissertation, and PhD thesis all focused on Liberia, catapulting me back to the country in 2002, 2006, and 2012–2013, respectively, for field research. I joined the Liberian Studies Association (LSA), learned how to cook Liberian cuisine, and perfected the lilting Liberian English that rolls off the tongue like an unstoppable locomotive. I developed a wanderlust that facilitated an extended four-year return to Monrovia beginning in 2007, at age twenty-five, to work with then President Sirleaf. In my personal and professional endeavours, I have encountered Liberians of varying backgrounds, perspectives, and ideologies, which enabled access to over 200 respondents for this book. As an academic, activist, and author, I represent a composite of the categories of Liberians I interviewed making me simultaneously an 'insider looking out' and 'outsider looking in' (Collins, 1985).

I spoke to Liberians with different citizenship statuses, some of whom, like me, have remained fiercely engaged with the country in both tangible and intangible ways. Although I spent the majority of my childhood and adolescence in the United States and large portions of my professional career in the United Kingdom, I opted for non-citizen residency abroad rather than naturalisation because I did not want to relinquish my legal Liberian citizenship. Nonetheless, I am acutely aware that my mother's compulsion to naturalise empowered my refusal to do so. I also recognise that Liberians like my mother naturalise for a variety of reasons whether prompted by force or choice. This book is primarily informed by my desire to interrogate why people opt for or out of certain citizenship statuses and what policies and practices support or invalidate those decisions – from an empirical point of reference.

Though a self-professed transnational and scholar of development, I have maintained a decidedly critical stance on non-resident forms of citizenship and mainstream notions of socio-economic change. This is precisely because Liberia has had a complicated relationship with its nationals abroad, with neoliberal development deployed historically and contemporarily to silence and suppress subaltern actors. While I do not claim to be neutral or objective, I have mitigated biases in writing this book by constantly validating positions and experiences that are different from mine, in and outside of field settings. In generously showcasing vignettes and verbatim quotes from interviews, I underscore how respondents conceive of themselves as Liberian political subjects, how they understand and experience development, and how they engage with each other and with post-war governments.

Conclusion

As revealed by the seamstress and businessman profiled in the introduction of this chapter, the demographic composition of interviewees within and across my selected field sites is all-encompassing. Because this book is principally concerned with how qualitative factors such as conflict, migration, and post-war recovery have influenced claims for and against dual citizenship in Liberia, I demonstrated why it was essential to converse with actors inhabiting different locales. Although my decision to seek out Liberians in capital cities could be considered a form of urban bias, or a blind spot, I pre-empted this critique by highlighting academic literature that frames cities as the most appropriate sites to measure contestations around citizenship and belonging. Nevertheless, I acknowledge that rural dwellers may have very different interpretations of Liberia's political economy of belonging and their role in the system, as would Liberians abroad who maintain very loose ties or no ties at all to Liberia although analysis in the book is concerned with the perspectives of transnational actors.

While Long's actor-oriented analysis examines the disparate ways in which actors respond to development interventions within rural settings in the so-called developing world, I demonstrate that the form of intervention relevant for my study on Liberia is a contested policy prescription, dual citizenship, with presumed development outcomes. As one of many actors captured in this chapter, Liberian diasporas disclose through their identities, practices, and relationships that citizenship can be simultaneously passive, active, and interactive. They also both challenge and substantiate certain theoretical approaches including conceptualisations of diasporic influences on homeland foreign policy and, by my extension, homeland domestic policy.

Reflecting on my positionality as a researcher who has occupied multiple spaces and places, I evaluated my own biases as a child of Liberian soil who made a conscious choice not to naturalise in the United States or the United Kingdom and how this decision influences my analysis of Liberia's political economy of belonging. The next chapter inspects contemporary Liberian citizenship construction and practice as a baseline for extensive analysis later in the book about why claims for and against dual citizenship have persisted in Liberia, in Africa writ large, and across transnational spaces.

2 | *The Political Economy of Belonging to Liberia*[*]

Introduction

As a twenty-first-century post-war, emigrant-sending African country, Liberia reflects global citizenship norms while simultaneously departing from them, and this unique positioning offers new opportunities to theorise citizenship across spatial and temporal landscapes. It is a country where one's citizenship could be called into question by a 1973 Aliens and Nationality Law that had, as of mid-December 2019, yet to respond to constantly shifting social processes as illustrated in the vignettes here:

Thirty-five-year-old Beyan[1] was born in Nairobi, Kenya, to two Liberian citizen parents, grew up in the United States and Gambia and returned to Liberia to work in 2005. He was eligible for *jus soli* Kenyan citizenship and US naturalisation but held fast to his Liberian passport for fear that his *jus sanguinis* Liberian citizenship might be revoked.

Forty-nine-year-old Teta[2] was born in Rivercess, Liberia, to a Liberian mother and a Lebanese father. Having immigrated to the United Kingdom at the age of twelve and naturalised in the mid-1990s, she was asked by the Liberian Ministry of Foreign Affairs to swear an oath of allegiance to Liberia and formalise her legal status when she returned to the country in 2008 to renew her passport. She suspected that her UK-born children, both of whose parents are *jus soli* Liberians, would never be able to obtain their *jus sanguinis* entitlements given the heightened controversies around claiming citizenship from afar.

---

[*] This chapter is derived in part from Pailey (2016).
[1] Pseudonym used to protect the identity of a permanent returnee respondent [PR7] interviewed in Monrovia on 25 June 2013.
[2] Pseudonym used to protect the identity of a diaspora respondent [DL6] interviewed in London on 12 June 2012.

Fifty-five-year-old Aisha[3] was born in Liberia to a Mandingo father of Guinean ancestry. She married an Indian national and entrepreneur in Monrovia who was ineligible for legal Liberian citizenship because of his race and together they had children who were entitled to Liberian citizenship by birth but whose citizenship was often questioned because of their non-'Negro' father.

Thirty-eight-year-old James[4] was born in Freetown to a Sierra Leonean father and Liberian mother but spent most of his life in Liberia. He was able to acquire a Liberian passport while growing up although his mother could not legally pass on citizenship to him. When James returned to Freetown in 2006 he was asked by the Sierra Leonean government to naturalise in the country of his birth because his accent and way of life were considered 'too Liberian'.

Throughout this chapter, I use the unique backstories of respondents interviewed for this book, like the ones previously profiled, to begin to identify the twenty-first-century features of Liberia's political economy of belonging. In it, I examine how actors across the five urban sites in my study conceive of citizenship, how their contemporary constructions of Liberian citizenship deviate or cohere according to their lived experiences and socio-economic positions, and how they practise citizenship in the everyday. The chapter provides empirical grounding for my conceptualisation of Liberian citizenship as identity (passive), practice (active), and a set of relations (interactive), simultaneously, as well as the foundation for explaining in subsequent chapters the impasse on dual citizenship. Citizenship, in my analysis, is not only a bundle of rights and privileges embedded in constructions of legal, national, and cultural identity, but it is also a set of practices and interactions embodied in the life-worlds and social locations of actors in Liberia and across transnational spaces.

Birthplace, Bloodline, Blackness, and Beyond

The introduction and suspension in passage of Liberia's 2008 dual citizenship bill was a manifestation of the ways in which Liberian citizenship is constantly being negotiated and redefined. During an

---

[3] Pseudonym used to protect the identity of a diaspora respondent [DL9] interviewed in London on 13 June 2012.

[4] Pseudonym used to protect the identity of a diaspora respondent [DL63] interviewed in Freetown on 11 April 2013.

interview with me in Monrovia on 19 June 2013, then Minister of Justice Christiana Tah reflected on the reconfigurations of Liberian citizenship across space and time as a consequence of crisis thus echoing Joppke (1999: 632) who defines citizenship as 'shared understandings and practices':

The definition [of Liberian citizenship] has taken on new meanings. And because we went through this period of transformation during the war, it took on another meaning, too. ... It goes to the extent that it incorporates experiences. Shared experiences. And this is an informal definition, and it's a definition that just emerged from the war.

While Liberian citizenship may have been construed as passive and constructed from 'above' before armed conflict, newer meanings of citizenship have emerged to include more active forms of citizenship from 'below', bringing about the reconfiguration to which Tah alluded. Therefore, the conception of Liberian citizenship amongst 202 Liberian actors in London, Washington, Freetown, Accra, and Monrovia sits on a continuum between passivity and activity, identity and practice. The list in Table 2.1 illustrates recurring responses to an open-ended question posed to all respondents about how they define a Liberian citizen.

Although the markers of a Liberian citizen in the table are not ranked, the most prevalent responses were: (1) born in Liberia; (2) has a Liberian mother or father; (3) naturalises in Liberia; (4) has heart, love, or affinity for Liberia; and (5) contributes to Liberia's development. The first five categories in Table 2.1 are passive thereby constituting identity, whereas the last four are active thereby constituting practice. As one Monrovia-based circular returnee man informed me, being a Liberian citizen is 'a decision and also an act'.[5] For instance, one who naturalises in Liberia expresses more active citizenship than someone merely born or raised in the country. The very act of naturalisation is agentic and involves making a conscious and deliberate choice to become a Liberian citizen. These sentiments echo Afrobarometer (2012) data in which 54 per cent of Liberians surveyed in-country strongly agreed that 'a person who came from another country, but who has lived and worked in Liberia for many years, and wishes to make Liberia his/her home' should be entitled to citizenship.

---

[5] [CR7] Interview in Monrovia on 18 June 2013.

Table 2.1 *Top ten conceptions of what constitutes a Liberian citizen*

Markers of a Liberian citizen	Cities where responses most frequent
Born in Liberia (*jus soli*)	All
Has Liberian mother or father (*jus sanguinis*)	All
Identifies as Liberian, feels and behaves Liberian culturally (speaks Liberian language or Liberian English; dresses in Liberian clothing; eats Liberian food)	All
Considers Liberia 'home'	London, Washington, Freetown, Monrovia
Raised in Liberia	London, Freetown, Monrovia
Has 'heart', love, or affinity for Liberia (and Liberians)	London, Washington, Accra, Monrovia
Has lived in Liberia extensively and/or currently resides fulltime in Liberia	All
Naturalises in Liberia	All
Shows allegiance, loyalty, and patriotism to Liberia (and Liberians)	London, Freetown, Monrovia
Contributes to Liberia's development (involved in capacity building and nation-building; abides by the laws of Liberia and its Constitution; pays taxes; invests in real estate and businesses; supports democratic governance and peace; engages in political processes)	All

As the sixth item listed, 'having heart' for Liberia (and Liberians) straddles both the passive and active ends of the citizenship spectrum since feeling deeply committed to a nation and its people may compel one to act on behalf of that geographic territory and its citizens. The multiple meanings of Liberian citizenship can thus be visualised as a continuum coupling passivity with identity and activity with practice. Whereas some respondents listed a single identity-based or practice-based criterion, such as 'born in Liberia' or 'contributes to Liberia's development', respectively, others listed multiple criteria from each end of the continuum. As illustrated in the table, Monrovia-based actors interviewed for this book were most emphatic with a composite list of markers that surpasses those of respondents in the four diasporic urban sites.

On the 'passive' side of the continuum, variants of the 'by birth' (*jus soli*) or 'by blood' (*jus sanguinis*) principles of citizenship were invoked most often by respondents in the five urban interview sites. 'Birthplace' and 'bloodline' occupy the passive end of the spectrum because they generally require minimal to no effort and are constituted by the conferral of automatic legal rights and privileges. When queried about who a Liberian citizen is, the majority of respondents conceptualised citizenship initially as a form of legal identity as then enshrined in the 1973 Aliens and Nationality Law and 1986 Constitution. Yet, it is clear based on Liberia's cultural and social milieu that all those born in the country regardless of their entitlements as 'Negroes' are not considered equal, just as Yuval-Davis (2000) and O'Connell Davidson (2013) argue – thus invoking Crenshaw's (1989) notion of intersectionality – that citizenship is largely differentiated by race, gender, class, and ethnicity.

This is particularly stark for Liberians of the Mandingo ethnic group whose ancestors migrated from the Mali empire in the fourteenth and fifteenth centuries, establishing trade routes in enslaved Africans, gold, and kola nuts connecting the hinterland to the Atlantic coast (Konneh, 1996a: 9, 56, 63; Konneh, 1996b: 142–143). Because of their constantly shifting trade and migratory patterns, faith in Islam, as well as cultural ties to several different West African countries, Mandingos have often been characterised as 'strangers' and therefore non-Liberian citizens (Konneh, 1996a: 15, 25; Konneh, 1996b: 142, 144, 150). Their participation in Liberian economic and political life is further begrudged and contested because they tend to dominate the public transport, retail, and consumable goods sectors of the economy in the same way that belonging and citizenship legitimacy pose a challenge for the Fulani and Hausa of Nigeria, the Serahule of the Gambia, the Bamileke of Cameroon, and the Luba of the Democratic Republic of the Congo (Konneh, 1996a: 135; Konneh, 1996b: 144, 151; Easterly, 2006: 83). Konneh's assertion (1996b: 141) that Mandingos have always 'stood at the margins' of shifting conceptualisations of Liberian citizenship was echoed by a number of informants. Previously mentioned in the introduction of this chapter and resident in London for fourteen years, fifty-five-year-old Aisha emphasised the importance of maintaining the *jus soli* principle of citizenship particularly for Liberian-born Mandingos because of her paternal connections to Guinea:

I think [a] Liberian citizen is, I would say, those of us who grew up over there [in Liberia]. Because we have had that problem, we as Mandingos in Liberia. People always say, 'You Mandingo, you foreigner'. But we say, 'We were born here [in Liberia]. We got just as much rights as, you know, as you people!' . . . Someone who was born in Liberia, I will consider them a citizen.[6]

'Negroes' phenotypically, Mandingos pass the race-based requirement for legal Liberian citizenship yet they are a stark example of how birthplace benefits, as enshrined in the then 1973 Aliens and Nationality Law and 1986 Constitution, remained contested at the time of my interviews.

Roots, blood coursing through one's veins, and psychological attachments embody the existential entitlements of those who identify as Liberian citizens by ancestry but who were not born in the country. For instance, a fifty-nine-year-old Washington-based respondent who had lived in the United States for thirty-one consecutive years quipped about how her American-born daughter, who had never touched Liberian soil, understands the cultural logics of Liberian dress better than she does:

[My second-generation daughter] thinks she's a Liberian. You see that girl tie her lappa like one Kru woman and set that thing on her head. I was sitting here one time, the girl, when she was going to do her laundry, and she took the laundry basket and put it on her head . . . she just sat it on her head, it's just like it was something that was just *in* her.[7]

The idea that one's Liberianness can be inherited through biological and cultural transmission, regardless of birthplace, was repeated heartily by other respondents. A sixty-five-year-old permanent returnee in Monrovia insisted that no one could negate the Liberianness of her American-born son who had spent his childhood and adolescence in Liberia but relocated to the United States in adulthood out of 'convenience':

He grew up here [in Liberia], he knows the streets, he knows all the corners, he knows the culture. But even in America, he's Liberian. He doesn't go eat

---

[6] [DL9] Interview in London on 13 June 2012.
[7] [DL56] Interview in Washington on 26 October 2012.

hamburger or McDonald's. He goes to the Puerto Rican, and Indian, and Chinese shops to look for palm butter. ... And his children, he's got two children by a white girl, they wake their father up in the morning and they say they want rice and cassava leaves. ... they've never been here [in Liberia] but they eat cassava leaves, palm butter, potato greens. Everything. They know everything about, you know, as much as they can about Liberia ... their blood comes from here [Liberia].[8]

Though the relevance of bloodline ties cannot be negated, some respondents argued that cultural links alone should not dictate an automatic entitlement to Liberian citizenship as a legal status with attendant rights and privileges. For instance, forty-nine-year-old Teta, mentioned previously and resident in the United Kingdom for thirty-seven years, reasoned that her UK-born children would have to earn the right to be considered Liberian citizens:

I wouldn't consider them [my children born in the United Kingdom] to be Liberian citizens ... if they don't live in the country [Liberia] and they have never lived in the country I don't think it [Liberian citizenship] should be their automatic right because their parents are Liberians.[9]

Teta echoed the sentiments of many interviewees in Monrovia who ardently supported the then provision within Liberia's Aliens and Nationality Law that someone of Liberian parentage born abroad would have to declare at the age of majority whether they wanted to maintain legal Liberian citizenship or the citizenship of the country of their birth.

Although there was contention about who should qualify for *jus soli* Liberian citizenship and whether or not a statute of limitation should be placed on *jus sanguinis* citizenship, most respondents debunked the notion that citizenship should be traced only patrilineally and this was largely based on post-war reconfigurations of gender norms in Liberia rather than on transnational forms of engagement or assimilation in the so-called Global North. This position was particularly salient for respondents who were born abroad to Liberian citizen mothers and non-Liberian citizen fathers. As a case in point, one forty-three-year-old female who had been a resident in London for twenty-two consecutive years was born in the United Kingdom to a Liberian citizen mother.

[8] [PR6] Interview in Monrovia on 24 June 2013.
[9] [DL6] Interview in London on 12 June 2012.

Although this respondent had lived in Liberia for half her life, having moved there before her first birthday, she complained about constantly having to defend her right to be called Liberian:

I say it's difficult because sometimes when I say to people, 'Well, my father was a naturalised Liberian and I was born in the UK [United Kingdom] and, you know, my maternal grandmother was actually Jamaican', they're like, 'You're not Liberian!', and I'm like, 'What gives you the right to say that, you know? Because I feel I am!' You know, I think I would define a Liberian citizen as someone who has some sort of ties, whether it's mother or father, to that country [Liberia] ... a true Liberian is someone who identifies with that country and who accepts that they've got roots there.[10]

Since President Tubman's Unification and Integration Policy, which generally incorporated as citizens people of 'Negro descent' resident in Liberia, the notion that Liberian women should be relegated to the private sphere alone, without the associated rights and privileges of citizenship, has been contested. As a case in point, the majority of respondents critiqued as overtly sexist and discriminatory Liberia's then legal provision still barring a Liberian citizen woman from passing on citizenship to her children born abroad.

Liberian Citizenship, Race, and the 'Negro Clause'

While there was consensus amongst respondents about the need to enfranchise Liberian citizen women fully, those who voluntarily interrogated the 'Negro clause' were more ideologically divided. Their assessments were based less on acknowledgement of pluralistic international conventions and more on lived experiences of non-black immigration to Liberia. For instance, Monrovia-based respondents, particularly homelanders and the 2008 dual citizenship bill sponsors alike, were more emphatic about maintaining the race-based proviso because of perceived contemporary socio-economic inequities between Lebanese, Indian, and Chinese merchants and resident Liberians, while their counterparts abroad were either ambivalent or more inclined to reject the 'Negro clause'. Contrary to President Weah's (2018) inaugural pronouncements on 29 January 2018 that the clause was unnecessarily 'racist', my findings illustrating popular domestic support have

[10] [DL15] Interview in London on 15 June 2012.

been further corroborated by Afrobarometer (2018) data in which two thirds of Liberians surveyed said the clause should be maintained and only citizens, and by extension blacks, should be entitled to own land.

Wide-ranging dissent about the 'Negro clause' is a function of historical and contemporary Asian and Middle Eastern immigration to Liberia. While Indian and Chinese migration is relatively recent – with no known empirical studies documenting this trend that I am aware of – Arab migration started in the early twentieth century and is therefore embedded in modern Liberian economic history (Dunn, Beyan & Burrowes, 2001: 203). As is the case in other locales in West Africa – and akin to South Asians in East and southern Africa – Lebanese merchants in Liberia, for instance, have historically dominated the retail industry as owners of consumable goods, building materials, and cement commercial chains dotted across the country (Dunn, Beyan & Burrowes, 2001: 203). As the most prevalent Arab immigrants in Liberia, Lebanese nationals could not obtain citizenship at the time of my interviews and until I finalised this book in late 2019 because they were not considered to be of 'Negro descent'. A thirty-year-old male homelander argued that the Lebanese, who have collectively resided in Liberia longer than Indian or Chinese immigrants, are culturally differentiated by their own choice and therefore should not be considered Liberian citizens:

Lebanese can never be Liberian by heart. . . . In a sense that the Lebanese, they have customs and traditions . . . I don't care, the Lebanese can live here [in Liberia], they can be born here but their roots can never be forgotten.[11]

Arguments for maintaining the 'Negro clause' were also often framed as an economic zero-sum game with Liberians inevitably losing in the event of its abolishment, as demonstrated by this fifty-three-year-old male homeland entrepreneur:

I believe Liberians are a very long way from gaining control of their economy which I believe is fundamental to our stability and peace. And until deliberate efforts are made – by not just this [Sirleaf's] government, any government for that matter – to see Liberians take control, meaningful control, of the

---

[11] [HL17] Interview in Monrovia on 12 June 2013.

economy I think it would be premature to have foreigners become citizens of Liberia, foreigners meaning people of non-'Negro' descent.[12]

Deeply embedded in Liberia's historical DNA, the 'Negro clause' was instituted at a time when repatriated blacks had fled economic servitude in the United States and Caribbean vowing to create a haven where they would be the sole owners of capital, land, and the means of production. For many Liberians, particularly those running private businesses like the aforementioned respondent, the time I conducted interviews in 2012–2013 was not ripe for removing the clause because people of black African descent did not own and control the economy.

Taking an opposing view, a Monrovia-based circular returnee man argued that some individuals of non-'Negro' descent, such as Lebanese nationals, are already politically and socially embedded in Liberia, contribute to development through their commercial activities, and should therefore be entitled to citizenship:

I'd consider them [the Lebanese] to be Liberians because I think they fulfil the conditions [of citizenship] – living here, being part of the culture. They're part of the political discourse because they influence the political decisions that are made ... because of their economic power. In my definition they are Liberians because any businesses they own pay taxes in Liberia.[13]

However compelling the argument appears to fully incorporate non-blacks as citizens by abrogating the 'Negro clause', staunch support for maintaining it persists even in transnational circles, as articulated by this thirty-one-year-old male resident of London:

If we move this ['Negro'] clause, they [non-blacks] will buy up every lick of the private sector. There's a whole bunch of landowners in Monrovia who will be eager to sell because they will see six zeros and their eyeballs will start turning and Liberia won't be Liberian anymore. It won't. That's why I'm in favour of it [the 'Negro clause'], and if that makes me a bigot or a pseudo racist or prejudice then, yeah, I am. This [Liberia] is my damn country and I got more right to it than you![14]

This respondent's visceral views are particularly curious because he admitted to being engaged to a South Asian woman in the United Kingdom, who, by virtue of her race, would not have been entitled to

---

[12] [HL18] Interview in Monrovia on 12 June 2013.
[13] [CR7] Interview in Monrovia on 18 June 2013.
[14] [DL29] Interview in London on 22 June 2012.

Liberian citizenship or to owning land in Liberia at the time of our interview in 2012. Yet, his ostensibly dogmatic outlook was supported by then Governance Commission (GC) chairman, Amos Sawyer, who had previously served as head of Liberia's constitutional review committee in the early to mid-1980s. He disclosed to me that his committee maintained the 'Negro clause' because of fears expressed by Liberians of all persuasions, including a traditional chief who said 'all the white people will take our land' if the clause were abolished.[15] While informants who supported the clause espoused an identity-based framework of citizenship, arguing that non-blacks are too culturally and racially differentiated as well as economically empowered to legitimately demand Liberian citizenship, those who opposed it adopted a practice-based framework of citizenship, arguing that non-blacks who actively participate in the economic life of the nation should be automatically entitled to the political entitlements derived from citizenship.

Liberian Citizenship as 'Having Heart'

Clearly entangled with Liberian citizenship, blackness was vigorously debated by respondents. Like the first five identity-based markers of citizenship listed in the table at the beginning of the chapter – which are passive and, therefore, foregrounded by rights and privileges – it stands in sharp contrast to the last four which constitute practices that remain active in orientation and, therefore, demand the fulfilment of duties and responsibilities. Connecting passivity with activity, the middle of the Liberian citizenship continuum includes those who have the 'heart' for Liberia, as a thirty-one-year-old London-based female respondent asserted:

[Y]ou do find people who are born in Liberia who don't have as much passion for Liberia compared to foreigners. I would say people who weren't born in Liberia but they found out about Liberia and they met Liberians and they've gone to the extent of investigating about Liberia and they've built that passion and do stuff for Liberia more than they do for themselves or their own country … if you've got the heart for Liberia you are a Liberian as well as those who are born there [in Liberia] …[16]

---

[15] Interview in Monrovia on 25 June 2013.
[16] [DL3] Interview in London on 9 June 2012.

The word 'heart' appeared as a recurring verbal motif in utterances from London to Washington, from Freetown to Accra, and within Monrovia, bringing us closer to what Barry (2006) and others call 'active citizenship' or citizenship as a 'public vocation' in which 'the (true) citizen plays a full and active part in the affairs of the community' (Dagger, 2000: 27). For instance, a thirty-year-old male homelander resident in Liberia all his life conceived of a Liberian 'by heart' as someone who prioritises Liberia's advancement above all other nations regardless of one's citizenship or residence status:

[I]f I have Liberia at heart and I know that, yes, indeed, I am from Liberia, my root is from Liberia, all other development, all other improvement to make sure that Liberia improves, to make sure that Liberia be part of those nations that are up there, those expertise, those knowledge that I have, I should come and invest it in Liberia. That means I have Liberia at heart. Whatsoever I will do I will always take Liberia first no matter where I am.[17]

This respondent echoed van Steenbergen (1994: 2) who defines the ideal citizen as 'active in public life and fundamentally willing to submit his [or her] private interests to the general interest of society'. Also employing the 'heart' trope was a fifty-nine-year-old woman resident in Accra on and off for fifteen years who argued that 'for a person to be a Liberian, the person must have Liberia at heart. I mean, the person should be thinking development, thinking nation-building, human capacity'.[18] This woman's 'heart' was tangibly exhibited in her humanitarian health work as she had organised the airlifting of dozens of poor, chronically ill Liberian children to different parts of the world for treatments and surgeries otherwise unavailable to them in the homeland. Similarly, a thirty-six-year-old female homelander equated 'heart' with jingoism and nationalist fervour, another common thread throughout my interviews: 'A Liberian [citizen] has a sense of patriotism, belonging to Liberia, and makes an effort to love his/her country thereby doing things that make Liberia progress or develop'.[19] Indeed, the articulation of Liberian citizenship as 'having heart' is analogous to a feeling that induces action. 'Having heart' also transcends legal status thus eliminating birthplace, bloodline, and blackness as defining markers of Liberianness.

[17] [HL17] Interview in Monrovia on 12 June 2013.
[18] [DL83] Interview in Accra on 7 May 2013.
[19] [HL7] Interview in Monrovia on 6 June 2013.

Liberian Citizenship as 'Contribution'

According to many respondents in the five urban sites, one who actively contributes to Liberia's development through political, economic, and social practice – that is, voting in national elections, paying taxes, investing in real estate or local enterprise, sending remittances, developing Liberian capacities – demonstrates more active citizenship than one who merely identifies as Liberian or considers Liberia 'home'. A significant number of respondents conceived of Liberian citizenship as a form of practice, bringing us to the extreme end of the continuum which is defined as 'contribution'. Most importantly, making a 'contribution' is a concrete demonstration of one's active participation in Liberia's political economy of belonging. For instance, respondents reasoned that a 'Liberian is somebody who lives Liberia, not somebody who talks about Liberia',[20] or someone who is 'prepared to give to Liberia, to serve Liberia, to be Liberia'.[21] On the extreme end of the 'contribution' spectrum is the notion that a Liberian citizen is 'one who is prepared to go to war for Liberia ... prepared to take a bullet for Liberia'.[22] More practically, however, some informants argued that personal and substantial investments in Liberia define a Liberian citizen. Exemplifying this, a thirty-four-year-old male resident in Accra for twelve years used rhetorical language to describe how 'contribution' could manifest in concrete action:

People must know that that country [Liberia] is the only thing we have, and must be willing to contribute. That is how I define a typical Liberian [citizen], contributing in any way possible to the society ... Do you have family there [in Liberia], are you helping the family there? Do you have a home there? Can people really appreciate who you are? These are contributions.[23]

Most respondents who coupled 'citizenship' with 'contribution' argued that those contributions, however varied, should profoundly impact Liberia and the lives of Liberians, wherever they happen to reside – essentially, Liberian citizenship as a set of relations. One thirty-eight-year-old homeland woman even insisted that contributions should be unconditional, refuting claims by some diaspora respondents that their

[20] [CR7] Interview in Monrovia on 18 June 2013.
[21] [PR1] Interview in Monrovia on 7 June 2013.
[22] [PR3] Interview in Monrovia on 11 June 2013.
[23] [DL105] Interview in Accra on 20 May 2013.

continued engagement with Liberia would be contingent upon the passage of dual citizenship legislation: 'You can't come and say, "Before I participate as a Liberian, the government should give me better housing; I need to be employed to get this"'.[24] Similarly, a forty-three-year-old male homeland development specialist stipulated that unconditional commitment to Liberia should be a criterion for citizenship:

I think anyone who has a vested interest and commitment to seeing this country [Liberia] grow, whether it's economically, whether it's politically, whether it's culturally, whether it's socially, but demonstrates a high level of patriotism, you know, the love for a land, the love for a fellow compatriot . . . Anyone who is coming and saying, 'Look, I don't care whether I am offered a job in the government or a public agency, I just want to invest. I want the opportunity to contribute [should be a citizen]'.[25]

Others were more emphatic about citizenship as 'contribution' to the political economy of belonging. For example, a forty-eight-year-old male homelander maintained that Liberian citizenship depends on not only residence in Liberia but also paying taxes regularly to the Liberian state:

You have to be here, you have to pay tax. . . . That binds you to the state-citizen responsibility, it's a part of the social contract. . . . If you are a resident you should have a vested interest. . . . It could be in terms of your investment in businesses. Investment in just . . . property. Even investment in how you stay engaged with the country in terms of even the political processes because all of those things add to who you are as a citizen. . . . It's about you, in your own way, contributing whatever it is to the growth and development of the country. . . . This is a community, so if you live in a community there are roles and responsibilities, there are duties binding upon you to ensure that that community lives and fulfils its mandate.[26]

By arguing that citizenship involves duties and responsibilities such as paying taxes, this respondent implicitly described citizenship as practices involving concrete contributions to state functionality. His views are corroborated by Afrobarometer (2012, 2015) data in which 70 per cent and 51 per cent of Liberians surveyed in 2012 and 2015, respectively, strongly agreed that 'citizens must pay taxes to

---

[24] [HL24] Interview in Monrovia on 17 June 2013.
[25] [HL3] Interview in Monrovia on 5 June 2013.
[26] [HL45] Interview in Monrovia on 24 June 2013.

government in order for the country to develop'. Although the respondent said only residence would facilitate meaningful participation in Liberia's political economy of belonging, he conceded that residence could be sporadic and circular. Moreover, physical residence as a requirement for citizenship was not only advanced by homeland Liberians. An experienced media consultant who had been shuttling between the United States and Liberia since 2006, one circular returnee asserted that 'what makes you a citizen of the country is to live and make [a] decision to be there [in Liberia], to be part of that culture. ... Because you can't be in the US [United States] and say "I'm Liberian", not wanting to come home. ... So, you have to come home and be Liberian'.[27] I suspect that this respondent's resolve to return to Liberia was primarily informed by his conception of what signifies a 'true Liberian citizen' – one who resides within the territorial confines of the nation-state, even if occasionally, and influences its development outcomes.

Nevertheless, the view that Liberian citizenship is based on domestic residence and includes both rights and responsibilities represents a position not shared by all actors interviewed for this book. For instance, a fifty-six-year-old man in Washington spurned the Liberian-citizen-as-Liberian-resident trope, instead arguing that a Liberian is 'anyone who dedicates his or her cause of life and everything to the Liberian cause ... you cannot say because that person is not in the country, he is not a Liberian or she is not a Liberian'.[28] Some respondents, particularly those abroad, stressed their legal entitlements to Liberian citizenship first, such as owning land, while only belatedly discussing obligations, such as paying property taxes, if at all. This skewed view of the political economy of belonging has been challenged by literature that critiques dual citizenship as only about claiming privileges and protections rather than also about fulfilling duties and obligations (FitzGerald, 2006; FitzGerald, 2012: 285–286; Spiro, 2012: 311, 318). Accordingly, one fifty-eight-year-old male respondent in Accra interrogated the tendency of Liberians to omit the 'responsibility' side of the citizenship equation altogether:

Let's ask ourselves, do we have citizenship only by name? Or you have citizenship based upon your responsibility and duty? If we say we are

[27] [CR7] Interview in Monrovia on 18 June 2013.
[28] [DL52] Interview in Washington on 25 October 2012.

a Liberian, what are we doing for Liberia as a Liberian? ... We cry [for] citizenship, we cry for rights. ... What right do you get without duty and responsibility?[29]

Although most respondents in the five urban sites affirmed that a Liberian citizen is someone who actively effects positive politico-socio-economic change in the homeland, interviewees in Freetown, Accra, and Monrovia were more explicitly wedded to this criterion. This could be attributed to the fact that domestic citizens and 'near' diasporas, particularly those residing in countries in the so-called Global South such as Sierra Leone and Ghana, are closer in proximity to development challenges and, therefore, understand more intuitively the imperatives of active citizenship embodying duties *and* obligations. This trend is particularly apparent in debates about whether or not citizenship should be based on residence. While most diasporic respondents dismissed residence in Liberia as a marker of citizenship, many homelanders, for instance, insisted that living in Liberia fulltime would be the only means of participating organically in the political, economic, and social life of the nation. Contrary to these assertions, however, I have observed that because of their elevated social locations some Liberian transnationals far surpass domestic counterparts in impacting homeland development, so residence in Liberia is not always an accurate yardstick of one's meaningful engagement in the political economy of belonging.

Just as the residence requirement appears to be a contested space of inquiry, so, too, is the citizenship as 'contribution' trope, proving that where Liberian citizenship is concerned dissent is the only constant. Some respondents claimed that Liberian citizenship is solely about legal, cultural, and national identity, and, by extension, rights and privileges, such as then Foreign Affairs Minister Augustine Ngafuan, who said, 'whether you contribute or not if you're a Liberian [citizen], you are Liberian. No one can take that citizenship from you. It's part of a reality that you refuse to contribute ... you are [still] a Liberian'.[30] However, C William Allen, then ambassador-designate to France, countered his colleague's assertion by providing the most comprehensive articulation of the Liberian citizenship continuum and, by extension, the political economy of belonging to Liberia:

---

[29] [DL101] Interview in Accra on 19 May 2013.
[30] Interview in Monrovia on 11 June 2013.

Well, I think being a Liberian comes from what I call the Liberianness of a person. And, it's something like character. It's something that is on the inside of you. What do you feel in your soul? What do you feel in your inner self? Do you feel Liberian? And I think when you come to grips with that then the outward expression of your Liberianness is what makes you a Liberian [citizen]. Do you feel patriotic? Do you love your country? Do you honestly want to contribute towards its reform and its reconciliation and its development? Do you remain psychologically engaged with Liberia? If some other country were to attack Liberia tomorrow … would you be willing to give your time, treasure, and talent to the defence of Liberia? Ok, now, time, we all cannot serve in the military but could you provide advice? Treasure, meaning would you be willing to contribute to the national effort, resources, money, to help that effort? I think these are the real things that make you a Liberian [citizen]. It's not what colour of passport you wave around.[31]

Allen's understanding of Liberian citizenship as manifested in contributions of 'time, talent, and treasure' couples identity with practice and rights with responsibilities, simultaneously. This particular framework is all-encompassing thereby illustrating clearly the multilayered meanings of Liberian citizenship and how it has come to be reconfigured over space and time as a political economy of belonging. In the next section, I employ Allen's reference to the biblical 'time, talent, and treasure' metaphor to assess whether or not conceptions of Liberian citizenship align with citizenship practices transnationally and domestically, particularly amongst Liberian respondents speaking in unofficial capacities for this book.

Time, Talent, and Treasure

Although there is some synergy, the practice of Liberian citizenship amongst respondents in London, Washington, Freetown, and Accra differs from that of respondents in Monrovia. This is unsurprising. While diasporic citizenship practices occur within a transnational sphere, domestic citizenship practices are locally entrenched. Amongst actors in the four diasporic urban sites, there was a continuum of citizenship pursuits largely contingent upon their socioeconomic positions abroad, as illustrated in Table 2.2 ranking transnational citizenship practices from most to least frequent responses.

---

[31] Interview in Monrovia on 4 June 2013.

Table 2.2 *Top ten ways of practising Liberian citizenship transnationally*

Transnational citizenship practices	Cities where responses frequent
(1) Sending remittances to Liberia (in goods, cash, and kind)	All
(2) Participating in Liberian diaspora organisations – fundraising, charity/development work in health and education (in Liberia and abroad)	All
(3) Paying the school fees of Liberians in Liberia	All
(4) Investing in businesses and real estate in Liberia	All
(5) Paying property taxes in Liberia	London, Washington, Accra
(6) Engaging in investment promotion on behalf of Liberia	London, Accra
(7) Visiting Liberia periodically	London, Washington, Accra
(8) Collaborating with the Liberian embassy (investment fora; 26 July celebrations; meetings with embassy staff; meetings with visiting government officials; *Liberia Rising 2030* Forum)	London, Washington
(9) Actively engaging in Liberia's political processes (voting in national elections; serving Liberian government in ad-hoc roles, that is, policy support, reconciliation initiatives, capacity building; advocating for governance reforms)	Washington, Accra
(10) Engaging in direct capacity building in Liberia and abroad (mentoring Liberians abroad; providing individual voluntary service to tertiary institutions in Liberia; facilitating educational exchanges between Liberian students and students abroad; providing individual pro-bono service to health institutions in Liberia)	London, Washington, Accra

London-based respondents were members of LASO, Liberia Rebuild Global Team, European Federation of Liberian Associations (EFLA), Union of Liberian Organisations in the United Kingdom (ULO-UK), and Mandingo Association. Washington-based respondents were members of RISE, Liberian Students Association in America, Liberian Community Association, Liberian Studies Association (LSA), Marylanders for Progress, Tubman High Alumni Association, BW Harris Alumni Association, Liberian Professional Network (LPN), Sinoe Reconstruction, Checago Bright Foundation, Coalition of

Concerned Liberians (CCL), EFLA, Union of Liberian Associations in the Americas (ULAA), Liberian Development Group, Bethel World Outreach Ministries International, United Bassa Organisation in the Americas (UNIBOA), and Grand Bassa Scholarship Foundation. Freetown-based respondents were members of Youth Vision, Liberians for Progress, Kru and Bassa Christian Association, and Kru Development Association. Accra-based respondents were members of United Liberian Association in Ghana (ULAG), Liberia Refugee Women Organisation, HealthPage Liberia, Rotary Club, Women of Glory, Liberian Students Association (LISA), Liberian Youth Group, Foundation for Peace and Justice, Liberian Refugee Welfare Council, and Association of Bong County Citizens in Ghana.

I compiled the list to illustrate recurring responses to an open-ended question posed to 'near' and 'wider' diasporas about how they remain engaged with Liberia and Liberians while abroad.

Liberian citizenship practices amongst respondents in London, Washington, Freetown, and Accra range from individual activities – that is, remitting money to relatives and friends in Liberia – to collective ventures – that is, pooling resources to sponsor students in Liberia – regardless of legal citizenship status in Liberia. At the level of individual transnational pursuits, a thirty-five-year-old respondent in London indicated that she sent remittances to Liberia for both consumption and income generation by supporting her mother in cultivating a fruit farm of pineapples and mangoes.[32] Moreover, there appears to be a healthy balance amongst respondents between individual citizenship practices and collective activities with Liberian diaspora organisations serving as conduits for interventions in the homeland. For instance, a forty-six-year-old man in London established an organisation that transformed from a social club to a full-fledged education charity, galvanising the support of many UK-based Liberians to sponsor an orphanage and build a school.[33] Employing similar tactics, a sixty-year-old Washington resident used his hometown association to raise funds for health sciences scholarships at tertiary institutions in Liberia:

When I was president for the United Bassa Organisation in the Americas (UNIBOA) ... under my leadership we sponsored ten students at Mother Patern College of Health Sciences, and out of the ten one dropped [out] and nine graduated and they are now working in the Liberian government as

[32] [DL25] Interview in London on 22 June 2012.
[33] [DL20] Interview in London on 16 June 2012.

nurses in the hospital. Presently, I'm the executive director for the Grand Bassa Scholarship Foundation. ... We're sponsoring students to go to the Community College; right now we have fifty students [enrolled].[34]

Transnational pursuits also vary from directly impacting Liberia through on-the-ground development outputs – investing in businesses and property in Liberia – to indirectly impacting the lives of Liberians, whether in Liberia or abroad, through humanitarian relief or capacity development. As evidenced by a surge in the number of houses constructed in Monrovia and its environs that I have observed throughout the years, land ownership appears to be the most popular means of planting roots firmly in Liberia for diasporas. This is certainly true for me as I supervised the construction of my very first (and only) home on the outskirts of Monrovia before relocating to the United Kingdom in 2011 to pursue my PhD. Many respondents disclosed that they had purchased land and/or already erected personal edifices in Liberia, such as a fifty-seven-year-old London-based man who boasted about a three-bedroom house in his ancestral county of Lofa.[35] Similarly, the forty-eight-year-old Freetown-based businessman profiled in Chapter 1 said he invested in real estate for personal and commercial purposes to mitigate affordable housing shortages in Liberia.[36]

Besides developing real estate, other respondents maintained substantial investments in agriculture, particularly cash crops, such as a sixty-one-year-old man in Washington who said he intended to replant rubber on a 500-acre farm that he owned.[37] Another respondent, a forty-three-year-old resident in London, said she used her transnational cargo business to earn an extra income, provide reliable shipping services to Liberians in the United Kingdom, and generate tax revenue for the Liberian government:

I think we've succeeded in this [shipping] business because people trust us and they know that when we say we're going to do something we do it. I think we've changed the whole ethics of doing business in Liberia because I say to people, 'You're going to get your things for 26th' and before 26 July [Liberia's independence day] they will have their things [in Liberia]. ... And we have to send money from here [London] to pay the duty and everything

---

[34] [DL55] Interview in Washington on 26 October 2012.
[35] [DL18] Interview in London on 16 June 2012.
[36] [DL79] Interview in Freetown on 19 April 2013.
[37] [DL50] Interview in Washington on 24 October 2012.

and, you know, I insist on going the proper way. The Liberian government says you need to pay your duty on goods you ship to the country. I charge people duty. When some people have come out and said, 'Oh, you don't need to pay duty to the Liberian government!', I am like, 'Look, whatever you're paying me is what is building the roads in Liberia right now. It's what is developing the country so if you don't want to see Liberia get off her feet, then you can go behind. I am not going to go, you know, [through] the back door. I'm going to do what exactly I'm supposed to do'.[38]

In paying taxes to the Liberian government, this respondent framed herself as advancing the tenets of Liberia's political economy of belonging by improving government–citizen relations and state functionality. In addition to owning the shipping company with her husband, the London resident also served as a distributor for pharmaceutical supplies to Liberia and invested in a cab service, a biofuels start-up company in rural Liberia, and large amounts of real estate. Other respondents said that they practised Liberian citizenship transnationally by impacting the lives of Liberians abroad through humanitarian relief, such as this Washington-based, American-born fifty-five-year-old woman who served in the leadership of the Liberian Community Association:

A lot of the work involved helping recently arrived immigrants get Temporary Protected Status (TPS). ... Some people needed housing, trying to put them in touch with lawyers who we thought could help them. And a lot of it was helping people who died, helping them get buried and all that stuff.[39]

By participating in relief efforts to address the material well-being of Liberians in Washington, this respondent bolstered the political economy of belonging by strengthening citizen–citizen relations.

Although respondents across the four diasporic urban sites engaged in the first four transnational citizenship activities listed in Table 2.2 at varying degrees – that is, diaspora organisational support, remittance transfers to Liberia, school fees payments, and investments in Liberia – careful analysis shows that the remaining six transnational citizenship activities were unique to particular diasporic groupings because of their varied positionalities abroad. For example, although some respondents in Freetown admitted to owning inherited or personally acquired

---

[38] [DL15] Interview in London on 15 June 2012.
[39] [DL34] Interview in Washington on 17 October 2012.

property in Liberia, few indicated paying property taxes unlike their counterparts in London, Washington, and Accra. As demonstrated in Chapter 1, this can be attributed to the fact that on average the socio-economic status of respondents in Freetown – most of whom had applied for local refugee integration in Sierra Leone – is much lower than those who settled in London, Washington, and Accra, with a few outliers here and there. As a case in point, the practice of Liberian citizenship varies considerably between relatively established professionals in Accra and Freetown and their locally integrated former refugee counterparts. Although the majority of Freetown-based respondents were closer in proximity to Liberia, few of them visited Liberia regularly primarily because of financial constraints. Some of their counterparts in London, Washington, and Accra, however, said they visited Liberia more frequently despite travelling longer distances and paying a higher premium.

Professional and/or educational attainment also impacts the citizenship practices of respondents across diasporic sites. Respondents in London and Washington admitted to engaging directly in capacity building and skills development in Liberia through short-term visits or educational exchanges, such as this fifty-six-year-old doctor based in London who travels to Liberia once a year to render voluntary medical services in Nimba, his county of origin:

I have taken equipment again to Ganta Hospital. I have also given some services to the Tappita Hospital, the new Chinese hospital. I went in there a year ago [in 2011] and helped to set up some of their equipment. ... The School of Nursing in Ganta, I took a hundred stethoscopes to them. I sometimes take equipment like sutures and other equipment to the hospitals.[40]

Similarly, the fifty-nine-year-old female health professional in Accra mentioned earlier provides transnational medical relief services for women and children in Liberia largely facilitated by her vast networks established while living abroad:

I was able to treat nine women, brought them in [to Ghana], they did all their chemo and everything and they are back in Monrovia and they are doing well right now. ... And then I also, seven years ago [in 2006], took on the children. I call them the vulnerable medical fragile children, Liberian children

[40] [DL30] Interview in London on 23 June 2012.

suffering. . . . So I fly them out [to receive medical care abroad] and in seven
years I've done 149 children.[41]

Other respondents in Accra – many of whom took advantage of United
Nations High Commissioner for Refugees (UNHCR)-sponsored skills
development schemes – revealed that they also transfer knowledge to
Liberians primarily in Ghana, such as a man who organised vocational
training in carpentry, masonry, and tie-dye for Liberians at the
Buduburam Refugee Camp.[42] Unlike respondents in Accra, London,
and Washington, most interviewees in Freetown collectively possessed
lower levels of education and did not engage in capacity building efforts
in Liberia or Sierra Leone. Unsurprisingly, the demographic profiles of
respondents in the four 'near' and 'wider' diaspora sites of this study
are indicative of continental trends in which African migrants who
travel to North America and Europe tend to be more educated and
well-off than their counterparts in the so-called Global South (Black
et al., 2006: 7).

 While some citizenship engagement patterns are based on socio-
economic positioning in the country of settlement, others are based
on networks cultivated in the homeland and abroad. For instance,
respondents in London and Washington appeared to have closer ties
with embassy officials in those locales and were, therefore, more
engaged with government-sponsored activities than their counterparts
in Freetown and Accra. This is expected. A large percentage of the
respondent pool in Freetown and Accra are former refugees whose
statuses would have been compromised by sustained political engagement with the Liberian government. Moreover, it is unsurprising that
some respondents in Washington indicated being more engaged in the
political process in Liberia than their counterparts in London and
Freetown given the historically politicised nature of US-based diasporas discussed in Chapter 1. One Washington-based male respondent,
a forty-four-year-old veteran political activist and staunch proponent
of dual citizenship, said that he had co-drafted with American congres-
sional members legislation for post-war bilateral support to Liberia
after the cessation of conflict in 2003.[43] Mirroring the profiles of their
Washington-based counterparts, respondents in Accra who admitted

---

[41] [DL83] Interview in Accra on 7 May 2013.
[42] [DL104] Interview in Accra on 20 May 2013.
[43] [DL44] Interview in Washington on 22 October 2012.

to being actively engaged in domestic homeland politics are elites who had previously worked for the Liberian government on short-term assignments or were entangled with the then ruling regime through their personal connections.

As evidenced by the previously illustrated examples, Liberians across the four diasporic sites practise citizenship differently, largely based on their social locations and established networks in Liberia and abroad. At this juncture, I shift the analysis from diasporas to consider the citizenship practices of homeland Liberians above all other Monrovia-based respondents primarily because they appear to be the most rooted as indicated in Table 2.3 ranking domestic citizenship practices from

Table 2.3 *Top ten ways of practising Liberian citizenship domestically*

Domestic citizenship practices	Most frequent Monrovia-based respondents
(1) Engaging in capacity building work (teaching at all levels – from elementary to tertiary – and conducting teacher training; engaging in organisational development, especially amongst non-governmental organisations (NGOs); mentoring young Liberians; providing scholarships)	All (homelanders, permanent and circular returnees)
(2) Investing in Liberia (real estate, businesses, stocks)	All
(3) Paying income and real estate taxes	All
(4) Involved actively in political life (voting in national elections; holding membership of political parties; conducting elections monitoring and registration)	Homelanders
(5) Engaging in community development activities (community clean-up campaigns; community peace initiatives, blood donation drives; sanitation, hygiene, and health promotion/awareness; reconstructing physical infrastructure; civic education; sports promotion)	All
(6) Contributing to humanitarian, emergency and development aid to Liberia (resettling	All

Table 2.3 (*cont.*)

Domestic citizenship practices	Most frequent Monrovia-based respondents
Liberians after war; demobilising ex-combatants; food distribution; grant writing; working with orphans)	
(7) Involved in advocacy, policymaking, and public service (advocating for participatory governance, human rights, women's empowerment, transitional justice, media development)	All
(8) Contributing to charity organisations through membership (Rotary Club, Paramount Young Women Initiative, United Methodist Youth Movement, Catholic Youth Secretariat, Lion's Club, Young Women's Christian Association)	All
(9) Writing and publishing creative works about Liberia	Homelanders
(10) Conducting empirically driven research on Liberia	All

most to least frequent responses. I compiled the list in the table to illustrate recurring responses to an open-ended question posed to homeland and returnee respondents about how they engage in post-war recovery. Although the manner in which homelanders practise Liberian citizenship mirrors returnees in many ways, the depth and breadth of their embeddedness in Liberia supersedes that of permanent and circular return migrants. This is attributed to the fact that on average homelanders have spent longer periods of time in Liberia and are enmeshed in the complicated web of social relations and mores, whereas returnees must reconstitute networks or create new ones no matter how economically empowered or politically connected they happen to be.

What primarily differentiates the citizenship practices of Liberian diasporas from their Monrovia-based counterparts, particularly homelanders, is distance and scale. Most respondents in the 'wider' diaspora were engaged in their host nations as citizens or legal residents, with the resultant rights and responsibilities, and, therefore, were less directly involved in Liberia because of their relative physical distance. Homelanders, on the other hand, demonstrated citizenship practices that appear broader in magnitude and more expansive in scale. For instance, homelanders were more consistently involved in the political life of Liberia, voting in national elections and other electoral processes while actively contributing to widespread political and governance reforms. For instance, a forty-seven-year-old homelander resident in Liberia his whole life was one of only two respondents I interviewed who had voted in all four national elections between 1985 and 2011.[44] Given Liberia's recurring political upheavals this is no small feat. Neither is navigating through a charged post-war environment littered with the competing interests of donors, national government, civil society, multinationals, and the UN, but that is precisely what two male homelanders had managed to do successfully. While one forty-eight-year-old transitional justice expert was involved in establishing Liberia's Truth and Reconciliation Commission (TRC) in 2005,[45] a forty-seven-year-old legal scholar and pro-bono law lecturer served in a number of appointed positions in natural resource governance, including as head of the Liberia Extractive Industries Transparency Initiative (LEITI).[46] Regardless of failed development outcomes discussed in subsequent chapters, these respondents' efforts to strengthen rule of law challenged the Liberian state to mend strained government–citizen relations with better governance.

Homelanders tended to be more entrenched in the economic life of Liberia as well, having paid income and real estate taxes for longer periods of time than their diaspora or returnee counterparts. While citizenship practices manifested in the political seemed to be largely dominated by male homeland respondents, economic activities presented fertile ground for women. One thirty-eight-year-old entrepreneur said that she managed multiple businesses by involving local communities in the process:

I have a material store where I do general merchandise. I have a power saw which I do pit sawing. ... Those places that we are doing the pit sawing,

[44] [HL29] Interview in Monrovia on 18 June 2013.
[45] [HL45] Interview in Monrovia on 24 June 2013.
[46] [HL6] Interview in Monrovia on 6 June 2013.

many of those villages, their bridges are not intact. To enable us to get the planks from those places that we are sawing, we are compelled to reconstruct the bridges. So, we reconstruct. It's expensive but I persuade them. I get to the place, speak the local dialect. . . . Though I want to get cash, but I make them feel included. . . . So, in that way, I use their trees, fell the trees, we produce planks. . . . My father got a farmland but apart from my father's land, in Suakoko [Bong County], people were selling their land so I bought three acres for the same purpose of doing farming.[47]

While agriculture and farming may interest a select few because of the association with back-breaking manual labour, many homeland Liberians, like their counterparts abroad, reported going into real estate for commercial purposes regardless of recurring land tenure disputes throughout the country. A forty-three-year-old development specialist said he invests in real estate to generate profit and create employment opportunities for Liberians who do not have the luxury of drawing on two incomes.[48] Through his real estate business, this respondent framed himself as improving citizen–citizen relations by employing his fellow Liberians thus participating fully in Liberia's political economy of belonging.

In addition to practising citizenship through economic activities, homelanders exhibited higher levels of engagement in community development, charity organisations, and the creative arts than their returnee or diaspora counterparts. Moreover, community outreach activities appear to be uniquely gendered and aged, with more women and young men engaged at this micro level. One of the youngest respondents, a twenty-three-year-old female university student, said that her work with a young women's organisation contributes to gender equality by providing 'scholarships to needy female students' and training them in entrepreneurship.[49] Inspired by her passion for gender justice, a slightly older female respondent had established the first organisation for women living with and affected by HIV/AIDS. The thirty-six-year-old activist recognised that women were being unduly stigmatised in communities largely dominated by men:

Well, the organisation was founded simply to give women and girls living with HIV a face, help them live a life of dignity even in the face of the

47 [HL24] Interview in Monrovia on 17 June 2013.
48 [HL3] Interview in Monrovia on 5 June 2013.
49 [HL37] Interview in Monrovia on 21 June 2013.

pandemic. ... So, we started with small loans, kind of, sort of a revolving fund and then we tried to keep in contact as much as possible with the women. ... Peer-to-peer counseling has done a lot in keeping a lot of women alive because if I am HIV-positive and I can get another woman who is HIV-positive to talk to me and say, 'Look, I've been through this and I'm here. You know, I think you can rise above it'. It has helped greatly in increasing the lives of women who live with HIV.[50]

Given their efforts to enrich the lives of women and girls in Liberia, the two previously mentioned female respondents contributed to Liberia's political economy of belonging by augmenting citizen–citizen relations through community engagement and development practice. Because of Liberia's patriarchal political milieu, the micro-level community development sphere happens to be where homeland women are most visibly active and, therefore, empowered to perform citizenship. It is a sphere occupied by young men as well, as demonstrated by a twenty-nine-year-old former youth volunteer whose monitoring activities at a local school exposed the financial improprieties of a corrupt business manager.[51] It is clear based on analysis of the social/community, economic, and political domains of homeland citizenship practices in Liberia that women and men, young and old, practise citizenship differently primarily based on their social locations and that these practices have a direct impact on the set of relations between the Liberian government and citizens as well as amongst citizens themselves.

In the next section, I explore in more detail my conceptual framing of Liberian citizenship as a set of relations by examining interfaces between the Liberian government through its embassies abroad and Liberians in 'near' and 'wider' diaspora sites as well as amongst Liberian actors in regional diaspora organisations.

Government–Citizen and Citizen–Citizen Engagements

While broadcasting its domestic and foreign policies abroad, the Liberian state's simultaneous engagement with its emigrant populations confirms important features of the political economy of belonging. As a case in point, the Liberian embassy's interactions with

[50] [HL7] Interview in Monrovia on 6 June 2013.
[51] [HL23] Interview in Monrovia on 4 June 2013.

Liberians in the United Kingdom exhibited loose government–citizen relations. The embassy lacked an official database and could only boast of registering 1,500 to 2,000 of the approximately 5,000 to 6,000 Liberians in the United Kingdom, according to then Ambassador Wesley Momo Johnson[52] who also indicated that aside from the 2,000 or so Liberian Londoners, large concentrations of Liberians reside in urban centres such as Sheffield, Manchester, Liverpool, Bradford, and Milton Keynes. Beyond serving as a channel for UK aid and investment links to Liberia, the embassy was constrained in its ability to reach Liberians in London, and by extension, the United Kingdom, especially those who were undocumented. Johnson suggested that Liberians in the United Kingdom previously viewed the embassy as an extension of a transatlantic surveillance system. However, he could not articulate a clear engagement strategy beyond the fact that the embassy assisted Liberians periodically who needed to regularise their status in the United Kingdom and served as a partner to Liberian organisations in the country.

That the embassy had limited penetration amongst Liberians was particularly stark in my interview with Prince Taylor,[53] then head of the ULO-UK, who said that his organisation had been asked by the embassy to gather demographic information on Liberians in the United Kingdom for a comprehensive database. Filling the void in embassy engagement, organisations like ULO-UK sustain Liberian citizen–citizen relations abroad thereby notably impacting the political economy of belonging. According to Taylor, ULO-UK and its member organisations facilitated access to social services for Liberians while collaborating with other UK-based diaspora organisations and were in the process of transitioning from a collection of social and recreation oriented clubs to organisations involved in development activities in Liberia.[54] ULO-UK's deliberate shift in focus from the social to the developmental is indicative of the reconfiguration of Liberian citizenship from identity to political and socio-economic practice.

Because of the citizenship practices of Liberian actors in the United States, the Liberian embassy in Washington demonstrated a more spirited engagement with nationals abroad than its counterpart in London. This is evidenced by previous ambassadors' efforts to establish

---

[52] Interview in London on 14 June 2012.
[53] Interview in London on 16 June 2012.   [54] Ibid.

a Diaspora Advisory Board[55] and a diaspora liaison at the embassy; the embassy's mediation role in a series of civil and criminal cases involving Liberians resettled in the United States; as well as its hosting of a diaspora/dual citizenship symposium during festivities marking Liberia's 165th independence day in July 2012. Moreover, the embassy's annual 26 July Independence Day celebration on its mani-cured grounds in Washington attracts hundreds of Liberians and friends of Liberia. As someone who attended festivities as a child with my parents and then later of my own volition as an adult, I can attest that '26', as we call it, is a mid-annual climax for Liberians in the metropolitan area, with some visiting from further afield in diasporic hubs such as New York, New Jersey, and Pennsylvania, or from as far flung as Minnesota. The success of '26' is partly due to the embassy's collaboration with Liberian associations in both the planning and execution of activities.[56]

Although the Washington embassy appeared committed to amplify-ing Liberia's political economy of belonging by nurturing government–citizen relations, engagement was primarily confined to its social and political networks with an expressed mandate to strengthen Liberian citizen–citizen relations abroad, such as the Liberian Community Association in the Washington Metropolitan Area. Then vice president Nee Allison[57] averred that the Association's activities at that time were not development-oriented and geared towards Liberia, per se, but rather social, cultural, and humanitarian in nature and focused on interventions in the Washington area, such as advocating on behalf of Liberians then registered under Deferred Enforced Departure (DED).[58] It was clear from Allison's account that while the Community Association was more politically active in the 1990s and early 2000s during Liberia's armed conflicts, it had adopted a rather neutral stance post-war, particularly amongst those who did not have regularised

---

[55] The Liberian Diaspora Advisory Board, of which I was a member, had a relatively short life span because of limited support from Monrovia. Former Ambassador Milton Nathaniel Barnes established the Board in 2009 to formalise relations between Liberians in the United States and the Liberian government thereby attempting to harness the financial, political, social, and cultural capital of Liberians for development in Liberia. Barnes was recalled by Sirleaf in 2010, however, amidst rumours that he had allegedly used his position to support a 2011 presidential bid.

[56] Interview with Gabriel IH Williams in Washington on 2 November 2012.

[57] Interview in Washington on 2 November 2012.   [58] Ibid.

statuses in the United States. This is supported by academic literature which states that diasporas have cycles of active engagement that often mirror the political climate in their countries of origin (Østergaard-Nielsen, 2001; Adamson, 2002; Brinkerhoff, 2008).

As I did not come across regional umbrella organisations comprising Liberians in Freetown, my interpretation of Liberian government–citizen relations was gleaned from interviews with embassy staff. Despite the fluidity of Liberian and Sierra Leonean identities, the Freetown-based Liberian embassy revealed weaker government–citizen relations than its counterparts in Washington and London. Then Ambassador Thomas Brima,[59] who would later pass away in 2014, admitted that because the embassy did not have a database of Liberians in Sierra Leone, it relied heavily on UNHCR statistics. It is apparent from our interview that the embassy lacked the infrastructure to document migration flows from Liberia to Sierra Leone, prompting the ambassador to speculate that about 4,000 Liberians resided in Sierra Leone since UNHCR discontinued refugee status for Liberians in June 2012. Because most Liberians who travelled to Sierra Leone seeking refuge from armed conflict were protected by UNHCR, any official connection to the Liberian embassy in Sierra Leone – and, by extension, the government of Liberia – would have jeopardised their refugee status. This, according to Brima, had severely constrained the embassy's engagement with Liberians in Sierra Leone. Yet, despite its hands-off policy with regard to refugees, the embassy had intervened on behalf of Liberians under the auspices of UNHCR, particularly those who had been unduly incarcerated for criminal offences.[60] That the embassy interfered when warranted was an indication that the Liberian government's engagement with its nationals in Sierra Leone, albeit circumstantial, was still anchored on an expressed responsibility to protect Liberian citizens abroad thus fulfilling a limited role in the political economy of belonging.

Brima's counterpart in Accra, however, did not operate on this abiding principle. Of all the embassies I approached across the four urban centres abroad, the one in Accra appeared the least engaged with Liberian migrants and the least successful in propelling the 'development diplomacy'[61] foreign policy agenda introduced by former minister

---

[59]   Interview in Freetown on 18 April 2013.   [60]   Ibid.
[61]   Visit www.mofa.gov.lr/public2/2press.php?news_id=179&related=7&pg=sp to read more about the 'development diplomacy' programme.

Olubanke King-Akerele, a returnee who had previously worked for the United Nations Development Programme (UNDP) in Dakar, Senegal. The embassy did not have a full record of Liberians in Ghana and instead relied on statistics from UNHCR which had a database of 47,000 Liberians in 2005 and as of May 2013 had 3,000 former Liberian refugees registered for local integration. Echoing the sentiments of his counterpart in Freetown, then Ambassador Rudolf Von Ballmoos,[62] who would later pass away in 2015, admitted that the embassy had been restricted in its response to the needs of Liberian citizens in Ghana because most were registered under UNHCR protection and therefore could not officially seek assistance from the embassy without jeopardising their refugee status. The ambassador could not articulate a clear engagement strategy for Liberians in Ghana beyond the embassy's one-off outreach event for over 1,000 Liberians in Accra and its environs in January 2013, executed by embassy second secretary Angela Lavela Von Ballmoos.[63]

While Liberian government–citizen relations were virtually non-existent in Ghana, citizen–citizen relations appeared to be more solid, especially amongst former refugee members of the ULAG. Established in 2010, ULAG responded to the needs of its then over thirty active members by providing financial support to Liberians in Accra and its environs and facilitating social gatherings for community cohesion, said president Julia Richards.[64] In many respects, ULAG mirrors the mandate of the Liberian Community Association in Washington yet it was less financially robust in 2013. ULAG's lack of fiscal capacity prohibited the kinds of development-oriented collective efforts undertaken by ULO-UK, for instance. Nevertheless, the Association helped to facilitate the *Liberia Rising 2030* town hall meeting in Accra in 2012 to solicit the views of Liberians in Ghana to feed into the country's second major post-war development agenda thereby demonstrating an ability to maintain satisfactory government–citizen relations while contributing in its own way to Liberia's political economy of belonging. Although ULAG appears to be apolitical, Richards revealed that she had also collaborated with the EFLA and the ULAA as a signatory to the petition in favour of dual citizenship by members of Liberia's diasporas. When EFLA delegates transited through Accra

---

[62] Interview in Accra on 23 May 2013.   [63] Ibid.
[64] Interview in Accra on 18 May 2013.

in 2010 on their way to Monrovia to lobby for passage of the 2008 bill, Richards organised their informal discussions with Liberians resident in Accra and its environs, indicating that ULAG also maintains strong citizen–citizen relations with other Liberian nationals abroad.

In this section, I have demonstrated that relations between the Liberian government and nationals abroad are either limited or expansive largely due to embassy engagement, or lack thereof, and the social locations (manifested in immigration status) of Liberians abroad. Regional diaspora organisations tend to fill gaps in government–citizen relations with their own brand of citizen–citizen engagement ranging from humanitarian relief abroad to transnational development practices in Liberia.

Conclusion

The respondents whose narratives are showcased in the introduction of this chapter – Beyan, Teta, Aisha, and James – would all be considered Liberian citizens on a continuum, as would their offspring, because their Liberianness is anchored by the fluidity of *jus soli* and *jus sanguinis* principles of citizenship. Although identities are foundational to the political economy of belonging to Liberia, it is the expression of those identities through practices (i.e., contributions of time, talent, treasure) and sets of relations that establish the system as active and interactive. As evidenced by the analysis captured herein, actual participation by an individual in Liberia's contemporary political economy of belonging is contingent upon one's social location and life-world thus inadvertently discounting those with little to no political, economic, or social capital. In essence, the transactional nature of the system creates citizenship tiers as it designates some Liberians more 'legitimate' or 'authentic' than others. Yet, as I argue throughout this book, exclusionary forms of Liberian citizenship have been contested across space and time and are therefore emblematic of a larger narrative of citizenship reconfiguration processes in Africa and beyond.

In this chapter, I have demonstrated that contemporary constructions of Liberian citizenship are part of a continuum – moving from passive, identity-based citizenship emphasising rights and entitlements (and based on birthplace, bloodline, and blackness) to more active, practice-based citizenship privileging duties and responsibilities – thereby transcending the legal definition enshrined in the country's

1973 Aliens and Nationality Law and 1986 Constitution at least until mid-December 2019. While homeland Liberians interviewed for this book embody citizenship practices that are domestically rooted and territorially confined to Liberia, diasporas and returnees engage in transnational pursuits that attempt to positively alter citizen–citizen and government–citizen relations abroad and within Liberia. I also illustrated that relations between the Liberian government and diasporas have been strengthened or weakened depending on the levels of engagement of embassies and the immigration status of nationals abroad. Whereas the homeland state provided limited to no privileges/protections to nationals abroad in London, Washington, Freetown, and Accra, thus shirking its role in the political economy of belonging, Liberians abroad interviewed for this book implied that they had more meaningfully fulfilled duties/obligations through their varied individual and collective efforts.

Building further on the analysis of Liberia's political economy of belonging, Chapter 3 explores how dual citizenship has come to be regarded as a viable policy prescription in Liberia, in Africa, and across transnational spaces.

3 | *Dual Citizenship and Its Discontents in Africa*

Introduction

Once a bastion of political advocacy against government repression, the University of Liberia came to a standstill in May 2013. A mob of students heckled and jeered at a delegation from the Union of Liberian Associations in the Americas (ULAA) attempting to host one of many town hall meetings discussing the merits of proposed dual citizenship legislation. Although a few students supported the delegation, pushing back at their naysaying counterparts, the forceful majority barred them from speaking. In the same month as the students' stand-off, one of Liberia's most notorious senators, Dan Morais, unleashed an anti-dual citizenship radio campaign that left the ULAA delegation scrambling to return to the United States to raise funds for lobbying more conciliatory members of the Legislature.

Two years later, controversies around the 2008 bill re-emerged when the majority of delegates at a 2015 constitutional review conference in Gbarnga, Bong County, rejected its passage and removal of the 'Negro clause'. These hard-line stances were largely corroborated by Afrobarometer (2012) data in which only 27 per cent of those surveyed in Liberia agreed with the statement that 'a person who wishes to hold dual citizenship, that is, to be a citizen of both Liberia and some other country' should be entitled to citizenship. When newly inaugurated footballer-turned-Liberian President George Oppong Weah (2018) proclaimed unwavering support for abolishing the 'Negro clause' and enacting dual citizenship in his very first address to the Legislature on 29 January 2018, he sparked controversy and catapulted a transnational conversation about citizenship into overdrive on social media and in public discourse.

Instead of reacting immediately, I read with keen interest the avalanche of rejoinders either rebuking or applauding the president's statements – from Liberians at home and those further afield in diasporic hotspots. Just as I had expected, however, most of the retorts were based on sentiments (i.e., how people felt about the laws) rather than evidence (i.e., what the laws actually meant in reality). They echoed the anxieties and aspirations of respondents interviewed for this book and reified the 2013 impasse between homeland anti-dual citizenship student activists and their ULAA pro-dual citizenship counterparts. This chapter suggests that interactions between disparate actors – as evidenced by the University of Liberia interface – can quickly morph into a head-on collision. In it, I examine how global liberal citizenship norms and dual citizenship diffusion in Africa have generated a politics of inclusion thus boosting dual citizenship advocacy for Liberia. Further, I argue that the bundle of visceral responses to dual citizenship as a proposed development intervention in Liberia has signified an interface wherein actors negotiate the discontinuities and continuities in their lived experiences of being Liberian. Such interfaces have had an ultimate bearing on post-war development outcomes as discussed in the three chapters that follow this one.

Globalisation of Liberal Citizenship Norms

Globalisation has fundamentally shaped the contours of citizenship construction and practice in Liberia, in Africa, and across the world. Polarised disputes about resident- and non-resident forms of citizenship, in particular, are mirrored in debates about globalisation, pitting those who advocate for the increased relevance of nation-states in regulating citizenship regimes against those who argue that countries are not the basic unit of analysis or the custodians of citizenship but one of many institutions whose powers extend transnationally, such as multilateral agencies, multinational corporations, and international non-governmental organisations (NGOs) (Isin, 2000: 2; Glick Schiller, 2009: 6). Therefore, it is important to explore the nuanced ways in which globalisation has simultaneously unsettled and entrenched residence-only ('bounded') citizenship as this will serve as the basis for my analysis later about the diffusion of dual citizenship in Africa.

On one hand, Marshall's (1950) idealistic brand of civil, political, and social citizenship is based on fixity or 'stasis, of the rights and duties attributed to, and available to, those living and working within a given territory by virtue of long-term membership within a given society' (Urry, 2000: 63–64). Nevertheless, citizenship brokered by processes of globalisation is based on flow or flux, 'concerned with the causes and consequences' of movement 'across borders of risks, cultures, migrants and visitors, respectively' (Urry, 2000: 63–64). Thus, globalisation has not undermined the institution of citizenship, per se, rather it has reconfigured 'the ways in which people think about their sense of citizenship, their sense of belonging and their sense of responsibility' (Desforges, Jones & Woods, 2005: 442). For example, individuals may form bonds of solidarity across transnational spaces in response to the negative consequences of economic globalisation while simultaneously maintaining their residence-based citizenship and calling for universalised notions of personhood (Falk, 2000: 7).

Moreover, activists employ the Universal Declaration of Human Rights (UDHR) to propel citizenship rights 'above the state' thereby stretching the philosophical tenets of citizenship from membership within a political territory to individual humanity and personhood (UN, 1948; Shafir & Brysk, 2006: 275, 277). Yet, the relevance of residence-based forms of citizenship is maintained despite the globalisation of ideas and the assumed universalisation of human rights. Although citizenship rights can be claimed and protected by law, however limited in scope, human rights cannot (Shafir & Brysk, 2006: 285). Furthermore, the principles of universal personhood are still highly contested. Although some assert that residence-based-only citizenship is more entrenched than ever before in spite of globalisation, others argue it has fundamentally lost its relevance and debates about fixity and flow in citizenship regimes are as relevant in discourses on globalisation as they are in debates about migration. The two sections that follow this one examine how the globalisation of ideas – embedded in human rights discourses and dual citizenship diffusion trends in Africa – impacted claims for and against Liberia's proposed dual citizenship bill of 2008.

Human Rights Rhetoric and Dual Citizenship Claims

Citizenship and human rights are often contradictorily applied. While human rights are entangled with the politics of inclusion, citizenship is embedded in the politics of exclusion, where people are often barred based on a number of social qualifiers such as race (in the case of Liberia and Sierra Leone), ethnic identity, gender, and birthplace nationality. Yet, there is an important discourse that frames citizenship and the right to a nationality as a human right among other rights. According to the UDHR adopted in 1948, 'everyone has a right to a nationality' and 'no one shall be arbitrarily deprived of his [or her] nationality' (UN, 1948). Therefore, any state that ratified the UDHR, regardless of its domestic laws, is required to uphold it by guaranteeing the right to citizenship. Similarly, the Convention on the Elimination of All Forms of Discrimination against Women (CEDAW) stipulates that women should be granted equal rights to citizenship under the law (UN, 1979). And the Convention on the Reduction of Statelessness requires a 'contracting state' to 'grant its nationality to a person born in its territory who would otherwise be stateless' (UN, 1961). The diffusion of ideas about rights that should be accorded to every human being has spread to every corner of the world – including Africa, generally, and Liberia, specifically.

In advocating for the expansion of citizenship rights in Africa to groups previously marginalised, Manby (2010: 1–2) also invokes human rights to argue that there should be provisions within African continental agreements on the right to a nationality. Nevertheless, African soft law treaties – such as the African Charter on Human and Peoples' Rights, the African Charter on the Rights and Welfare of the Child, and the Protocol to the African Charter on Human and Peoples' Rights on the Rights of Women in Africa – are relatively silent on nationality and citizenship (OAU, 1981; OAU, 1990; AU, 2003; Manby, 2010: 10). Regardless of this, however, the globalisation of human rights discourse emboldened claims for dual citizenship in Liberia by which proponents argued that revocation of citizenship without due process severely impinges upon one's human rights.

Globalised notions of citizenship as a human right have also engendered a transnational conversation about Liberia's citizenship architecture with non-Liberians weighing in. For example, the American Bar Association (ABA) (2009: 5, 15, 17–18) argued in 2009 that provisions within Liberia's then 1973 Aliens and Nationality Law compelling someone to renounce a previous citizenship at the time of naturalisation was a deterrent for diasporas and other African citizens who wished to become Liberian citizens. Furthermore, Section 21.51 – which affirmed that a naturalised citizen would revoke her/his legal Liberian citizenship if s/he travelled to her/his country of first nationality and resided there for up to two years or any other foreign country for up to five years – created classes of citizens and denied a naturalised citizen the right to travel or seek employment abroad (Government of Liberia, 1973). Equally harsh was Section 21.58 of the Law which declared that any Liberian who naturalised abroad automatically lost her/his claim on property owned which would go to the state uncompensated if s/he did not have a Liberian citizen spouse or child to inherit said property (Government of Liberia, 1973; ABA, 2009: 16).

Feminist discourses about the rights of women may have also influenced advocacy to expand Liberian citizenship as defined by gender. The 2008 proposed dual citizenship legislation clearly stipulated that Liberian citizen women should be able to pass on citizenship to their children born abroad, thus opening the scope for citizenship to be granted to a larger number of *jus sanguinis* Liberians beyond the age of majority. Others have likewise contended that denying a person citizenship because her/his father did not reside in Liberia prior to her/his birth discriminates against children whose fathers fled Liberia during intermittent warfare, a major point of contention for Liberians abroad who advocated for dual citizenship (ABA, 2009: 14). Similarly, denying a person citizenship because s/he, having been born outside of Liberia to a Liberian citizen father, was not resident in Liberia at the age of majority discriminates against children who were exiled during armed conflicts and did not return to Liberia before reaching the age of majority (ABA, 2009: 14). Legal scholars and advocates have urged lawmakers to eliminate the aforementioned provisions from the Aliens and Nationality Law because parents whose children fall within these categories would be disinclined to repatriate capital to or invest in Liberia if their children were stateless (ABA, 2009: 14).

The rights rhetoric has further legitimated an interrogation of citizenship based on race, although the proposed dual citizenship legislation of 2008 maintained the 'Negro clause' as did its successor in 2019. Nevertheless, the clause remains seemingly inconsistent with Article 5 of the Liberian Constitution, which prohibits ethnic discrimination, as well as the International Convention on the Elimination of All Forms of Racial Discrimination (ICERD), which Liberia ratified in 1978 (UN, 1969). Although the 'Negro clause' was enacted in the spirit of pan-Africanism, detractors have called it antiquated given the contributions of previously mentioned non-black residents of Liberia in the service, retail, trading, agriculture, and mining sectors (ABA, 2009: 14). They have advocated for either abrogating the race-based clause, thereby amending the 1973 Aliens and Nationality Law and 1986 Constitution concurrently, or carefully defining the terms 'Negro' and 'Negro descent', in a way that accounts for international norms (ABA 2009: 14). Yet, I argue that examining Liberia's 'Negro clause' through a purely legalistic or human rights lens negates important historical and sociological considerations, like how the race-based provision centres blackness as an explicit property of citizenship thereby challenging white supremacy and unsettling the very foundation of citizenship as nested in a predominantly white, liberal state (Pailey, 2020).

Beyond race, the framing of citizenship as a human right has intensified appeals to expand Liberia's legal definition of citizenship to include groups that would otherwise have been disenfranchised, particularly *jus soli* Liberians who naturalised abroad and *jus sanguinis* Liberians who wished to maintain both their birthplace and bloodline citizenships. In essence, the globalisation of ideas manifested in notions of citizenship as a human right has strengthened citizen–citizen relations and engendered principles of inclusion thus advancing pro-dual citizenship sentiments. Next, I discuss how the battle to harmonise citizenship laws across Africa also emboldened Liberia's dual citizenship crusade.

Dual Citizenship Diffusion in Africa

African governments have increasingly factored diasporas into domestic development and post-war recovery efforts. This explicit acknowledgement of transnationals as partners in progress has manifested in legal instruments and frameworks such as dual citizenship. Within the African Union (AU) a majority of member states maintained different types of non-resident citizenship provisions embedded in law prior to 2020, as indicated in Table 3.1. For instance, while Algeria, Cape Verde, Comoros, Gabon, and Lesotho enabled carte blanche dual citizenship, eSwatini (formerly Swaziland) and São Tomé and Príncipe only permitted dual citizenship for *jus soli* citizens (Manby, 2016; GLOBALCIT, 2017). Conditions applied in other contexts as well. For example, Egyptians and South Africans could hold dual citizenship only if they obtained permission from the homeland government before acquiring another citizenship (GLOBALCIT, 2017). Similarly, the loss of citizenship for *jus soli* Guineans and Ivorians was subject to authorisation by their governments during a fifteen-year period from the time of eligibility for military service (GLOBALCIT,

Table 3.1 *Africa's dual citizenship trends as of 20 December 2019*

Regions/ dual citizenship provisions	Dual citizenship permitted	Dual citizenship permitted/ prohibited in certain circumstances	Dual citizenship prohibited
Central Africa	Burundi, Chad, Congo Republic, Gabon	Central African Republic, São Tomé and Príncipe	Cameroon, Democratic Republic of the Congo, Equatorial Guinea
East Africa	Comoros, Djibouti, Kenya, Rwanda, Seychelles, Somalia, South Sudan, Sudan (except with South Sudan)	Madagascar, Mauritius, Uganda	Eritrea, Ethiopia, Tanzania
North Africa	Algeria, Morocco, Tunisia	Egypt, Libya, Mauritania	N/A
Southern Africa	Angola, Lesotho, Malawi, Mozambique, Zambia	Botswana, eSwatini, Namibia, South Africa, Zimbabwe	N/A
West Africa	Benin, Burkina Faso, Cape Verde, Ghana, Guinea Bissau, Mali, Niger, Nigeria, Sierra Leone	Côte d'Ivoire, Gambia, Guinea, Senegal, Togo	Liberia
Totals	**29**	**18**	**7**

In February 2019, the Zimbabwean cabinet approved amendments to the Citizenship of Zimbabwe Act to permit dual citizenship for *jus soli* Zimbabweans in order to align it with the 2013 Constitution. However, at the time of finalising this book in December 2019, the alignment process was incomplete.
Sources: Manby, 2016; GLOBALCIT, 2017

2017). And while Malagasy, in general, who naturalised elsewhere could regain their homeland citizenship after fifteen years of military service, a Malagasy woman, in particular, would renounce her citizenship if she lived outside Madagascar, married a foreigner, and obtained the citizenship of her spouse automatically (GLOBALCIT, 2017).

Apart from the peculiar contexts listed in this section briefly and beyond my expansive analysis of Liberia throughout this book, I refrain from exploring in any depth how other African countries came to allow or prohibit non-resident forms of citizenship. This is primarily because of the dearth of available case study material as well as the constantly changing legal regimes around citizenship and dual citizenship in the continent. Suffice it to say that, like other regions of the so-called Global South, Africa experienced a diffusion of dual citizenship in the past three decades with important implications for Liberia. As a disclaimer, I have designated Liberia in Table 3.1 as a country that banned dual citizenship prior to 2020; nevertheless, because it allowed *jus sanguinis* Liberians to conditionally hold dual citizenship until the age of majority as of my completing this monograph in mid-December 2019, the country actually occupied a hybrid space between permitting dual citizenship in certain circumstances and prohibiting it entirely. For the sake of my analysis, the table does not factor in a subsequent ruling by the Liberian Supreme Court that automatic revocation of citizenship without due process is unconstitutional.

Before exploring the normalisation of dual citizenship in Africa, I would like to speculate briefly how Cameroon, Democratic Republic of the Congo, Equatorial Guinea, Eritrea, Ethiopia, and Tanzania became outliers. These six countries exemplify threats posed to citizenship regimes not only by the legacies of settler colonialism (i.e., Equatorial Guinea) but also by the protracted nature of post-independence secessionist politics (i.e., Cameroon), conflicts and/or refugee displacements (i.e., Democratic Republic of the Congo, Tanzania), and post-secession border disputes (i.e., Eritrea, Ethiopia).

Although the previously mentioned six countries and Liberia represented exceptions rather than the rule prior to 2020, dual citizenship has mushroomed despite stiff opposition across the continent. In her noteworthy examination of dual citizenship diffusion in Africa, Beth

Elise Whitaker (2011) illuminates the contested nature of legislating transnational forms of belonging. Through comparative analyses of Senegal, Ghana, Kenya, and Ethiopia, she discloses how each country underwent political and legal wrangling which resulted in different outcomes for nationals abroad. For example, dual citizenship in Senegal was instituted from 'above' at independence in 1960 by political elites including first president Léopold Sédar Senghor who held dual Senegalese and French citizenship. Bolstered primarily by political and economic motivations, its provisions on non-resident citizenship are some of the most liberal in Africa enabling diaspora voting and parliamentary representation. In contrast, Ghana's 'bottom-up' dual citizenship passage was largely brokered by nationals abroad in the era of political liberalisation. Although diasporic rights and privileges were recognised in the mid-1990s, implementation of dual citizenship only began in 2002 with restrictions then on emigrants holding public office and voting from abroad. Kenya's transnationals agitated intensely from 2002 onwards until dual citizenship provisions were finally incorporated in the country's new constitution of 2010. While politicians considered remittances an important channel for homeland development, they engaged in tactical delays because of border security fears and concerns that diasporas could eventually wrest control from them. And although Ethiopia did not recognise dual citizenship until the point at which I completed this book in December 2019, foreign nationals of Ethiopian descent had fought for the right to apply for and secure special identity cards that granted them certain nonpolitical allowances. Whitaker's study demonstrates, as does this book, that diasporas have the capacity to mobilise and influence domestic policies in origin countries yet they must reckon with homeland political actors who sometimes wield considerably more power.

Beyond Whitaker's four continental case studies, a subregional analysis is instructive for Liberia since it was the only country in the fifteen-member Economic Community of West African States (ECOWAS) that had not officially instituted dual citizenship as of mid-December 2019. While Senegal was the first country in the region to authorise non-resident forms of citizenship, Benin, Burkina Faso, Cape Verde, Guinea, Mali, Nigeria, and Togo legislated dual citizenship in the latter part of the twentieth century. Côte d'Ivoire, Ghana, Gambia, Sierra Leone, Guinea Bissau, and Niger followed in succession in the first two decades of the twenty-first century. As ECOWAS attempts to facilitate economic integration and streamline the free movement of persons – in accordance with the AU's macro-level goals of implementing the African Continental Free Trade Area (AfCFTA) and advancing a borderless Africa – it is presumed that harmonising citizenship laws will facilitate the regionalisation of capital flows of trade and investment. For example, Siaplay (2014: 3) uses a random effects economic model to argue that ECOWAS countries which recognise dual citizenship 'have positive and statistically significant association with foreign direct investment net inflows, gross capital formation, and household consumption', although he does not make claims that dual citizenship is cause for these trends.

Nonetheless, dual citizenship is often touted as having definitively positive results based on assumptions about subregional developments. Then Liberian senator Sumo G Kupee divulged to me in 2012 that the 2008 bill he co-sponsored was inspired by continental experiences, with his colleagues warning him that there would be staunch opposition along the way:

I've spoken to parliamentarians in Accra. I've spoken to parliamentarians in Sierra Leone. And they shared the same difficulties they had. . . . And again, especially my colleagues in Ghana. They said it was really tough and because looking at where Ghana was coming from at the time, grossly underdeveloped, and they had these citizens coming from London, there was this same apprehension from local Ghanaians and their counterparts, you know.[1]

Kupee's admission foreshadows the fact that while dual citizenship passage may be inevitable for Liberia, delays have actually been in keeping with the circumstances of its regional neighbours. Corroborating the protracted process of enacting dual citizenship in Sierra Leone, Ansumana Jaia Kaikai, then deputy minority leader of Parliament and chief sponsor of that country's dual citizenship bill, explained to me in his Freetown office in 2013 that it took the president's full endorsement to finally pass the Dual Citizenship Act of 2006 nine years after it was introduced in 1997:

I had noted that there were several Sierra Leoneans that were living overseas and that they were being disadvantaged because they had taken dual citizenships in other countries other than Sierra Leone. And because our Constitution prohibited dual nationality [citizenship], I felt that our country

---

[1] Interview in Monrovia on 4 December 2012.

was not, our laws were not favouring, we were disadvantaging our citizens and nationals that were residing overseas, and who had, because they wanted to make their stay in other countries liveable, so they had taken those citizenships as it is required of the laws of those countries. ... Well, we came to realise, as I said earlier, among those reasons, that in fact there were Sierra Leoneans with access to our roots. I mean, there were people, Americans, Jamaicans, etc., Europeans, with their roots from Sierra Leone, either by way of parentage, who wanted to be associated with their home country. So, I thought it fit that I should make it my point of duty to have the president endorse it [the dual citizenship bill] ... which he did, and not too long after that it went through cabinet and then it came here [to Parliament], became law.[2]

One of the unique elements of Sierra Leone's Dual Citizenship Act is that it enables African Americans to become citizens through mitochondrial DNA testing, as evidenced by the US actor Isaiah Washington (2011), who requested and was granted Sierra Leonean citizenship in 2008. This practice is not uniquely Sierra Leonean, however. During its commercially driven 'Year of Return' in 2019 marking the 400th anniversary of the beginning of the transatlantic slave trade, Ghana granted citizenship to over one hundred people of African descent in a bid to cement itself as a diasporic hub. One could argue that because of their historical trajectories, Liberia and Sierra Leone are more appropriately placed for such posturing. For policy-makers in Sierra Leone, staking such a claim has been a priority. During a meeting with a delegation representing the Gullah from the US state of South Carolina who trace their lineage to Sierra Leone, Kaikai said he used the occasion to apply pressure on then President Ahmad Tejan Kabbah to pass the Dual Citizenship Act. Kaikai, who had lived in the United States as a permanent resident for twenty-three years before relocating to Freetown, claimed that the nine-year limbo for the Act was well worth the wait since Sierra Leonean diasporas have become more engaged in politics:

It [dual citizenship] actually has given lots of chance to Sierra Leoneans to participate in the governments of the country. The amount of members of Parliament [who have dual citizenship] has increased, the amount of cabinet members [who have dual citizenship] has increased ... The amount of non-political operations [by diaspora groups] had increased.[3]

[2] Interview in Freetown on 19 April 2013.   [3] Ibid.

Although Kaikai could not identify concrete development outcomes emanating from these transnational political engagements, there were other spill-over effects of the Act which undoubtedly influenced Liberia's introduction of dual citizenship legislation in 2008 and 2019. For instance, Ernest Bai Koroma, then president of Sierra Leone, announced an Executive Proclamation shortly after assuming office in 2007 that diasporas constituted Sierra Leone's fifth region, prompting a concept note that established an Office of Diaspora Affairs in Statehouse in 2008.[4] This is consistent with other diaspora agencies that have sprung up across Africa, including the Council of the Moroccan Community Living Abroad (created in 2007), the Ministry of Foreign Affairs and Senegalese Abroad (founded in 2014), Ghana's Office of Diaspora Affairs in the presidency (established in 2017), and the Ethiopian Diaspora Agency (created in 2019). During my tenure working with President Sirleaf, I was seconded to Sierra Leone's Office of Diaspora Affairs for a week-long study tour in 2010 and subsequently applied for and secured a US$.5 million grant to incubate a similar division within the Liberian Ministry of State.[5] Hence, the Liberian president began referring to diasporas as Liberia's 'sixteenth county' in the same way that Somalilanders abroad are considered the seventh region of the semi-autonomous territory of Somaliland and Africans outside of the continent are recognised by the AU as its sixth region.

As I have indicated, Liberia's 2008 bill was clearly inspired by citizenship reconfiguration processes across Africa. Yet, even in countries that have adopted dual citizenship, transnational claims for legitimacy are still disputed. Particularly relevant here is a study of *ressortissants* Guinéens – which has come to connote Guineans living abroad although the literal translation is Guinean nationals generally – and contestations over their political citizenship (i.e., privileges and obligations) against a backdrop of rising tensions between the

---

[4] This information was culled from a semi-structured interview I conducted in Freetown on 18 April 2013 with Karamoh Kabba, Sierra Leone's then deputy minister of political and public affairs who oversaw the Office of Diaspora Affairs.

[5] Much to my chagrin, I was told by the World Bank that instead of allocating funds to procure the proposed unit's hard and soft infrastructure (including equipment and staffing), the majority of the grant budget had to be earmarked for what I assumed would be foreign consultants writing superfluous policy documents.

government and homeland trade unions (Schroven, 2016). Between 2006 and 2007, national protests and strikes were instigated to push for economic reforms and regime change following years of mismanagement and deteriorating living conditions. This incited solidarity demonstrations by *ressortissants* in front of Guinean embassies in Washington, Paris, and Brussels which were welcomed by homelanders (Schroven, 2016: 85). As tensions flared in Guinea, however, less welcome were *ressortissants* residing in West Africa, Europe, or North America who, in radio commentaries, urged their homeland counterparts to prolong the strikes and make particular demands on the government (Schroven, 2016: 83). 'They are not Guineans!', accused homelanders, arguing that *ressortissants'* interference in political discourse from afar was illegitimate because their residence abroad protected them from hardship and insecurity (Schroven, 2016: 87–89).

Conversely, however, there have been challenges to governments that attempt to browbeat dual citizens into choosing one citizenship over another. In Kenya, for example, ambassador-nominee to South Korea, Mwende Mwinzi, was victorious in her 2019 suit against the National Assembly for insisting, after having already confirmed her, that she relinquish her *jus soli* US citizenship before assuming diplomatic duties. The Assembly cited Section 31(2) of the Leadership and Integrity Act which required state officers to abandon any non-Kenyan citizenships before taking up diplomatic posts. Mwinzi, whose mother is American and late father was Kenyan, argued convincingly that it would be unconstitutional to force her to renounce a US citizenship that she did not choose, especially since Kenyan diplomats were not considered state officers under law. Her case raised major concerns about whether Kenyans with dual citizenship would be eligible for government jobs in the future, particularly state-level positions, while also inspiring Ghana's Diaspora Engagement Policy Bill of 2019 which proposed to amend the Constitution by allowing dual citizens to occupy public offices previously unavailable to them such as members of Parliament, justices of the supreme court, including chief justice, ambassadors and high commissioners, amongst others.

Having clarified how dual citizenship diffusion in Africa motivated Liberia's lawmakers to introduce measures of their own, I now turn to the 2008 bill itself.

The (Liberian) Passport Can Change but the Heart Cannot?

Given that dual citizenship represented a manifestation of the reconfiguration of Liberian citizenship across space and time and a site of extreme post-war contestation at the time of my interviews in 2012–2013, what follows is an in-depth analysis of how Liberians across five urban field sites reacted to proposed legislation in this regard.

Of the 202 respondents surveyed, 123 (61 per cent) advocated for dual citizenship in principle; 30 (15 per cent) supported dual citizenship with caveats; 37 (18 per cent) rebuffed dual citizenship outright; 9 (5 per cent) admitted feeling ambivalent about dual citizenship; and 3 (1 per cent) provided no response. The latter included one policymaker who said that he would have to thoroughly study the issue in more detail for an informed opinion, as well as one policymaker in Monrovia and another embassy official in Accra who did not have the opportunity to offer opinions because of time limitations during our interviews. Although the percentages are not representative of the opinions of Liberians worldwide, they reveal qualitative trends in how Liberians across my respondent pool actually evaluate dual citizenship as a development enabler, spoiler, neither, or both simultaneously. Additionally, I recognise that the numbers could have been drastically altered had I interviewed more homelanders in Monrovia and 'near' diasporas in Freetown and Accra, as these actors represent the staunchest opponents of dual citizenship.

Based on statistical analysis of my actual respondent pool, however, it is clear that the vast majority of interviewees – 76 per cent – conceive of Liberian citizenship as territorially fluid and of dual citizenship as potentially enabling both structural transformation and social cohesion. This is evidenced by their endorsement of dual citizenship as a policy prescription for Liberia in principle or with caveats. Conjuring up the ubiquitous 'heart' trope, thirty-eight-year-old Freetown-based James, previously profiled in Chapter 2, argued:

If a man must contribute to his nation, most especially like Liberia, the man must go out [of the country]. And if the man goes out, he acquires knowledge that can help Liberia. If you will stop a man from being a citizen in another country that will be contributing to the man's development and indirectly contributing to the nation, Liberia, then it means you'll be hindering the development in Liberia. .... I support dual citizenship [one] hundred per cent because the book [passport] can change but the heart cannot change.[6]

James's dual Liberian–Sierra Leonean parentage undoubtedly presaged his liberal attitudes about the synergies between dual citizenship and development. Other respondents insisted that Liberians who migrate, naturalise abroad, and maintain transnational ties contribute not only to the rich tapestry of the country's amalgamated identities but also to the political economy of belonging, and, therefore, should be able to maintain their *jus soli* or *jus sanguinis* Liberian citizenship. Employing Liberia's future development as her framework of analysis, one thirty-six-year-old female respondent based in London argued that dual citizenship would facilitate the fulfilment of civic responsibility amongst Liberians abroad:

People are preparing to come back [to Liberia] and I think if you make people feel excluded, or on the outside, or as outsiders coming in, you know, you're trying to get people on board, all this 'lift Liberia'[7] and stuff like that. I think people need to share ownership of that vision and if they feel that they are going to be dipping in and out or come when they're ready, you know, then that commitment will not be strong. People will commit if they feel that something is theirs.[8]

However, respondents who supported dual citizenship with caveats argued that the proposed bill should clearly articulate provisions about the rights *and* responsibilities of would-be dual citizens in order to curb abuse. A forty-two-year-old woman in London, who did not naturalise in the United Kingdom despite being eligible for citizenship, shared her misgivings emphatically:

It is nice to have dual citizenship to know that you still have allegiance to your country of birth or country of natural, you know, heritage. But I think the bill is yet to be qualified because of national security, foreign affairs and things like that, you know, the interest of the nation, so that the interest of the

---

[6] [DL62] Interview in Freetown on 11 April 2013.
[7] *Lift Liberia* was the colloquial phrase adopted for the 2008–2011 Poverty Reduction Strategy (PRS) based on a national naming competition that I spearheaded in 2008 to engage Liberians in-country in selecting a pithy idiom that would exemplify the government's determination to reduce poverty. Visit www.emansion.gov.lr/2press.php?news_id=789&related=7&pg=sp for more information.
[8] [DL8] Interview in London on 13 June 2012.

nation is not compromised when it comes to, you know, who's doing what and what status has this person got.[9]

Although the 2008 bill did not explicitly define the privileges of potential dual citizens, such as holding public office, the Dual Citizen and Nationality Act of 2019[10] clearly stipulated that they would be ineligible for particular elected and appointed positions – including president and vice president; speaker of the House of Representatives; president pro-tempore of the Senate; chief justice and associate justices of the Supreme Court; cabinet ministers; Armed Forces of Liberia (AFL) chief of staff and deputy chief of staff; inspector-general of the Liberia National Police (LNP); ambassadors, and so on (Government of Liberia, 2008c; Government of Liberia, 2019a). Limitations were more than likely catalogued in the new bill and referendum Proposition #1 because of widespread concerns about national security and divided loyalties, as articulated by the previous respondent. I suspect also that restrictions on holding elected and appointed office were extended as an olive branch to insecure members of the Legislature who view would-be dual citizens as possible threats to their political fiefdoms.

Interviewees who expressed ambivalence about dual citizenship were agnostic, conveying effectively the pros and cons of the 2008 bill without siding with any one view. Ranked in order from most to least frequently cited, Table 3.2 summarises major reasons given for adopting or renouncing dual citizenship, which appear to be diametrically opposed to one another.

I must clarify here that no single category of respondents unanimously rejected or favoured dual citizenship, further reinforcing the contested space citizenship occupies amongst Liberians across varying spatial landscapes. Therefore, it is important to mention some critical trends across my five urban field sites.

Of the thirty-two informants in London, twenty-seven supported dual citizenship with only five expressing reservations or uncertainty. While the regional head of the Union of Liberian Organisations in the United Kingdom (ULO-UK) and two diaspora respondents argued that

---

[9] [DL10] Interview in London on 13 June 2012.
[10] The 2020 referendum proposition based on this Act varied slightly, however, barring would-be dual citizens from holding all national elected offices and the following additional appointed offices: all heads of autonomous commissions, agencies, and nonacademic/research/scientific institutions (Government of Liberia, 2019b).

Table 3.2 *Catalogue of pros and cons of dual citizenship for Liberia*

Pros	Cons
(1) Liberians were forced out of the country involuntarily by war and may have naturalised abroad because of circumstances beyond their control	Liberians are not patriotic or nationalistic, and will exploit dual citizenship for their own selfish interests
(2) Denying citizenship would negate the past and present development contributions of Liberians abroad (i.e., remittances, skills transfer, humanitarian relief)	Those who fuelled Liberia's crises had the luxury of stoking conflict in the comfort and security of their homes abroad and could do so again if granted dual citizenship
(3) Liberians abroad would be encouraged to participate fully in future homeland development (i.e., brain gain/circulation, investment, paying taxes, establishing middle class)	Liberia would become a farmland of extraction where would-be dual citizens would cultivate Liberia and send revenues from that cultivation abroad, similar to foreign multinationals
(4) Other countries (particularly within the subregion) have enacted dual citizenship legislation and Liberians have benefitted from the protection and citizenship of more pluralistic nations	Liberia's development priorities and challenges are innumerable and enacting dual citizenship is neither a priority nor a matter of urgency for homeland actors
(5) Enacting dual citizenship would legislate what already exists in practice, that is, de facto dual citizenship, thereby encouraging those who carry two passports illegally to come out of hiding	Dual citizenship would privilege an already privileged social class (i.e., diasporas/transnationals) thereby increasing inequality in Liberia and replicating the nineteenth-century settler/indigene divide in the twenty-first century
(6) Dual citizenship would facilitate family reunification and encourage second-generation Liberians abroad to become more connected to the country	National reconciliation and healing through the Truth and Reconciliation Commission (TRC) recommendations must be addressed before dual citizenship can be meaningfully debated

Table 3.2 (*cont.*)

Pros	Cons
(7) Dual citizenship would enable free movement to and from Liberia without visa hurdles	Dual citizenship would enable violation of Liberia's already weak penal laws thus facilitating transnational crime (i.e., corruption, fraud, money laundering) with impunity
(8) Revocation of *jus soli* and *jus sanguinis* citizenship is unconstitutional because citizenship is the birth right of all Liberians	Dual citizenship will dilute the tenets of what it means to be 'truly Liberian'
(9) Liberia needs to wean itself off the assistance of foreign agents and replace them with capable Liberian development actors who may have naturalised abroad	Dual citizenship would create divided loyalties and one cannot 'serve two masters' at the same time
(10) Liberians abroad would be able to influence governance positively through active participation in the political process (i.e., voting, holding public office, etc.)	Transnational and diasporic Liberians cannot have the same rights and privileges as resident Liberian citizens (i.e., owning property, voting in national elections, holding public office, etc.) because their relationship with the Liberian state is distant and contested

they would uphold a bill with clearly defined stipulations, two other London-based actors were more ambivalent. In Washington, the breakdown was similar, with twenty-six of the thirty-three respondents endorsing dual citizenship while three had misgivings. Unlike London, however, four Washington-based informants completely dismissed dual citizenship as a development intervention. The slight contrast in perspectives on dual citizenship between London and Washington respondents is reflected in their citizenship profiles, where more Liberian-born interviewees in Washington (eleven) retained their legal Liberian citizenship while abroad than their London-based counterparts (six).

Of the twenty-one informants in Freetown, eighteen backed dual citizenship carte blanche. One expressed support with hesitation while another respondent denounced the policy prescription altogether. Liberia's then ambassador to Sierra Leone, Thomas Brima, noted his ambivalence about the 2008 bill. Unlike his counterparts in the United Kingdom and the United States, Ambassador Brima's personal views differed from the de facto official policy line by the then executive branch of the Liberian government. He shared his concerns with me in 2013 that dual citizenship could be subject to abuse and manipulation if it were not regulated thoroughly: 'I don't think it will improve anything. I think it will just give [a] chance for people to exploit two situations at their advantage'.[11] His admission that he did not fully agree with President Sirleaf's pro-dual citizenship posturing points to unofficial variations in perspectives despite official executive branch endorsement of the 2008 proposed legislation. This mirrors the range of divergent opinions amongst actors in Liberia and those abroad about the merits and demerits of dual citizenship.

Many Liberians interviewed in Freetown stated that they would not opt for naturalising in Sierra Leone if dual citizenship were enacted because being a Liberian is just like being a Sierra Leonean with very few distinct markers of identity. Implied in their views is the build-up of a sharp consciousness about the obligatory nature of participating in Liberia's political economy of belonging. Respondents argued that being a Liberian entails more than just carrying a passport or being born within the country's territorial borders; rather, it means making concrete contributions to the country's post-war recovery process. This level of acute awareness could be attributed to the fact that Liberians in Sierra Leone have a deeper appreciation of the importance of citizen participation in development outcomes because they reside in a country where post-war recovery is lived and experienced first-hand, unlike their counterparts in the United Kingdom and the United States.

In Accra, twenty of the thirty-three informants championed dual citizenship for Liberia while four supported it with reservations and one appeared undecided. Within the pool of diasporas, Accra represents the site where rejection of dual citizenship was most apparent with seven respondents snubbing the development intervention as unpatriotic. Strong opposition to dual citizenship is very likely because while national

---

[11] Interview in Freetown on 18 April 2013.

identity in the United Kingdom, the United States, and Sierra Leone appears more heterogeneous and malleable, it remains homogeneous and entrenched in Ghana despite the country's enactment of an all-inclusive dual citizenship act in 2000 which came into force in 2002. Therefore, respondents in Accra had a seemingly stronger sense of long distance nationalism (Anderson, 1992) than their counterparts elsewhere with many subscribing to the notion that citizenship is essentially confined to a unitary nation-state. Many Accra-based actors asserted that their Liberianness has been strengthened almost by compulsion because they reside in a country that explicitly delineates 'foreigner' from 'native', regardless of one's acquired citizenship status. Elaborating on this, a female entrepreneur and fourteen-year resident of Accra said:

I love my country [Liberia], come what may. And I don't see the need of becoming a Ghanaian when we are all ECOWAS [Economic Community of West African States citizens]. There's no need for that ... They [Ghanaians] protect themselves. I think it's a good thing, unlike we Liberians, we don't do that. We love strangers more than our own or ourselves. So, actually, no matter what it's their [Ghanaians'] country, you have to accept anything. ... Because you either take it or you leave it.[12]

Moreover, actors in Accra were similar to their counterparts in Freetown in admitting that they would pursue non-African citizenships if given the opportunity because of the perceived socio-economic benefits of naturalisation in the so-called Global North. Although one twenty-eight-year-old opted for local integration to attend university in Ghana, she visibly scoffed at the thought of naturalising in Ghana or any other African country for that matter:

Why should I get another African country citizenship when my country is an African country? ... But when you look at the Western world there are so many facilities, there are things that I can have in America, London, that I cannot have in my country. So, if America is requesting for a citizenship before I can get those things, I prefer having the [US] citizenship because if I come to my country I won't have that thing they are offering me.[13]

Nevertheless, a fifty-one-year-old self-professed pan-Africanist[14] said that if dual citizenship were enacted in Liberia she would opt for

[12] [DL110] Interview in Accra on 24 May 2013.
[13] [DL98] Interview in Accra on 18 May 2013.
[14] [CR9] Interview in Monrovia 27 June 2013.

another African passport rather than naturalise in Europe or America, proving that the socio-economic positions and lived experiences of individuals often shape their personal choices and political stances. Having moved to the United States after the 1980 coup in Liberia and resided there for twenty-eight years, this Monrovia-based circular returnee retained her legal Liberian citizenship, although most of her immediate family had become American citizens.

In stark contrast to the perspectives of informants in London, Washington, Freetown, and Accra, the majority of whom explicitly approved of blanket dual citizenship for Liberia, the greatest resistance to dual citizenship came from homelanders in Monrovia. This was subsequently corroborated by Afrobarometer (2018) survey data in which two-thirds of Liberians in-country said they oppose dual citizenship as a policy prescription, support limiting citizenship to people of 'Negro descent', and believe that only citizens should own land. Of the fifty homeland interviewees, twenty-two categorically rebuffed dual citizenship as a conceptual framework, legal instrument, and development intervention for Liberia. The majority of those who denounced the policy prescription were Liberians who admitted to physically residing in the country throughout the course of their lives. This supports my hypothesis that actors who never physically left Liberia might have slightly different conceptions of citizenship, and the rights and responsibilities therein, than those who travelled for short stints or lived abroad for longer periods of time. Sometimes employing symbolic imagery from slavery to describe citizens as 'slaves' and nation-states as 'masters', those who condemned dual citizenship said that Liberians who naturalised abroad had abandoned Liberia for a 'second master' thus exhibiting no loyalty to Liberia or divided loyalties at best. Invoking the 'heart' motif, one thirty-year-old male homelander emphatically scorned the 2008 dual citizenship bill on the grounds that it would facilitate divided loyalties if passed:

You cannot serve two masters. There is no way that one man can serve two masters. You cannot have two captains running one ship. You will always have the head captain, he's there to make the final decision ... If you have ten children or fifteen children there is no way you can love every one of them equally. Even if you have two wives, there is no way you can love two of them equally. You will always have love for one and it will exceed the other. So, there is no way one can love two countries at heart.[15]

---

[15] [HL17] Interview in Monrovia on 12 June 2013.

This particular position is theorised by Turner (2000: 141) who makes an interesting distinction between 'hot/cool loyalty' and 'thick/thin solidarity'. For instance, it is speculated that while cosmopolitan (dual) citizens exhibit 'cool' loyalties to any particular nation-state and 'thin' patterns of solidarity with a particular group of nationals governed within a nation-state, their non-cosmopolitan (single-citizen) counterparts exhibit 'hot' loyalties and 'thick' patterns of solidarity, respectively. In addition to spurning the presumed divided loyalties underpinning dual citizenship, homeland respondents also argued that Liberia's 2008 proposed bill would exacerbate an already-widening gap between rich and poor and encourage fraud and corruption by would-be dual citizens. These concerns will be explored in detail in subsequent chapters of this book.

Although a majority of the fifty homelanders snubbed dual citizenship, twelve defended the 2008 bill arguing that Liberians should not be penalised for seeking better opportunities abroad. These homeland actors claimed that dual citizenship would encourage Liberians who naturalised abroad (and their children) to reconnect with the country and become even more involved in post-war reconstruction. This perspective is indicative of the fact that the movement of people, ideas, and capital across territorial boundaries has impacted Liberians residing in the country as I mentioned earlier in this chapter about dual citizenship diffusion in Africa and will do so once again in Chapter 5 about how migration has influenced Liberian citizenship construction and practice. So, rather than representing a composite opinion about dual citizenship, homeland interviewees happened to be divided along ideological lines precisely because of their encounters with the globalisation of liberal citizenship norms and migration. While only two homelanders vacillated about dual citizenship, fourteen argued that if the proposed legislation were passed airtight provisions would have to be included and, most importantly, enforced to curb abuse and violation of Liberian laws. These actors had additional qualms about the premature timing of the bill considering Liberia's weak legal infrastructure and the challenge of protecting the rights and privileges of those with Liberian citizenship solely.

Variations in perspectives on dual citizenship were also apparent amongst returnee respondents, further illustrating the contested nature of Liberian citizenship across space and time. While six of the ten permanent returnees approved the bill and one admitted to supporting dual citizenship with a few reservations, three categorically rejected the proposed legislation. Of those who advocated for dual citizenship, one fifty-five-year-old US-born respondent admitted that she practised de facto dual citizenship because of her doubly inscribed identity:

I feel that I am a Liberian and I feel that I am an American by birth. And I feel that these two countries are not in war, they're not in conflict. I'm not aspiring to be president or any high government official, personally. So, what is the conflict? I know it's against the Liberian law [to carry both US and Liberian passports] but I also know that people turn the other way a lot. And why should I inconvenience myself by giving up one citizenship or the other? Both are valued to me.[16]

The respondent's admission that she covertly held two passports even though it was forbidden at the time of our interview in 2013 provided ammunition for homeland Liberians who framed dual citizenship as a channel for transnational crime. These views will be scrutinised further in Chapter 6 where I talk about the duality of diasporic interventions in homeland post-war development.

Unsurprisingly, the only consistent pattern of perspectives about dual citizenship in this study came from circular returnee respondents, all of whom – except one who expressed ambivalence – admitted to preferring dual citizenship carte blanche. One forty-four-year-old man born in the United States to Liberian citizen parents discussed why Liberians of his ilk should be able to legitimately wield two passports:

As a post-war country, we should be clamouring, we should be clawing, screaming, fighting tooth and nail to make sure that everyone who even has an inkling of wanting to be considered Liberian, particularly if they have something to offer, we should be fighting to get them to be Liberian. There is no reason why we should have a nuclear physicist or two, or three, or four, an endocrinologist, a general surgeon or four, or five, or six, whatever, out there who by simple virtue of their partial parentage or perhaps during the war years, they were born outside this country but they actually want to identify with Liberians. There is no reason why we should not be pulling those people in.[17]

Such an impassioned, personalised appeal reinforces the argument that dual citizenship is of significant importance to actors who lead transnational lives, as they would be the primary beneficiaries of legislation

16 [PR2] Interview in Monrovia on 7 June 2013.
17 [CR2] Interview in Monrovia on 5 June 2013.

in this regard. As illustrated by the previous respondent's strong defence of dual citizenship, Liberians' motivations for seeking other citizenships are varied, complex, and largely based on migration experiences, constraints, and opportunities, as I will explain in detail in Chapter 5.

The most revealing manifestation of citizenship as a contested space of inquiry for Liberia was that one of the sponsors of the 2008 proposed dual citizenship bill, then senator Taylor, admitted her ambivalence about the development intervention while her other co-sponsors emphatically endorsed it. Taylor said she had misgivings about the bill's unintended consequences given its implications for her own political future in Liberia. She, therefore, questioned the motives of Liberian diaspora proponents of dual citizenship:

What they're actually clamouring for is political ownership of Liberia. It's not economic; it's not developmental. That's how I feel. Because they want to determine who becomes president in Liberia ... So, they're looking for political capital; I don't see them looking for development or the interest in Liberia as we want to see. ... So, can you imagine people want to stay in America to take advantage of the opportunities there, live in the luxury that they have, they don't care what's happening here [in Liberia], but when it's time to vote all of them will rush home and say, 'Oh, I'm a Liberian citizen'. ... I don't want somebody living in America ... then you come and say ... 'Let [a] thousand of us go decide, ok, Senator Taylor will not be president for Liberia. Let's make sure we get George Weah' because you like George Weah. ... So, I'm one of those that have really taken a step back because we need to be a little careful because I don't want to do something that in the end will hamper the lives of my children. ... I'm not withdrawing as a sponsor [of the 2008 bill], but I think until we get the issues a little bit clearer we need to really look at it.[18]

Taylor's comments made in 2013 are particularly paradoxical now since she serves as Weah's vice president and as of mid-December 2019 there appeared to be a wedge in their relationship. Given her suspicions about diasporic support for him in 2013 as a threat to her professional ambitions, it is ironic that in 2017 she formed a merger to run as Weah's vice-presidential candidate and they won. Most importantly, Taylor's comments unsettled the very foundation upon which dual citizenship legislation was proffered: consensus by its sponsors.

---

[18]   Interview in Monrovia on 6 March 2013.

Since proponents of the 2008 bill disagreed about its potential merits, then it is no wonder that Liberians at home and abroad clashed over what it signified for them.

The inconsistency in perspectives about dual citizenship amongst legislative branch sponsors of the 2008 proposed bill is also mirrored in the divergent viewpoints of their executive branch counterparts. Whereas two of the eight executive policymakers lauded dual citizenship as an important development imperative, four others remarked that provisions in the 2008 bill would have to restrict the privileges of would-be dual citizens, such as serving in the AFL or holding high public office. One policymaker wavered on the issue, neither completely rejecting nor approving dual citizenship. Another abstained from offering an opinion. It was evident from high-ranking official interviewees that the Liberian government, particularly its executive branch, lacked a unified policy position on dual citizenship.

Based on the divergent life-worlds and social locations of Liberian actors consulted for this book, it is clear that dual citizenship was far from a topic of consensus during the time of my interviews and thereafter. This is not entirely shocking, however, since the conception and practice of Liberian citizenship across space and time have remained disputed.

Conclusion

As illustrated in the introduction of this chapter, the University of Liberia face-off between student activists and diaspora lobbyists indicates how homeland actors had just as much power in stalling the 2008 dual citizenship bill as their transnational counterparts had in pushing for its introduction and passage. It is important here to recount that actors may consciously and unconsciously display their diametrically opposed lived experiences and socio-economic positions in interface situations. While international norms manifested in discourses about human rights influenced a measured acceptance of the merits of dual citizenship for Liberia, the transmission in Africa of transnational belonging has had varied outcomes for the country. The different views about dual citizenship as espoused by Liberian respondents demonstrate the discontinuities within their life-worlds and social locations. Viewed as both promise and peril for diasporic and domestic actors, respectively, dual citizenship represented an instrumental tug of war in which homelanders preferred to protect their privileges while transnationals wished to expand their rights.

In the empirical chapters that follow, I explain how Liberia reached such a gridlock on dual citizenship. I argue that three key historical and contemporary factors – namely, conflict, migration, and post-war recovery – configured and reconfigured citizenship across space and time thereby sharpening the features of Liberia's political economy of belonging as well as influencing claims for and against the country's 2008 dual citizenship bill.

4 | *Give Me Your Land or I'll Shoot!*

Introduction

On 15 December 1821, King Peter (Zolu Duma), paramount chief of Cape Mesurado on the coast of pre-settler Liberia, was allegedly held at gunpoint. His assailants, Eli Ayers and Robert Stockton, were white agents of the American Colonisation Society (ACS) whose obsession with repatriating free blacks was really a smokescreen for averting slave revolts in the Southern United States. King Peter, like all the other African kings Ayers and Stockton had approached to secure land, was intransigent. Use of force and the threat of violence, they reasoned, would be the only means of pacifying him. As the uncorroborated account goes, a frustrated Stockton brandished two pistols, gave one to Ayers with instructions to shoot if provoked, aimed the other at King Peter's temple, and insisted that he and five other chiefs relinquish parcels of land by deed in exchange for US$300 and tradeable goods such as rum, tobacco, and guns.

When black settlers arrived at the Cape in 1822, however, King Peter apparently attempted to return compensation for the land complaining that he had been duped. This incident – which has become legend in Liberian historiography – would mark the first documented conflict between indigenes and settlers over land ownership, a major tenet of Liberia's political economy of belonging. In this chapter, I argue that Liberian citizenship has been constructed and reconstructed because of conflicts[1] precipitated by four major interfaces between a range of actors, including (1) the 1847 founding of the nation-state, its pre-settler antecedents and post-independence state-building and nation-building architecture; (2) the toppling of True Whig Party (TWP) rule

---

[1] According to Levitt (2005), Liberia experienced more than eighteen deadly conflicts between 1822 and 2003.

in 1980; (3) armed conflicts between 1989–1997 and 1999–2003 which ruptured and sealed government–citizen and citizen–citizen relations simultaneously; and (4) post-war contestations over income, land tenure, and transitional justice. I maintain further that these four sites of conflict reveal a crisis of citizenship dating back to Liberia's state formation beginning in the mid-nineteenth century and, therefore, underpin contemporary claims for and against dual citizenship.

Just as Liberia's citizenship construction has undergone a series of iterations, so too have its state-making processes, primarily triggered by conflicts of varying degrees and scales. Conflict, in my analysis, includes both physical and structural violence, coined by Johan Galtung (1969) to convey the social structures and institutions that inhibit individuals from meeting their basic needs or from actualising their fullest capabilities (Sen, 1999: 291). While I employ Long's notion of the interface, I also incorporate Galtung's conflict triangle with the elements of attitude (A), behaviour (B), and contradiction (C) representing each node. According to Galtung (1996: 70–73), conflict signifies a dynamic process in which the 'incompatibility of goals' of different actors (contradiction) fuels their perceptions and misperceptions of themselves and each other (attitudes) thereby influencing actions (behaviour) that may range from opposition to accommodation, as will be seen in the analysis that follows.

From Black Migrant Settlement to Unification and Integration

The first interactions between Liberia's indigenes and settlers exemplified a clash of life-worlds and social locations. Through a series of interfaces in the nineteenth century, white ACS agents and black repatriates encountered sixteen ethno-linguistic groups[2] who already occupied the hinterland and coast, and had been engaged in small-scale warfare over territory, trade (human and commodity) and political legitimacy (Levitt, 2005: 25). Whereas ACS operatives and their settler counterparts espoused an individualistic, free-market approach to territory, indigenes believed that they were the communal custodians of land. According to Liberia's Land Commission, the practice of treating

---

[2] The Bassa, Dan, Dei, Gbandi, Gio, Gola, Grebo, Kissi, Kpelle, Krahn, Kru, Lorma, Mandingo, Mano, Mende, and Vai comprise the sixteen indigenous groups.

all undeeded land as public and easily acquired privately was a misguided policy adopted by the settlers and ACS because until the country's 2018 Land Rights Act was passed there was no clear reconciliation between public and pre-existing customary land rights (Government of Liberia, 2013a: 6; Government of Liberia, 2018).

As indigenes defended their territorial integrity in pre-independence Liberia, the settlers launched counter-offensives, pushing further inland, appropriating more land, and establishing political dominion. They came to an eventual truce in 1822 and a subsequent peace settlement in 1825 though relations between the two sets of actors would remain hostile, particularly over trade, land tenure, taxation, and political jurisdiction, well after a constitution was drafted in 1845. Liberia became an independent republic two years later with the coastal counties[3] of Montserrado, Grand Bassa, and Sinoe comprising its initial territory. According to the Liberian Truth and Reconciliation Commission (TRC) (2009a: 49–50) preliminary findings, conflict between settlers and indigenes was inevitable precisely because of their competing contexts:

The new settlement was anti-slavery, pro-trade, predominantly Christian and highly centralised; whereas, most coastal native groups were pro-slavery, commercial tradesmen, non-Christian and lived under decentralised authority structures. Hence, the likelihood of any form of union between the settlement and native nations was highly unlikely.

While settlers appeared oblivious to the sophisticated writing systems, well-developed trade routes, and administrative governance structures of the indigenes they encountered, indigenes scoffed at settlers' penchant for centralised social organisation and legitimate hatred of human bondage (Kieh, 2012a: 169). Reflecting on this stalemate, a male circular returnee informant argued that Liberians' nineteenth-century xenophobic tendencies have twenty-first-century manifestations 'because there's this fear of the stranger. ... I think it's a historical thing. ... That fear is ingrained in Liberians' psyche, so deep that people express it anywhere, anyhow'.[4] It would be inaccurate, however, to assume that all interactions between indigenes and settlers were antagonistic. For instance, Liberty (1977: 37, 39) insisted

---

[3] These were the first three of Liberia's current fifteen political subdivisions.
[4] [CR7] Interview in Monrovia on 18 June 2013.

that there was significantly more 'interpenetration' between coastal and hinterland inhabitants – marked by either 'coercion' or 'voluntary accession' – than otherwise assumed. While some ethno-linguistic communities, most notably the Bassa, Dei, Gola, Grebo, Kru, and Vai, resisted settler rule in a series of deadly conflicts well into the early twentieth century, others such as the Gio and Kpelle were more conciliatory (Levitt, 2005: 6). Furthermore, trade in palm oil, tobacco, rice, rum, cotton goods, beads, and cassava connected settler coastal towns to inland indigenous communities and indigenous knowledge in medicinal relief saved settlers from the worst bouts of malaria (Clegg, 2004: 242).

Nevertheless, the free blacks who had been barred from citizenship in the United States and Caribbean adopted a narrow definition of legal, national identity that excluded all non-blacks and most indigenes, women, and non-Christians, just as ancient Greek citizenship had excluded women and the enslaved. Though a response to the invisibility of their previous lives abroad, the 'legalised personhood' and 'documented existence' of black repatriates infringed upon the life, liberty, and land tenure of indigenes (Clegg, 2004: 247). This form of repressive citizenship had loopholes, however. For a small number of indigenes, intermarriage and apprenticeship became the channels through which citizenship could be acquired. In 1838, for example, an apprenticeship law was enacted enabling settler families to take in indigenous children. In exchange for their domestic labour, these children were given clothing and food; upon reaching the age of majority they were considered 'civilised' and, therefore, eligible for legal Liberian citizenship (Gershoni, 1985: 27–28). An 1841 act further conferred citizenship on indigenes who 'abandoned all the forms of, customs, and superstitions of heathenism' and adopted 'the forms, customs and habits of civilised life', that is, what Liberty refers to as 'black whitemanism' (Liberty, 1977: 154–155; Clegg, 2004: 242). In the 1870s, selected indigenes were appointed 'referees' or 'delegates' in the Legislature as advisors followed by more meaningful participation in the political process in the twentieth century (Dunn, Beyan & Burrowes, 2001: 340–341). Tiers of citizenship soon developed, however, with the 'settler, commercial, coastal, and political elite' at the top, followed by the 'small business persons and farmers', recaptives, and select indigenes (Levitt, 2005: 91). While concessions on citizenship were welcomed, the Liberian state virtually overlooked indigenes in the hinterland who remained relatively independent until the early 1900s (Burrowes, 2004: 2).

Partial and Qualified Citizenship under Barclay

As Liberia tackled the challenge of 'white acceptance of black supremacy' internationally, it embarked in the early twentieth century on internal efforts to integrate indigenes formally into the body politic (Liberty, 1977: 203). Through territorial expansion in 1904, President Arthur Barclay attempted to ward off encroachment by French and British imperialists as well as establish a consistent stream of revenue for the administration of the hinterland. According to Liberty (1977: 256), during this period black migrant settlers were buoyed not by a sense of innate superiority, per se, but rather by desperate attempts to remain sovereign; nevertheless, Mamdani (1996) would liken their efforts to a form of 'decentralised despotism' or indirect rule best exemplified elsewhere in Africa by British colonisers. Employing the tools of state-building, Barclay extended Liberia's geographic ambit through military might and a system of centrally controlled taxation. Under the 'Barclay Plan', as it came to be known, Liberia was divided into administrative units under the auspices of district commissioners who maintained law and order according to the Liberian Constitution, reporting directly to the president, and traditional chiefs who governed according to customary law (Liberty, 1977: 245–247). The chiefs had a semblance of autonomy although the administration of traditional customs could not contradict the Constitution in any way. Violently resisted by ethno-linguistic groups such as the Gbandi, Grebo, Kpelle, and Kru, a series of norms were instituted under the 'Barclay Plan' through the construction of military outposts in strategic locations in rural Liberia with the backing of the Liberian Frontier Force (LFF),[5] established in 1908 to squash rebellion in the hinterlands: (1) indigenes who were educated, converted to Christianity, and adopted 'Western standards' of conduct and appearance could qualify for legal Liberian citizenship; (2) a 'hut tax' was imposed on households in the hinterlands and administered through local chiefs who received 10 per cent

---

[5] Established through financial and administrative support initially from the British, followed by the Americans, the LFF would later metamorphose into the Armed Forces of Liberia (AFL) in 1962.

commission; (3) Poro and Sande secret societies were banned; and (4) forced indigene labour, particularly for roadworks, became wide-spread (Government of Liberia, 1949; Liberty, 1977: 220–222, 258–260, 288–289; Dunn, 1979: 31; Jaye, 2003: 68–69; Levitt, 2005: 147–180; TRC, 2009b: 114–115).

Effectively, the 'Barclay Plan' failed to meaningfully integrate indigenes or incorporate them into Liberia's twentieth-century political economy of belonging. Hinterland residents, often referred to as 'uncivilised natives' in official policy documents, were performing citizenship through their payment of taxes yet treated as subjects within a bifurcated state in the same way that European colonialism privileged the 'civilised' thus making the 'uncivilised ... subject to an all-around tutelage ... with a modicum of civil rights, but not political rights' (Mamdani, 1996: 17). Although inhabitants of pre-settler Liberia had established trade relations with Europe in the 1500s, leaders of post-independence Liberia began full integration into the international capitalist system in the twentieth century thereby adversely impacting the institution of citizenship (Kieh, 1992: 36). For instance, it was during the administration of President Charles DB King between 1920 and 1930 that indigenes were conscripted for road construction projects throughout the country and also forcibly shipped to the cocoa producing Spanish colony of Fernando Po to work under labour conditions akin to chattel slavery (Kieh, 1992: 32–33). Considered subjects rather than citizens, hinterland inhabitants were easily expendable and could be used as commodities to attract foreign capital. The Fernando Po crisis, as it came to be known, triggered a formal inquiry by the League of Nations condemning Liberia and prompting the impeachment and later resignation of King and his vice president in 1930 (Kieh, 1992: 33; Dunn, 2009: 20–21). This calamity foreshadowed Liberia's enduring struggle to match pro-capitalist economic growth with pro-citizen holistic development.

There were two clearly defined categories of Liberians in the first half of the twentieth century, those governed nationally by the Liberian nation-state (often settler in orientation, urban, and considered 'civilised') and others governed locally by chieftain authorities (often indigenous in orientation, rural, and considered 'native') (Liberty, 1977: 149; Moran, 2006: 75). As previously mentioned, most 'Negro' inhabitants of the Liberian territory were not considered full citizens and were therefore excluded from formal rights and privileges until

Tubman's Unification and Integration Policy was adopted in the mid-twentieth century.

Conditional Full Citizenship under Tubman

Although President Tubman stretched the contours of Liberianness wider than Barclay, he failed to consolidate a strong national identity because the conferral of citizenship was conditional and based on the adoption of a 'civilised life', as indicated in his 1944 inaugural address (Government of Liberia, 1944; Tubman, 1944):

In the administration of our population inhabiting the hinterland, our aim and purpose shall be to educate them into good and useful citizens, capable of knowing their duty, status and rights as citizens, and competent of exerting, enjoying and asserting them: to have them love their native land and feel proud to be called Liberians. For it is to these fellow citizens of ours, inhabitants of the hinterland, that we must look very largely for the future maintenance and perpetuity of the state; for we are aiming at developing a civilised state, the civilisation of which will be as weak as its weakest pagan link if due precaution not be taken. ... It seems to me that if a woman possesses the same qualifications of a man in the state which entitles him to enjoy the suffrage, the mere and only fact of difference in sex should not reasonably form a bar to her enjoying that privilege. ... We shall therefore persevere in our endeavour to extend to the women of Liberia full participation in the affairs of government and its political activities including the right of woman suffrage.

Thus, Tubman expanded the parameters of Liberia's political economy of belonging with a series of seemingly progressive policies. He extended voting rights, among other privileges, to male and female property owners of 'Negro descent' who paid taxes (Dunn, Beyan & Burrowes, 2001: 341). This was coupled with equally measured, concessionary reforms affecting indigenes: (1) indigenes were entitled to a small number of elected positions within the Legislature although settlers retained the offices of the speaker of the House of Representatives and president pro-tempore of the Senate; (2) infrastructure such as road networks, water, and sanitation services were extended to former hinterland territories; and (3) basic social services such as access to healthcare and education were accorded indigenous citizens, albeit at a lower standard (TRC, 2009a: 52; TRC, 2009b: 120; Kieh, 2012b: 9). In 1964, Tubman altered further Liberia's political subdivisions by introducing four new counties that made former hinterland areas equal to that of coastal regions administered by settler elites (Dunn, Beyan & Burrowes, 2001: 341).

In hindsight, one could argue that Tubman, of non-Monrovia privileged pedigree, was forward thinking despite the constraints of his time. However, scholars have argued that his main objective was to solidify his own power base through territorial expansion of the settler state and this could only happen through appeasing indigenes and non-elites (Kieh, 1992: 33; Sawyer, 2005: 16). Moreover, Tubman's words of unprecedented conciliation to hinterland inhabitants were contradicted by patronising and offensive references to their presumed paganism and lack of civilisation. For the descendants of settlers like Tubman, being 'civilised' was often conflated with being a citizen, demarcated by the ability to speak English fluently, membership in a Christian church, employment in the formal economy as a wage labourer, residence in urban centres such as Monrovia, and the consumption of Western products (Burrowes, 2004: 69; Moran, 2006: 78). Throughout the twentieth century, a ward system replicated the nineteenth-century apprenticeship law in which children of indigenous families were shuttled to Monrovia to be raised and educated by settler families (Sirleaf, 2009; Waugh, 2011: 25–27). While the process of assimilation enabled the adoption of settler names, conversion to Christianity, and formal incorporation into a highly stratified social structure, it also alienated indigenes from their rural counterparts (Waugh, 2011: 26–27). Effectively, becoming a 'civilised' citizen was akin to relinquishing formal ties with one's indigenous heritage.

Some have argued that the Unification and Integration Policy was nothing more than pacification intended to create a cult around Tubman, support his patronage networks, and facilitate unencumbered exploitation of Liberia's natural resources by foreign multinationals. Because citizenship was tied to private property ownership, the Policy negated indigenous forms of communal land ownership and alienated men and women who did not have the resources to acquire land and pay taxes on that land. As such, the Policy neither completely overhauled the institution of Liberian citizenship nor did it effectively equalise transactions within the political economy of belonging to Liberia. Furthermore, although Tubman sought to create national cohesion, his administration was characterised by political repression, where opponents were either jailed or forced into exile; economic elitism, in which a few families controlled the export-based economy that relied heavily on the extraction of mineral and agricultural resources such as rubber, iron ore, gold, and timber without value addition; de facto one-party state entrenchment bolstered by 'selections' rather than 'elections'; and social alienation embedded in hierarchies of skin colour, ethnicity, and class coupled with religious intolerance against non-Christians (Jaye, 2003: 73–77; Kieh, 2004: 60–67; Levitt, 2005: 181–190; Afrofusion, 2012). The end of Tubman's twenty-seven-year reign upon his death in 1971 would usher in the most agentic forms of citizenship practice Liberia had seen to date. The expansion of citizenship rights and privileges facilitated increased political activism culminating in a 1980 coup that decisively ousted settler rule.

1980 Coup Pushes Boundaries of Liberian Citizen Agency

In addition to overthrowing a TWP dynasty, the 1980 coup symbolically transformed Liberian citizenship by making it an institution that all Liberians of 'Negro descent' could access from 'below' for the first time. As product of a cauldron that had been bubbling for over one hundred years, the Global South-leaning William R Tolbert Jr, Tubman's successor, had eschewed Liberia's asymmetrical alliance with the United States – what D Elwood Dunn (2009) calls the 'limits of reciprocity' – and opened up the domestic political space considerably to non-elite trade unionists, civil servants, students and educators, local entrepreneurs, and military personnel hence alienating members of the top echelons of his party (Levitt, 2005: 192). A number of interconnected factors in the late 1970s contributed to the dismantling of TWP power, among which was the agency of Liberians made manifest after long periods of pacification and coercion (Konneh, 2002: 76–79; Levitt, 2005: 191–197; TRC, 2009b: 129–139; Waugh, 2011: 34, 58, 61–63; Kieh, 2012b: 175; Burrowes, 2016a: viii).

First, Liberia's economy experienced a nosedive because of the downward spiral of global commodity prices in exports such as palm oil, rubber, iron ore, and timber. Eclipsed by the oil crisis, the country's economic meltdown led to inflation, food insecurity, and increased rural to urban migration. Second, large numbers of indigenes began attending universities in Liberia and abroad through government-sponsored scholarships and upon their return they assumed positions within the civil service though rarely at high managerial levels. Third, although President Tolbert attempted to adopt gradual political reforms he appointed members of his family to strategic positions within the executive branch of government, including the ministries of defence and finance, leading to public rumblings about patronage and nepotism. Fourth, civil unrest came to a head on 14 April 1979, when state security forces attacked, arrested, wounded, and killed street demonstrators after the government proposed an increase in the price of imported rice reportedly designed to benefit the president and his allies who owned farms dotted across Liberia. Although the planned inflation was partly a result of World Bank pressures to repeal subsidies on imports, it may also have been intended to encourage consumption of Liberia's locally produced staple crop. Nevertheless, it did not accompany positive structural changes in the living conditions of the majority of Liberians thus adversely tipping the scales of Liberia's political economy of belonging. Therefore, the 'Rice Riots', as they were popularly called, mirrored simultaneous labour strikes advocating for higher salaries and better working conditions.

When Tolbert spent an estimated US$200 million in hosting the Organisation of African Unity (OAU) Summit in Liberia in July 1979 amidst economic decline, there was widespread and visible discontent amongst an increasingly politicised populace (Kieh, 2012b). Similarly, the emergence of opposition groups – such as the Movement for Justice in Africa (MOJA), the Progressive Alliance of Liberia (PAL), and the Progressive People's Party (PPP) – permitted to register and operate freely – unsettled TWP hegemony for the first time in over twenty-five years since opposition parties had been banned in the 1950s (Dunn, 2009: 92; Kieh, 2012b: 145). As Liberian Ambassador to the United Kingdom Wesley Momo Johnson recounted to me in 2012, it was his exposure to the relatively egalitarian political systems in the United States while a student there in the 1970s that galvanised him to join Liberian opposition movements in the 1980s:

[I discovered] this is real freedom here [in the United States]. Why [do] we have one and only one political party in Liberia? It can be better! Then we organised PAL, which is the Progressive Alliance of Liberia, Bacchus Matthews, Samuel Jackson, Oscar Quiah, Marcus Dahn, all of us were there … and we began to challenge the government on the one-party state. And so, by 1984–1985 we became a registered party called PPP, Progressive

People's Party, and then from there we became United People's Party (UPP) which we are still today. Fortunately for us Ellen [Johnson Sirleaf] ... was a serious supporter of us and she saw a vision for the country that it can be better.[6]

Imbibing the spirit of indigenous resistance, marginalised groups of Liberians began to make claims to citizenship that essentially set the stage for the infamous 12 April 1980 coup. In addition to assassinating President Tolbert and declaring military rule, Samuel Kanyon Doe and a group of non-commissioned AFL soldiers executed thirteen members of his cabinet as an apparent symbol of the end of settler supremacy (Sawyer, 1987; Dunn, Beyan & Burrowes, 2001: 90–91). A Krahn man of limited education, Doe was celebrated as a channel through which indigenous Liberians could finally access the tenets of full citizenship and partake in the political economy of belonging. He subsequently suspended the 1847 Constitution and instituted a more inclusive military government, the People's Redemption Council (PRC), hiring a number of indigenous civilians who had returned to Liberia with terminal degrees from US universities; those of settler lineage were also incorporated in various ministerial posts (Sawyer, 1987; Konneh, 2002: 78). Months after the coup, the PRC also abolished the controversial 'hut tax' (Dunn, Beyan & Burrowes, 2001: 170).

Doomed to follow the mistakes of his predecessors, however, Doe became increasingly agitated with students, labour unions, clergy, and opposition leaders who resisted his dismissal of popular dissent. He developed an inner circle comprising members of his own ethnicity, the Krahns, invested heavily in the military, confiscated property, imposed curfews, and restricted the movement of civilians (Konneh, 2002: 78). After appointing in 1981 a National Constitution Commission to draft a new Constitution that would return the country to civilian rule in 1986, it became clear that Doe was not fundamentally interested in upending the status quo (Sawyer, 1987). Dismissing the Commission's draft constitution, which limited presidential powers amongst other recommendations, Doe co-opted a Constitutional Assembly, whose members had political ambitions, to revise the draft by increasing the terms of office for president from four to six years in exchange for increasing the terms of office for senators from six to nine years and representatives from four to six years (Sawyer, 1987; Kieh, 2012b:

[6] Interview in London on 14 June 2012.

166). When a 1985 election should have returned Liberia to democratic normalcy, Doe allegedly rigged the ballot boxes to win the presidency by a 51 per cent majority (Konneh, 2002: 79; Williams, 2006: 77). Although Doe's coup ultimately expanded Liberia's citizenship architecture and pried open its political economy of belonging, his subsequent reign as de facto head of state ironically muzzled the political practices of citizens he claimed to have liberated from settler domination.

On 12 November 1985, Thomas Quiwonkpa, one of Doe's trusted allies, was assassinated after attempting to depose the military regime (Dunn, Beyan & Burrowes, 2001: 275). Reprisals against ethnic Mano and Gio civilians in Quiwonkpa's Nimba County ensued until a general amnesty was adopted in 1986 (Konneh, 2002: 79). Following the aborted coup, Liberia was marked by entrenched authoritarianism, economic decline, and the politicisation of ethnicity. President Doe responded to repeated protests with violence; amassed personal wealth from millions of dollars in foreign largesse thereby neglecting public spending on important social services; and gradually increased the number of Krahn members in his cabinet (Konneh, 2002: 80–81). In dodging his duties to preserve Liberia's political economy of belonging, Doe set the stage for an absolute rupture of the system. One respondent in my study, a sixty-three-year-old Washington resident, recalled how the 1985 attempted coup by Quiwonkpa torpedoed Liberia into chaos and prompted him to leave his relatively comfortable life in Monrovia:

It was the [attempted] coup d'état [of 1985] that really drove some of us from there [Liberia] because there was a lot of instability, anticipated instability, that we knew was going to happen. ... Before the coup took place everything was fine. I was working as assistant minister, special assistant. I was working as director for research and planning. And then we realised that the country was getting harder and harder because there was a flight of capital. All the companies were leaving, they had packed up and they had left, so I just decided, 'Well, I think I will go to a greener pasture' ... because I had anticipated that something bigger was going to happen.[7]

As foreshadowed by this respondent, Liberia's government–citizen relations would be transformed through conflict once again with intermittent warfare beginning in 1989 and ending officially in 2003. Contrary to the mainstream literature that characterises Liberia's

---

[7] [DL58] Interview in Washington on 27 October 2012.

wars as localised and 'civil', it is clear from the various actors involved that the armed conflicts had international dimensions. They were also indicative of state collapse, representing not only continuations of the tragically flawed state formation project started in 1822 but also failed efforts to construct egalitarian forms of citizenship from independence onwards.

Two Uncivil Wars, Rupture and Melding of Citizen Relations

On Christmas Eve in 1989, Charles Taylor, a former cabinet official in Doe's administration, launched an insurgency from Côte d'Ivoire to topple his former boss. According to George Klay Kieh Jr (1992: 130), 'Taylor's strategy for winning support was anchored on the exploitation of the grievances of the various groups who were essential to the success of his military campaign'. Backed by external forces such as Burkina Faso, Côte d'Ivoire, Libya, and Liberian exiles in the United States, Taylor's multi-ethnic National Patriotic Front of Liberia (NPFL) comprised large numbers of Gio and Mano dissidents (Kieh, 1992: 131; Konneh, 2002: 83; Kieh, 2004: 69). A number of other insurgent groups emerged, but it was a splinter faction from the NPFL, the Independent National Patriotic Front of Liberia (INPFL), whose leader, former Taylor ally Prince Johnson, would lure Doe to the Freeport of Monrovia in 1990, torture, and kill him while taping the gruesome assassination for wider dissemination. Akin to the brutal murder of President Tolbert a decade before, Doe's death represented a symbolic levelling of illegitimate government authority by disgruntled citizens.

Fuelled and funded in part by the exploitation of Liberia's timber and diamonds, the first war ebbed and flowed between 1989 and 1997. Fearing a regional crisis, the Economic Community of West African States (ECOWAS) deployed an ad-hoc peacekeeping mission, ECOMOG, which eventually became a party to the conflict by allying itself with various warring factions (Jaye, 2003). Nevertheless, ECOMOG assisted in bringing the war to an end in 1996 with the signing of the Abuja II Peace Agreement, the last of seventeen agreements total, followed by elections in July 1997 that ushered in Taylor's presidency (Konneh, 2002: 85; Kieh, 2011: 53–54). Countering the one-dimensional analysis marked by some of the literature on Liberia's first war, Kieh (2004: 60–67) adopts a multidimensional causal framework, arguing convincingly that armed conflict was precipitated by historical, political, cultural, economic, social, and military factors already discussed earlier in this chapter. Kieh's 'crises of underdevelopment' analysis supports my contention that Liberia's contemporary conflicts are underpinned by unresolved historical crises of citizenship.

After two years marking a cessation of armed conflict, Taylor's reign of terror and subsequent foray into Sierra Leonean hostilities incited two rebel groups to stage a second war in 1999. Comprising former combatants from the first Liberian uprising and anti-Taylor enthusiasts, the Liberians United for Reconciliation and Democracy (LURD) launched an offensive from neighbouring Guinea (Waugh, 2011: 264–268; Hazen, 2013: 105–110). Backed by the Guinean and American governments and supported by financial contributions from Liberians abroad, LURD also sustained itself through looting and diamond extraction (Hazen, 2013: 113–118). The splinter group Movement for Democracy in Liberia (MODEL) began its incursion into Liberia in 2003 and was hoisted up by political support from Liberians abroad as well as the military and economic assistance of then Ivorian President Laurent Gbagbo (Hazen, 2013: 121, 131–133). Although Taylor had an advantage in terms of supply networks of guns and money, MODEL and LURD gained the upper hand when his arms and revenue stockpiles began to dwindle in 2003 (Hazen, 2013: 107). With mounting international pressure to step down and MODEL and LURD on his heels approaching Monrovia, Taylor was deflated and defeated when he agreed to seek political asylum in Nigeria in August 2003, leading to the signing of a peace agreement which ushered in a transitional government in 2005.

Liberia's intermittent armed conflicts represented a disintegration of the political economy of belonging as well as a continuation of the depravity of Tubman's Open Door Policy, during which a programme of plunder was adopted. State resources were bartered off to the highest bidder with gross domestic product (GDP) per capita falling by 90 per cent between 1987 and 1994 (Government of Liberia, 2008a: 15; Government of Liberia, 2011a: 57). Between 1990 and 1994 alone, it is estimated that more than US$500 million was accumulated yearly by leaders of armed factions and their associates from exports in rubber, diamonds, and other natural resources; Taylor reportedly accrued US$75 million annually (Sawyer, 2005: 38). His subsequent reign beginning 1997 reflected a further perversion of Open Door. The presumed gains in foreign exchange earnings from exports in iron ore and rubber were compromised by the high importation costs of most of Liberia's food products, including rice, as well as mineral fuels and other petroleum products (Kieh, 1992: 46). Like some of his presidential predecessors, Taylor proved early on that he was more interested in capital accumulation than strengthening government–citizen relations. For example, when workers employed by Liberia's first major foreign investor, Firestone,[8] demonstrated against the rubber giant's arbitrary decision in 1997 to deduct 38 per cent of their monthly salaries to replace money that had been allegedly stolen in the company's safe deposit box during the first Liberian armed conflict, Taylor unleashed his security personnel to indiscriminately attack 7,000 unarmed demonstrators thus stifling dissent (Kieh, 2012b: 206). In 1999, he signed a deal with an Indonesian-owned corporation, Oriental Timber Company (OTC), which had a dismal environmental record, and granted it logging rights to close to half of Liberia's rainforest (Sawyer, 2005: 38). Liberia's warlord president operated a post-war economy of seismic proportions; while smuggling Sierra Leonean diamonds to fuel that country's armed conflict, he was reportedly wheeling and dealing with the likes of South African diamond producer De Beers, Al-Qaeda, the American evangelist Pat Robertson, and lesser known but equally pernicious Dutch, Ukrainian, and Italian businessmen (Sawyer, 2005: 38–39). This prompted the United Nations (UN) to impose sanctions on Liberia's diamonds in 2001 and timber in 2003, respectively, precipitated by investigations by Liberian environmental campaigner Silas Kpanan'Ayoung Siakor of the Save My Future Foundation in collaboration with the UK-based natural resources watchdog Global Witness (Global Witness & the International Transport Workers Federation, 2001).

Although the vast literature on armed conflict emphasises poverty, inequality, bad neighbourhoods and governance, weak state institutions, and natural resource dependency as causal factors, Call (2010:

---

[8] Firestone has the world's largest industrial rubber plantation in Liberia, a sprawling 118,990 acres adjacent to the country's only international airport, Roberts International Airport (RIA) (Pailey, 2007a). In 1926, Liberia contracted a US$5 million loan from the Finance Corporation of America, sponsored by US-based Firestone Tire and Rubber Company, at an interest rate of 7 per cent. In exchange, Firestone leased one million acres of land for ninety-nine years at six cents per acre to extract unprocessed rubber under what some have called slavery-like conditions.

353–356) argues that grievances against Taylor's exclusionary behaviour after the 1997 elections – manifested in the repression and assassination of political opponents, media suppression, and exclusion of former foes within the security forces – led to war recurrence in Liberia. Kieh (2009) also concludes that failures of the post-war transitional and peace-building processes led to overall deprivation. Moreover, young ex-combatants who underwent demobilisation without the necessary reintegration were socially excluded and marginalised further because of their war-time status, proving that state collapse and its aftermath affect citizens in disparate ways.

When Two Elephants Fight, the Grass Suffers

By its very definition, citizenship signifies a certain level of agency and empowerment, of men and women making sense of their natural environment (Castles & Davidson, 2000: 21). It is supposed to bring about order, however, as the Liberian proverb states, 'when two elephants fight, the grass suffers'. Essentially, Liberians were forced to redefine what it meant to be citizens in the absence of a functioning government during the two wars. In fact, most respondents interviewed for this book left Liberia for short stints, extended periods, or indefinitely during protracted armed conflict, fundamentally altering how they identified with their country and with each other. The breakdown of order constituted a collapse of Liberia's political economy of belonging thus leading to mass exodus, said one Washington-based fifty-three -year-old female respondent: 'We wouldn't have left [Liberia] in those numbers were it not for the fact that there was no rule of law, no respect for property because there were soldiers getting in peoples' houses, toilets are busted out, you know, glasses busted out of the windows'.[9] Echoing this respondent's sentiments, then senator Wotorson, chief sponsor of the proposed dual citizenship bill of 2008, lamented to me in 2013:

Liberians by nature love their country and they never like to part from their country . . . the drafters of Liberia's Constitution did not foresee that we were going to have a destabilising civil war that would displace our citizens, most of them involuntarily, to countries, some of which were hostile, in a hostile

---

[9] [DL47] Interview in Washington on 23 October 2012.

environment, and for which reasons their [citizenship status] choices were limited.[10]

Yet, Liberia's violently contested state formation and political consolidation processes were marked by crises of citizenship that foreshadowed outbreaks of armed conflict in the twentieth and twenty-first centuries.

From the country's inception, rural dwellers were limited in their participation in the political and economic life of the nation-state. They could hardly boast of experiencing full citizenship with attendant rights and responsibilities even after calculated reforms instituted by Tubman, Tolbert, and Doe. It is no wonder, then, that Liberia's protracted armed conflicts were launched from ungoverned rural spaces – Nimba County in 1989 and Lofa County in 1999. What differentiated the wars in Liberia from those in neighbouring Côte d'Ivoire and Sierra Leone was the wanton destruction of essential infrastructure such as roads, bridges, power plants, and the Mt Coffee hydroelectric facility built in the 1960s (Government of Liberia, 2011a: 57). According to Liberian environmental activist Alfred Brownell, urban infrastructure represented easily expendable 'monuments of hatred'[11] in the eyes of young combatants because they could not access these fully in their pre-war communities. Although there was forced conscription during Liberia's conflicts, Utas (2005: 151; 2009: 270) reveals how disaffected young men and women joined a number of competing armed factions of their own volition primarily to unseat 'rural gerontocratic leadership' and 'an elitist urban leadership made up of autocrats'.

Based on his extensive field research on young ex-combatants in Liberia, Utas's findings support my arguments that while the wars ruptured government–citizen relations for some, they provided the impetus for others to access forms of citizenship that had been previously denied by structural forces. Systematically disenfranchised, Liberia's urban and rural youth used the wars to rage against what they perceived to be state machinery, said Gabriel IH Williams of the Liberian embassy in Washington during his interview with me in 2012:

The [Liberian] society over the years has been structured in such a way that it hasn't given back to its own people where you have feelings. Look at the war,

---

[10] Interview in Monrovia on 6 March 2013.
[11] Insights gleaned from an informal discussion in Monrovia in June 2013.

how these young kids came and destroyed everything. They have no stake in it. We're not the only country that had war, look at Sierra Leone next door, look at Ivory Coast [Côte d'Ivoire], the people got their lights on. What did we do in Liberia? We cut down the poles.[12]

In addition to the demolition of physical infrastructure by disillusioned young people, Taylor's counter-revolution followed by the LURD and MODEL insurgencies effectively reconfigured citizenship for the vast majority of Liberians in the most profound ways. During the first war alone, a quarter million people died, hundreds of thousands sought refuge within the subregion, and millions of others were internally displaced. Moreover, unprecedented waves of emigration prompted an official breach of government–citizen relations for many. One forty-six-year-old Accra-based respondent, for instance, vowed to never resettle in Liberia because of the trauma and loss he experienced during the initial armed conflict.[13] Profiled in Chapter 2, fifty-five-year-old Aisha said she grew increasingly frustrated with how the first war continuously threatened her safety and livelihood which triggered a move to Gambia from 1996 to 1998 followed by permanent settlement in London:

I got tired. I kept waiting for the [first] war to finish, you know ... You work, you think things are getting better, when you look again another one [war] starts and everything is gone. ... I think most of us didn't understand civil war. We had been through coups, so we thought it was the same thing; it will blow over [in] one month, you know. ... So, we said we'll hang around ... I'm a Mandingo and anyway business is in our blood. That's what we do best. So, I said, ok, next thing, let me start trading, you know. I took the kids to Ivory Coast [Côte d'Ivoire], put them in the international school there. I was trading backward and forward. And then when you look again, I don't know what faction it was or whatever happened, all my market went again. It happened three, four times. I said, no, look I'm getting tired of this. I'm not going anywhere and this thing [war] is not going to end just now. So, I just decided to leave [Liberia].[14]

Having lost faith in a state that was already on the brink of implosion and thus incapable of fulfilling its role in the political economy of belonging, many Liberians opted for naturalisation abroad, argued

---

[12] Interview in Washington on 2 November 2012.
[13] [DL96] Interview in Accra on 13 May 2013.
[14] [DL9] Interview in London on 13 June 2012.

a thirty-two-year-old man who spent thirteen years in Nigeria before relocating to London:

People didn't trust the system in Liberia, even when peace was coming back to Liberia ... there's another war again. And my mom was like, during the war, 'Let's get out of this country [Liberia] and go because this thing [war] will still continue'. And when I left I think there were [a] series of wars still ... and that shows that at the time people were not trusting the system. So, they felt like, 'Let me get the citizenship [of another country], let me be surviving, let me see how I can move on with my life'.[15]

According to a forty-four-year-old Washington-based male respondent who left Liberia a few months before the first war, some Liberians abroad 'acquired these [foreign citizenships] circumstantially ... for survival reasons'[16] or as insurance in the event of future crisis. As a case in point, the majority of Liberian-born respondents in this study who naturalised in other countries did so during or after the second war.

Discussed in more depth in Chapter 5, revocation of legal citizenship ties to Liberia, however, does not imply Liberians became any less Liberian 'by heart' during armed conflict. While warfare undoubtedly erodes government–citizen relations for many, it does not necessarily disrupt citizen–citizen relations. For instance, some respondents interviewed for this book said the armed conflicts presented opportunities for them to shelter and feed fellow citizens in-country or practise citizenship from afar, as long-distance nationalists, advocating for the cessation of war and sending humanitarian aid to relatives and friends who got stuck in the crossfire. Then senator Kupee, one of four co-sponsors of the proposed dual citizenship bill of 2008, quipped in his 2012 interview with me that 'there are two things Liberians were looking up to [during the wars]: God and Western Union'[17] because faith in religion and remittances was the only reliable means of survival for those who could not leave the country. For the vast majority of informants in my study, citizenship was not fundamentally tied to an abstract notion of personhood or statehood, but rather belonging to a community and being accountable to and responsible for that community – essentially, a set of citizen–citizen relations embedded in the political economy of belonging to Liberia.

---

[15] [DL12] Interview in London on 14 June 2012.
[16] [DL44] Interview in Washington on 22 October 2012.
[17] Interview in Monrovia on 4 December 2012.

Some Liberians abroad, however, undermined citizen–citizen relations by stoking the flames of war under the guise of removing Doe in the late 1980s and Taylor in the late 1990s. This phenomenon is now so widespread that a growing body of literature has emerged on diasporas as conflict generators, countering the literature on diasporas as development actors. Nevertheless, not all politically active Liberians abroad were wedded to the idea of violent regime change. A fifty-five-year-old respondent based in Washington recalled how during initial Association for Constitutional Democracy in Liberia (ACDL) meetings in the late 1980s she served as a lone voice against deposing Doe through unconstitutional means:

I didn't feel that he [Taylor] needed to invade his own country in order to get his, whoever was in charge, get them out. I thought he should have tried to use the Constitution because he could have gotten on a ballot, gotten petitions, or whatever, but he didn't do that. . . . So, that was my position and that was something that I had a difference of opinion with the other people because at the time it was, 'We want to have one voice and the voice should be support Charles Taylor to get rid of Doe', and I said, 'I can't do that'.[18]

Symbolic of dialectic change, Liberian diasporas would support LURD and MODEL in pushing for Taylor's ouster exactly a decade after some of them supported his own insurgency against Doe. The pitfalls of practising transnational citizenship to incite conflict were not lost on Liberians who did not have the wherewithal to leave the country during crises. Liberians' tactile experiences of armed conflict caused by the ruthless and rootless Taylor, and coupled with the searing memory of seeing some Liberians with other citizenships escape carnage, serve as a major indictment of non-resident forms of citizenship, argued this Accra-based male respondent:

When the war started those who had other citizenships, they all fled. They all left, and those of us who didn't have, we had to stay there [in Liberia] and go through [the war], even though some of the problems were caused by them. But they all could leave and could be evacuated.[19]

Indeed, it is because of the lived experience of war that some Liberians either reject dual citizenship entirely or insist on instituting measures to curb abuse if a bill to that end were enacted. In fact, a fifty-seven-year-

[18] [DL34] Interview in Washington on 17 October 2012.
[19] [DL104] Interview in Accra on 20 May 2013.

old male respondent based in London said that Liberia's wars engendered deep reflection about the tenets of active Liberian citizenship and of profound engagement within the political economy of belonging:

> It's today because of the war that we are talking about dual citizenship. The number of people that died, the family conflict, the kind of, you know, things that we have destroyed, our resources, where we're coming from, our culture have all been dismantled. We now need to have a better attitude about, 'This is my country, whatever happens, whatever political changes it should not result into violence'.[20]

As evidenced by the sentiments captured in the previous quote, Liberia's post-war milieu has been infused with debates about the trajectory of citizen participation in peace-building and post-war reconstruction. Principally, twenty-first-century conflicts tend to revolve around the unequal distribution of income, land, and transitional justice thereby underpinning claims for and against dual citizenship. This is why the term 'post-conflict' is a misnomer for Liberia, as struggles over citizenship and belonging remain embedded in post-war experiences of conflict-generating inequalities.

Post-war Inequalities Re-inscribe Pre-war Crises of Citizenship

Liisa Malkki argues that 'in the aftermath of violent conflict, many elements are reconfigured: relations of power, techniques of government, modes of organisation, livelihoods, identities and collective memories, and the relations between people and places' (1995, as quoted in Long, 2001: 231). This is primarily manifested in the incompatibility of goals between Liberians whose perceptions and misperceptions of each other influence their actions and interactions. What often differentiates Liberians in the post-war period is whether or not one identifies as a diaspora, returnee, or homelander. These categories pit one group against the other in interface situations that often mirror nineteenth- and twentieth-century conflicts discussed previously. For the sake of analysis, I take on the most extreme views espoused by respondents interviewed for this book because I draw on historical comparisons of tense interface encounters between settlers and indigenes.

---

[20] [DL18] Interview in London on 16 June 2012.

Although there are slight remnants of the settler–indigene divide in post-war Liberia, multiple factors such as intermarriage, migration, exile, and return have blurred these lines, instead creating two diametrically opposed markers of citizenship differentiated by war-time experiences or lack thereof. On one hand, those who travelled abroad during intermittent crises are often framed as not being 'Liberian enough' because they did not suffer the dredges of war, said this thirty-six-year-old female respondent who relocated to London a few years before Liberia's first armed conflict:

> It's interesting because we hadn't experienced 'the war', there were times when people would make that almost a criteria of being [a] Liberian [citizen]. And I'm like, 'Hello!', you know, 'I don't think I need to dodge bullets to qualify as a Liberian'.[21]

Contrary to the sedentarist bias that frames stasis as 'the natural order of things' (Malkki, 1992), the most strident supporters of dual citizenship were diasporic Liberians like the previous respondent who interrogated physical rootedness, particularly within conflict contexts, as somehow more desirable or authentic. Yet, direct war-time experiences embolden claims to an 'authentic' Liberian citizenship that explicitly excludes those who fled Liberia, argued homelander and then minister Augustine Ngafuan in 2013:

> There are a lot of people here [in Liberia] who feel that they did not run away from the country. They ate the Borbor John ... the greens that they took from the swamp when they couldn't get potato greens. Whatever they got in the swamp they ate and they survived ... they went through check-points, and they were here for all the wars. ... They take some of their brothers that come from the diaspora as those who chickened out. 'When those times of difficulties existed, you were more than glad to run away and not to face the burden with us. Now that the country has gotten stable and opportunities are coming, then you come and say you are a Liberian [citizen]'. .... Local people, some of them, detest diasporans too much.[22]

These extreme (mis)perceptions about diasporas and returnees are completely unfounded and often create feelings of alienation, argued one forty-four-year-old circular returnee male respondent who relocated to Monrovia with his entire family in 2012:

[21] [DL8] Interview in London on 13 June 2012.
[22] Interview in Monrovia on 11 June 2013.

Well, the first and the only person who has said to me, 'Welcome home!' was the Lebanese. I've never gotten the welcome home, even from Liberian members of my family. Now, I don't think it's because they necessarily have some deep-seated animosity towards me but I do think it is because – whether most Liberians want to admit it or not – I do believe there is some low-level animosity, envy, or whatever you want to call it, that they have towards returnees. There is an assumption that we are returning with all this wealth and that we don't understand all that they went through during the war years and the post-war years, and that we are returning with this chip on our shoulder.[23]

As a rejoinder to this respondent's claims, Ngafuan admitted that the 'contempt diasporans in government have for local people', for instance, foments resentment.[24] While returnees are caricatured as pompous and egomaniacal with settler sensibilities, those who remained in Liberia are often stereotyped as unskilled and incapable of handling the demands of post-war recovery, said this twenty-four-year-old male homelander:

[O]ne other thing I observe about our society is that we are like, let me use the term 'xenocentric' [xenophobic, ethnocentric]. We believe in foreign policies, foreign activities, foreign education, and foreign stuff more than our own. So, if a Liberian, in Liberia, that acquires a certain degree, for a typical example from the University of Liberia or any other university like the United Methodist University, and someone coming from the United States, like Harvard University or the University of Georgia, you will find out that the person coming from abroad will be given more credence, more preference, than the person in Liberia with the Liberian diploma or the Liberian degree.[25]

The respondent's complaints echo those expressed by homeland Rwandans and Somalis, respectively, captured in other accounts about waves of return migration to Africa (Longman, 2017: 8, 22; Galipo, 2019: 16–17, 79). In Liberia's case, the distorted opinions of homelanders as parochial and incompetent – essentially 'incomplete' citizens – conjures up nineteenth- and twentieth-century notions of the 'uncivilised' indigene. The markers of 'civilisation' in Liberia's post-war period are too often defined as international education, extensive

---

[23] [CR2] Interview in Monrovia on 5 June 2013.
[24] Interview in Monrovia on 11 June 2013.
[25] [HL16] Interview in Monrovia on 12 June 2013.

travel experiences, and networks abroad. However baseless, these social categories of differentiation often informed how appointments were doled out in the public, private, development, and humanitarian sectors during Sirleaf's two terms in office. They unfairly favoured returnees. Although the ideologically driven perspectives I have high-lighted herein were embedded in some national policymaking discussed in the next section, it would be misleading to assume that all Liberians espouse these overly zealous views. As then justice minister Christiana Tah told me emphatically in 2013, 'everybody who is here [in Liberia] is not unfriendly towards Liberians who come in [from abroad], and everybody who comes in do[es] not come with an air of arrogance'.[26]

Post-war Policies on Income, Land Tenure, and Transitional Justice Fuel Conflict

Post-war conflicts between Liberian actors who operate domestically and transnationally were often fuelled by misguided national policies that re-inscribed age-old struggles over citizenship and undermined the political economy of belonging. These conflicts were particularly acute in relation to the distribution of salaries. For example, the administration of President Sirleaf created multi-tiered income levels reminiscent of the hierarchies of the nineteenth and twentieth centuries. According to Kieh (1992: 128), prior to the 1980 coup, members of the ruling class and urban dwellers earned an average annual income of US$600 while their rural counterparts earned only US$70. Similarly, through the Sirleaf government's establishment of emergency capacity building programmes such as the Liberia Emergency Capacity Building Support (LECBS), the Transfer of Knowledge through Expatriate Nationals (TOKTEN), and the Senior Executive Service (SES), funded by philan-thropist George Soros, the United Nations Development Programme (UNDP), and Humanity United, respectively, Liberian returnees were often paid wages far exceeding those of their homeland counterparts as a top-off of their civil servant salaries (Government of Liberia, 2010a; Government of Liberia, 2012a). As a case in point, on average diaspora returnees in managerial positions were paid US$3,500 (untaxed) monthly under the SES programme while their equally qualified home-land counterparts could make up to US$2,000. While the SES and

---

[26] Interview in Monrovia on 19 June 2013.

TOKTEN programmes were more transparent, with wages of the different tiers of income published, the LECBS, quickly phased out because of a lack of funding, was shrouded in secrecy. As a beneficiary of LECBS for one year who was privy to confidential information about remunerations, I recognise my own complicity in reproducing the same systems of inequality that I condemn. With this acknowledgement in mind, I can attest that there was a wide variation between what some officials were paid compared to others in addition to receiving their government of Liberia salaries and amenities such as assigned vehicles, gasoline vouchers, and top-up phone cards. In many cases, the allocation of these incomes appeared to be based more on the president's discretion than on a transparent measurement of the core competencies of beneficiaries or their actual contributions to post-war recovery.

Although the Civil Service Agency (CSA) tried to standardise pay scales during my time in the Office of President Sirleaf from 2007 to 2011, the proposed reforms were often met with half-hearted commitments. I attribute this to a lack of political will from the president and the reluctance of some high-level appointees since they benefitted from a lacklustre approach to genuine reforms. Some returnees in Liberia's semi-autonomous agencies earned up to US$15,000 a month, as was the case with former European Union (EU)-funded Auditor-General John Morlu (Government of Liberia & European Commission, 2007: 117, 154). Liberia's adoption of the international system of unequal remuneration, in which agencies such as the UN and World Bank pay so-called 'expatriate' staff inflated tax-exempt salaries while compensating so-called 'local' staff at much lower domestic rates, hastened hatred of returnees and compromised the productivity of homelanders. One twenty-nine-year-old homeland man who handled salary arrangements within an international organisation in Liberia revealed how domestic senior staff earned less than many of their US citizen Liberian subordinates:

We have [a] couple of Liberians who were employed on US citizenship. .... They get paid more. They are hired because they are foreign nationals living here so they got a lot of allowances. And I can say for sure that they're not paying taxes. Some of their money is not going back to Liberia.[27]

---

[27] [HL23] Interview in Monrovia on 14 June 2013.

It is clear from the examples detailed herein that the bloated salaries of diaspora returnees were indicative of international income inequalities that have widened across the globe, thereby creating a clash of life-worlds and social locations. While some returnees justified their excessive earnings as an incentive for the 'sacrifice' of return migration, homelanders, such as this forty-three-year-old man, spurned the unequal treatment as unconscionable:

How can you be in a post-conflict country where poverty is at its peak, and you feel proud that you make 15 to 20,000 [US] dollars a month? And there's nothing wrong with it because you're qualified and, you know, you're being paid for a professional service. ... So, I think there are some inconsistencies around values, around principles, and how it translates into professionalism and our quest for what we call 'giving back to a country'. So, I think there's a total disconnect between our commitment, you know, as patriotic citizens and our quest and ego for affluence.[28]

This respondent's obvious scorn for exorbitantly paid returnee bureaucrats is especially ironic since he served as country director of an international organisation that compensated him well above his Liberian colleagues. Other respondents with more legitimate grievances argued that given the relative deprivation of most Liberians in-country, a real 'sacrifice' by repatriates would entail moving one's family to Liberia, relinquishing a mortgage abroad, and investing wholeheartedly in the post-war economy instead of transferring money to maintain a transnational lifestyle. These actors were describing how returnees could demonstrate their genuine commitment to meaningfully participating in Liberia's political economy of belonging.

Besides income disparities, unequal land tenure is also indicative of Liberia's post-war crisis of citizenship. Though no longer a *criterion for citizenship*, land ownership now defines a *right of citizenship*. Because of Liberia's two intermittent armed conflicts, which fuelled both rural to urban and international migration, land was often left unclaimed for long periods of time and then appropriated by squatters devoid of legitimate deeds. With the return of Liberians from abroad, some of whom revoked their citizenship and, therefore, legally relinquished entitlements to property once owned, land tenure had become increasingly tenuous during the time of my interviews. A twenty-three-year-

[28] [HL3] Interview in Monrovia on 5 June 2013.

old female homelander reflected on how land crises could often turn violent very fast between two competing claimants at the interface:

You have a land, and this person abandon[s] this land for close to twenty-five years. Other people took the land and built houses on it and other people started investing in this land. All of a sudden, you say the person came from America and want[s] to gain their land back. ... Other people feel bitter, other people feel because they're not of that [high] class so other people want to override them. ... It can be very brutal. ... It's not something to see. Land issue is a very serious thing.[29]

The young woman was alluding to incidents in which Liberians would attack each other with clubs and cutlasses over conflicting land entitlements, mobs would descend on surveyors representing the Ministry of Lands, Mines, and Energy, and unscrupulous opportunists would sell and resell plots of land to multiple people.

   The land crisis became so grave that Sirleaf's government established in 2009 a Land Commission, which later became the Land Authority in 2016, and although it is beyond the scope of this book to examine reforms undertaken in detail, suffice it to say that the Commission discovered a number of anomalies that it attempted to resolve, such as the appropriation of customary land by private citizens, unannounced evictions, the exercise of unlawful eminent domain by government, failure by individual owners and commercial bodies to pay applicable land taxes, and the inability of the government to enforce and collect property taxes (Government of Liberia, 2013a). With less than 20 per cent of Liberia's land privately titled and registered, the Commission/Authority adopted measures to reconcile statutory and customary land tenure systems, such as the Community Rights Law of 2009 and the Land Rights Policy of 2013 which eventually advanced to a Land Rights Act legislated on 19 September 2018 under President Weah (Government of Liberia, 2011a: 4; Government of Liberia, 2018). Although the Land Commission's (Land Authority's) reforms were admirable, the Sirleaf administration undermined its efforts by leasing millions of acres to foreign multinationals for timber and palm oil extraction, as well as other agro-industrial ventures, without consulting affected communities (Siakor & Knight, 2012; Pailey & Siakor, 2018). The overreliance on concession wealth and

---

[29] [HL37] Interview in Monrovia on 21 June 2013.

unauthorised seizures of communal land eroded government–citizen relations and pitted local communities against multinationals (Pailey, 2014a: 4).

Liberians abroad who own large tracks of unused land in the country also lamented the haphazard approach to land management. One fifty-three-year-old US-born and Washington-based woman, whose Liberian citizen parents acquired prime property in Monrovia and elsewhere, took serious exception to eminent domain as symbolic of the Liberian government's abdication of its responsibilities within the political economy of belonging:

Most of us would have been at home [in Liberia]; we wouldn't have left the country. .... So, all of a sudden, you're saying to me, and again, this is going back to your question of property, you know, being abandoned, you're saying to me, 'Well, you abandoned your property, so we have the right of eminent domain. We're gonna take that over and we'll sell it off to the highest bidder or to whomever', which, and seen in parenthesis, is the Lebanese who have the money. So, then, you know, the Liberians are saying, 'You know, wait a minute. I was at home perfectly fine until you all started shooting in the air. And I don't feel like I should have stayed there [in Liberia] and gotten shot up, so I left!'[30]

Although this respondent raised valid points about her family's property being abandoned as a result of the breakdown in government–citizen relations beyond their control during armed conflicts, her defensive posture about eminent domain calls into question whether or not the *commands* of citizenship – that is, owning land – should somehow supersede the *demands* of citizenship – that is, land development and payment of taxes. With the successful passage of the 2018 Land Rights Act, it remains to be seen how the new law would actually mitigate land disputes since it reinforces Article 22 of the 1986 Constitution permitting non-citizen 'benevolent' entities to own land for humanitarian and educational purposes solely (Government of Liberia, 1986).

In addition to land tenure, another post-war governance issue indicating a crisis of citizenship is transitional justice which has effectively pitted 'perpetrators' against 'victims' although the two categories are often blurred (Weah, 2012). As one thirty-five-year-old male homelander disclosed to me, 'a victim cannot be a citizen'[31] because

---

[30] [DL47] Interview in Washington on 23 October 2012.
[31] [HL47] Interview in Monrovia on 25 June 2013.

victimhood connotes an absence of agency and without justice agency cannot be restored. Disagreeing with this respondent's analysis, I believe victimhood and agency are not incompatible and that even the most marginalised groups can possess the knowledgeability and capability to act, as exemplified by the actor-oriented analysis adopted for this book. Nevertheless, I recognise that the Liberian government's refusal to implement the more contentious aspects of the Truth and Reconciliation Commission (TRC) recommendations prior to 2020 revealed a crisis of citizenship and engendered a polarised discourse on post-war impunity.

One of the provisions within the Comprehensive Peace Agreement (CPA) ending the second Liberian armed conflict was the passage of a Truth and Reconciliation Act in 2005 establishing a TRC (TRC, 2009a; TRC, 2009b). Mandated to systematically chart the root causes of Liberia's two wars; investigate gross human rights violations, violations of international humanitarian law and other abuses; and determine who bore the greatest responsibility and their impacts on survivors of the conflicts, the TRC began full operations with public hearings in 2008 and released its findings and recommendations in 2009 (TRC, 2009a; TRC, 2009b). Although the Commission was authorised to evaluate the periods January 1979 through 14 October 2003, in its findings, however, there is unequivocal admission that Liberia's contemporary armed conflicts date back to the antecedents of state formation in 1822 (TRC, 2009a: 2; TRC, 2009b: 17). It further identified four major conflict issues, which, in my analysis, are underpinned by asymmetrical government–citizen and citizen–citizen relations: voice and accountability, and the lack thereof; land and property-related disputes; the dualism of Liberian identity and politicisation of ethnicity; and the marginalisation, alienation, and manipulation of youth (TRC, 2009b: 211–213).

Unlike the more tepid South African TRC, which served as a model, the Liberian TRC in 2009 radically proffered a series of controversial and punitive recommendations aimed at addressing asymmetries of power between government and citizens and amongst citizens, such as the establishment of an extraordinary criminal court for over one hundred individuals deemed to have committed gross human rights violations, including Charles Taylor and Prince Johnson; the barring from public office (lustration) of those recommended for prosecution (both for war crimes and domestic criminal prosecution) in addition to a special category of individuals publicly castigated for financing and supporting warring factions, including then sitting President Sirleaf, for a period of thirty years; the seizure and restitution of individual and corporate assets acquired by means of economic pillage during the wars; reparations for designated survivors administered through a Reparations Trust Fund; the transformation of Liberia's national motto from 'the love of liberty brought us here' to 'the love of liberty brought us together'; and the enactment of dual citizenship legislation and diaspora transnational voting (TRC, 2009b: 347–353, 359–362, 369–379, 396–397, 400). Essentially, the TRC recommendations mentioned herein were an attempt at restoring Liberia's political economy of belonging thus strengthening citizen–citizen and government–citizen relations through processes of accountability and justice.

Illustrating the contested nature of the recommendations and the politicisation of the Commission after 3 years of collecting over 20,000 statements from more than 17,000 individuals throughout Liberia and in select diaspora centres such as Ghana and the United States, 3 of the 9 commissioners abstained from affixing their signatures on the final report signifying dissent (TRC, 2009b: xxvi, 186–187). Although most Liberians at home and abroad hailed the TRC recommendations as a vindication of their losses, with some activists mounting domestic and international support for the establishment of a war and economic crimes court in Liberia,[32] those implicated have made full implementation impossible either through political intimidation and threats of renewed violence or by completely ignoring the report altogether. At the time of my completing this book in late 2019, the only TRC proposal fully applied was the establishment in 2009 of the Independent National Commission on Human Rights (INCHR) which had yet to fulfil its mandate by implementing all recommendations (TRC, 2009b: 388–389). As of mid-December 2019, other recommendations were still under consideration, such as proposed dual citizenship legislation and a comprehensive review of Liberia's

---

[32] For example, Hassan Bility, founder of the Monrovia-based Global Justice and Research Project, has since 2012 investigated and documented war-related atrocities while aiding prosecutions and convictions of alleged Liberian war criminals residing abroad. A staunch supporter of post-war transitional justice, he operates under the conviction that Liberia will one day establish its own war crimes court.

national symbols. In endorsing transnational citizenship as a reconciliatory imperative for Liberia, the TRC was able to balance its portrayal of diasporas by acknowledging in an earlier part of the report their past role in fuelling conflict while subsequently recognising their previous and potential contributions to post-war recovery (TRC, 2009b: 396).

In this section, I argued that a crisis of citizenship re-emerged in Liberia's post-war milieu which harkened back to unresolved pre-war societal fissures that impacted a gridlock on dual citizenship from 2008 to 2018.

Conclusion

In reading 'against the grain' I suspect King Peter's perspective about his encounter with Eli Ayers and Robert Stockton in pre-independence Liberia would have been fundamentally different had we access to his written account. But for the sake of taking this chapter's analysis to its logical conclusion, it is evident that the chief's reportedly coerced sale of indigenous land in 1821 marked the first in a long series of crises of citizenship which simultaneously weakened and enhanced Liberia's political economy of belonging. Four major interfaces of conflict ultimately followed thereby shifting Liberian citizenship from passive and fixed to active and reconstructed. While strained government–citizen relations engendered dissent and divergence – that is, the imposition of the 'hut tax'; protests against intended hikes in the price of rice; the mid-1980s thwarted constitutional review process – improvements in those relations also ushered in intervals of consent and convergence – that is, the Unification and Integration Policy; repeal of the 'hut tax'; the Land Rights Policy of 2013 and Land Rights Act of 2018.

I traced the defining moments in which Liberian actors employed a variety of domestic and diasporic tactics such as protest and opposition to hold their governments and each other accountable with responses ranging from repression to conciliation. Just as the Haitian Revolution of 1791–1804 and French Revolution of 1789–1799 were fought on the grounds of citizenship, so too were Liberia's multiple upheavals, beginning with the indigenous wars of resistance in the nineteenth century and climaxing in twenty-first-century post-war rivalries over income, land tenure, and transitional justice. This chapter demonstrates that a decade-long impasse on dual citizenship reveals how Liberian citizenship has changed across space and time through conflict and crisis and is still undergoing transformation in the post-war era.

In Chapter 5, I examine migration as a major factor in the evolution of Liberia's political economy of belonging thus prompting the introduction and suspension of dual citizenship legislation.

5 | *Between Rootedness and Rootlessness**

Introduction

A permanent returnee based in Monrovia, fifty-five-year-old Denise[1] is a product of the exceedingly complex historical and contemporary migratory patterns to and from Liberia. Born in the American South to two Liberian citizen parents, one of whom was in medical school at the time of her birth, Denise and her brother once held dual citizenship as minors. Not the de facto kind practised by some Liberian transnationals prior to 2020, but the de jure kind sanctioned by the country's then 1973 Aliens and Nationality Law. As a child, Denise shuttled between Liberia and the United States with ease as a *jus soli* US citizen and *jus sanguinis* Liberian citizen. In preparation for a return trip to Liberia in the early 1960s, Denise's parents attempted to obtain US visas for her and her brother. Halting them in their tracks, the US immigration officer at the time said, 'But, we don't give our own citizens visas', to which Denise's father replied, 'They're not your citizens!' The immigration officer offered a cheeky, yet measured, retort, 'I beg your pardon, sir, but until they are old enough to choose, they are American citizens!' Thereafter, Denise and her brother carried two passports – American and Liberian – because they belonged to both nations legally, at least until reaching the age of majority. Despite the impasse on dual citizenship decades later, however, Denise continued to use both her birthplace and bloodline travel documents.

As the previous vignette illustrates, Liberia's history is steeped in processes of migration, mobility, and flux. Whereas movement in the nineteenth century was directed inwards, the late twentieth and early

---

* This chapter is derived in part from Pailey (2018).
[1] Pseudonym used to protect the identity of a permanent returnee respondent [PR2] interviewed in Monrovia on 7 June 2013.

142

twenty-first centuries were characterised by unprecedented outflows in which emigration touched the lives of nearly all Liberians. In this chapter, I argue that historical and contemporary migration to and from Liberia simultaneously challenged and reinforced the merits of Liberia's legal citizenship framework thus influencing the ten-year suspension of proposed dual citizenship legislation. First, I present a brief overview of the migration literature relevant for this book. Second, I trace Liberia's historical and contemporary migration trends, paying close attention to the migratory patterns of the actors I interviewed. Third, I explore how the challenges embedded in processes of migration influenced claims for dual citizenship. And lastly, I examine the citizenship status of respondents, their motivations for naturalising abroad or not, and how this maps onto nomadic and sedentarist metaphysical thinking about resident- and non-resident forms of citizenship. In order to maintain a focused discussion, this chapter examines international migration to and from Liberia rather than internal migration within Liberia, primarily because immigration and emigration influenced public discourse and policymaking on dual citizenship more significantly than internal migration.

Contestations over Movement and Stasis

Citizenship is entrenched in philosophical debates about movement and stasis. According to Cresswell (2006: 25), there are two paradigms framing mobility and emplacement. On one hand, contemporary social thought depicts nomadism, mobility, and rootlessness as 'progressive, exciting, and contemporary' while sedentarism, stasis, and rootedness are seen as 'reactionary, dull or of the past'. Furthermore, movement is embedded in social and political history in which 'people have always moved, whether through desire or through violence' (Malkki, 1992: 24). The 'nomadic metaphysic', as it is called, 'links mobility to forms of subaltern power ... central to the practices of transgression and resistance' (Cresswell, 2006: 46), and appears closely aligned with arguments in favour of transnational forms of citizenship, generally, and dual citizenship for Liberia, specifically. It can thus be argued that those who interpret naturalisation abroad as a legitimate response to protracted conflict view Liberian citizenship through a nomadic metaphysical lens, such as this Monrovia-based male homelander:

[H]istorically Liberians were never a people to want to take on anyone else's nationality. ... Yeah, we have Liberians that travelled abroad many, many, many years ago. Some took on foreign wives and it never crossed their minds to take on citizenship of other countries or [that] of their spouses. There is a reason why Liberians now do that and it's an understandable and justifiable reason. ... A lot of Liberians travelled, left Liberia, and that exodus started in 1980. In 1990, it escalated to levels unthinkable. When I lived in the United States then, between 1980 and 1982 and 1990 and 1998, especially early on in [19]'82, if it was possible for me to take on or to get residence or US citizenship, to, in fact, allow me to go to school cheaper, I would have, alright? But at the time, that wasn't the case. In 1990, because of the war, I became a resident [in the United States]. We all filed for political asylum [in the United States]. Some people did what they had to do because they were in foreign lands, not because of their own choosing but because they had to survive as best as they could.[2]

On the other hand, there is an alternative school of thought referred to as the 'sedentarist metaphysic' in which 'people are often thought of, and think of themselves, as being rooted in place and as deriving identity from that rootedness' (Malkki, 1992: 27). Embedded in nationalist discourse and entangled with arborescent metaphors, the 'roots' paradigm portrays mobility as pathological, dysfunctional, and threatening (Malkki, 1992: 27–28; Cresswell, 2006: 27, 31). It has fundamentally influenced the securitisation of migration wherein heightened preoccupations with containment have emboldened modern nation-states to adopt restrictive citizenship and visa regimes as well as border controls (Dannreuther, 2007: 101, 105–107, 110–111; Duffield, 2008: 146, 152–155). According to this model, 'mobility is often the assumed threat to the rooted, moral and authentic existence of place' and mobility involves 'the absence of commitment and attachment and involvement' (Cresswell, 2006: 31). It informs the thinking of opponents of dual citizenship for Liberia; while they may see migration within the context of conflict as involuntary, they often view naturalisation abroad as a voluntary abdication of commitment to Liberia, its citizens, and the political economy of belonging. As a case in point, one twenty-eight-year-old Monrovia-based circular returnee described herself as 'deeply rooted' even though she had only returned to Liberia in 2011 after twenty-one years abroad. Having naturalised in the United States just before relocating to Liberia, this respondent evoked the

---

[2] [HL18] Interview in Monrovia on 12 June 2013.

'heart' trope while ironically questioning the logic of dual citizenship on the grounds of its rootlessness:

If people have dual citizenship they are basically in a win-win situation because it almost forces them not to be deeply rooted somewhere. It's just like if they are in Liberia, if something pops up they can just pick up and leave to go somewhere else. So, there is this level of, like, non-attachment to a place. So, I think that, and in the case of Liberia, having people not be deeply rooted and not be attached to this place could possibly be dangerous. ... I think right now for Liberia, we need people that are deeply rooted here ... because I think where your heart is, is where your energy is going to be.[3]

Akin to the circular returnee quoted earlier, those who adopt a sedentarist metaphysic often assert that naturalisation is an illegitimate revocation of Liberian citizenship as legal, cultural, and national identity.

Yet, war-induced displacement, particularly of refugees, unsettles sedentarist biases as do forms of nomadism based on pastoralist lifestyles exhibited by, for example, the Tuareg of West Africa, Maasai of East Africa, and Bedouin of North Africa. Just as mobility is seen as unnatural in the sedentarist metaphysic, displacement caused by violence can also be viewed as rupturing the 'natural order of things', in which case refugees fleeing armed conflict cannot be considered aberrations in the same way that nomadic people are far from deviant. In her empirical study on Burundian Hutu refugees in Tanzania, Malkki (1992: 35–36) discovered that while refugees settled in urban centres juggled multiple identities through partial assimilation, those inhabiting camps staunchly held onto an essentialist construction of national identity bounded by a single geographic territory. Camp refugeeism became a symbol of cultural purity and a status signifying 'the ultimate temporariness of exile and of the refusal to become naturalised, to put down roots in a place to which one did not belong' (Malkki, 1992: 35). Although 79 per cent of Burundian exiles in Tanzania opted for naturalisation in 2007 (SA3, 2007), more than a decade after Malkki's *Purity and Exile* was published about the politics of integration, in her 1995 seminal book as well as in my more recent investigation detailed herein, keeping one's *jus soli* or *jus sanguinis* citizenship and

---

[3] [CR10] Interview in Monrovia on 27 June 2013.

refusing to assimilate or naturalise signified authenticity and rootedness for some, however imagined.

Just as the sedentarist and nomadic metaphysics challenge understandings of mobility and emplacement, contemporary migration flows, whether internal or international, disrupt widely held assumptions that migration is unidirectional and permanent (Leitner, 2003: 450–451). Migration may occur in stages with multiple intermediate destinations over a protracted period. It can also be circular or cyclical with migrants moving regularly between two or more locales representing hostlands and homelands, as is evidenced by the circular returnees profiled in this book. While migration may change from temporary to permanent it can also involve return migration after a long period of exile. These trends are indicative of the migratory flows to and from Liberia which can be considered circular in nature rather than unidirectional, from pre-settler origins to post-war manifestations. Quite often, migration can also be 'mixed' in terms of motivations with the nature of flows essentially a combination of both compulsion and choice (Van Hear, Brubaker & Bessa, 2009: 1, 3–4). In the same way that contemporary Liberian citizenship sits on a continuum of passivity and activity, so too do migration motivations and flows sit on a continuum 'ranging from "choice" or "more options" at one end to "little choice" or "few options" at the other' (Van Hear, Brubaker & Bessa, 2009: 3). Mixed migration accounts for nuanced structural forces at play while simultaneously revealing the agency of migrants. This level of analysis serves as the bedrock of my discussion later in the chapter about whether or not naturalisation can be considered a compulsion or a choice. What follows is an examination of how historical and contemporary movement across diverse spatial landscapes configured and reconfigured Liberian citizenship and impacted views about dual citizenship.

This Land of Migration, Not 'Liberty'

Long before the arrival of black settlers in the nineteenth century, there was significant migration to the territory that is modern-day Liberia. As a case in point, most of Liberia's sixteen ethno-linguistic groups are not 'indigenous' at all although I use the term to denote them throughout this book for lack of a more precise descriptor. Instead, they actually migrated in several waves, with the Gbandi, Gio, Kpelle, Lorma,

Mandingo, Mano, Mende, and Vai arriving between the twelfth and seventeenth centuries from far-flung West African territories such as contemporary Burkina Faso, Côte d'Ivoire, Guinea, Mali, and Sierra Leone (Guannu, 1983: 9–10; Konneh, 1996a: 7–11). Other early documented waves of migration began at the end of the fifteenth century when Mande-speaking peoples cascaded up the Niger River inhabiting present-day Liberia and Sierra Leone (Gershoni, 1985: 2; Burrowes, 2016b: 142–150). The Mane warriors, whose descendants are the Gbandi and Lorma, constituted another wave of migration as they settled in what is now northern Liberia and southern Sierra Leone thereby pushing the Golas further south into the forest belt (Gershoni, 1985: 2; Burrowes, 2016b: 46–49; 142–150, 179–182). Traditionally seafarers who travelled along the West African coast and across the Atlantic Ocean to Europe as early as the nineteenth century, the Krus from southeastern Liberia also exhibited migratory patterns that gradually spread from an area between the central coast of Liberia to the San Pedro River into modern-day Côte d'Ivoire (Gershoni, 1985: 2; Burrowes, 2016b: 46–49). Migrants were particularly attracted to the coast because of interactions with Portuguese seamen who began making regular expeditions to trade with the local people in the mid-fifteenth century; in exchange for brass, glass, clothes, and iron supplies, the local populations traded in enslaved Africans, skins, gold, and ivory (Gershoni, 1985: 3; Burrowes, 2016b: 151–153, 157–162).

By the time repatriated blacks arrived on the coast of pre-settler Liberia in the mid-nineteenth century, 250 years of migration had preceded them with various ethno-linguistic communities virtually established in their confederations of clans and chieftaincies offset by hierarchies, rivalries, and alliances (Liberty, 1977: 282; Gershoni, 1985: 3–4). Between 1822 and 1867, the American Colonisation Society (ACS) facilitated the emigration of 18,963 blacks to Liberia, including the free-born and formerly enslaved in the United States and Caribbean as well as Congo River basin recaptives (Liberty, 1977: 100, 275). Although recaptured blacks trickled into pre-settler Liberia, the 1850s marked a surge in their immigration; between 1858 and 1861, nearly a dozen ships carrying enslaved Africans en route to Cuba and other places in the Americas were intercepted and diverted to the shores of Liberia and by late 1860, between 3,600 and 6,000 recaptives had arrived (Clegg, 2004: 245; Moran, 2006: 2). These numbers were augmented in 1865 by 346 emigrants from Barbados after the abolition of slavery on that island in 1834 (Burrowes, 2016a: 33; Banton, 2019: 11).

Consequently, citizenship in post-independence Liberia was circumscribed by experiences of migration with the ultimate privileging of rootlessness. Therefore, it is unsurprising that the earliest presidents of Liberia were born in the United States, the Caribbean, and Sierra Leone (Guannu, 1989). As one twenty-nine-year-old male homelander pointed out to me in 2013, what underpins his family's history, and that of Liberia's, are 'various shades of immigration':

> I've always had this opinion that defining Liberian citizenship is a very, very difficult thing because I think Liberians don't have a unique identity that you can easily look at and say, 'This guy is a Liberian' ... you have a lot of Mandingos who have relatives in Guinea. ... They are Liberians. They can easily mingle in Guinea; they could easily pass on as citizens in Guinea. You have some people of the Kissi tribe who have relatives across the border in Sierra Leone. ... They can easily mingle as Sierra Leoneans; they could easily mingle as Liberians. We also have some Liberians, way back, when we were much younger, people used to laugh at the Ghana Kru and Nigerian Kru. But, actually, there are Kru people who ... most of the Kru people, some of them will tell you, 'I was born in Ghana, then I came on this side [to Liberia]'. ... Even my own situation, my grandfather, my paternal grandfather, came from Ghana and settled here [in Liberia] and then he had a Kpelle woman who had my father. And now, my mother is a Kru. So, sometimes identifying myself as a Liberian can be a little bit tricky. ... And then, historically, most of the tribes came from right around West Africa. So, if you came from around West Africa and settled here [in Liberia], other people came from maybe the Congo basin, or they came from the United States, they settled here [in Liberia], after a period of time, if there are other people who [are] settling on that side and coming here [to Liberia], how do you define yourself as more a Liberian than those who are just settlers like you are?[4]

That this respondent referenced his own embodied history to characterise Liberian citizenship as emblematic of different kinds of mobility is particularly insightful. His hybrid cultural lineage also resonates with mine: my maternal great-grandfather was apparently born in Kingston, Jamaica, having migrated to Buchanan, Grand Bassa County, at the turn of the twentieth century; I also have paternal connections to the

---

[4] [HL23] Interview in Monrovia on 14 June 2013.

Kroos of Sierra Leone who inhabited the Atlantic coast as seafarers. Thus, Liberia's migratory flows and their bearing on citizenship construction are extremely complicated, with claims to autochthony almost appearing questionable. Whereas Liberia's first citizens were 'rootless' immigrants with no filial ties to the land, the institution of citizenship became increasingly defined by rootedness – residence and land ownership – in the ensuing one hundred years of the republic before the decoupling of residence and citizenship altogether. After a 1980 coup overthrew settler rule, the citizen-as-rooted-resident trope no longer held sway since Liberians fleeing subsequent crises still considered themselves citizens, albeit from afar.

Moreover, the nation-state of Liberia became fundamentally multi-territorialised with a sizeable number of Liberians scattered throughout the globe yet still fully engaged transnationally as a result of armed conflict. For example, in the 1990s and early 2000s, Liberia, like Somalia, represented one of the top refugee producing countries in Africa with record highs in internal migration (Black et al., 2006: 5). Table 5.1 shows that while there was a gradual decrease in the numbers of registered Liberian refugees worldwide between 1993 and 2005, the numbers of internally displaced persons (IDPs) spiked one year before each of Liberia's armed conflicts ended (1996 and 2002, respectively).

Various sources estimate that hundreds of thousands of Liberians fled the homeland during wars to the Economic Community of West African States (ECOWAS) subregion, as indicated in previous chapters, as well as to other destinations around the globe, particularly the United Kingdom, Sweden, and Norway in Western Europe and Providence, Rhode Island, Minneapolis/St Paul, Minnesota, Philadelphia, Pennsylvania, and Staten Island, New York, in the

Table 5.1 *United Nations High Commissioner for Refugees (UNHCR) refugee/asylum/IDPs population statistics for Liberia*

Category/year	1993	1996	1999	2002	2005
Refugees	150,153	120,061	96,317	64,956	10,168
Asylum seekers	N/A	1	29	10	29
IDPs	N/A	320,000	90,584	304,115	237,822

Source: UNHCR, 2004

United States, though the exact number/size of Liberians in these regions is disputed. That the United States hosts, apart from West Africa, the largest population of Liberians outside of Liberia can be attributed to a number of factors, namely, the historical links between Liberia and America; the temporary migration of Liberian elites to the United States pre-armed conflicts; and that it not only boasted the largest resettlement programmes for Liberian refugees but also continued to renew programmes such as Temporary Protected Status (TPS) and Deferred Enforced Departure (DED) until beneficiaries won a hard-fought pathway to permanent residency in December 2019. Additionally, America offered naturalisation as a durable solution to two categories of Liberians: asylum applicants who could prove political persecution in Liberia and those who demonstrated considerable family ties to the United States who could be reunited. According to Gabriel IH Williams of the Liberian embassy in Washington, the generations of Liberians who eventually settled in the United States are indicative of pre- and post-war patterns of migration:

People who are older, fifty, sixty, seventy years or older, many of them came here [to the United States] for education and then over time they over stayed, especially during the 1960s coming through the 1970s. And then you have all of the civil upheavals that we had in Liberia beginning with the 'Rice Riots' in the late 1970s that culminated into the 1980 military coup, so many of those people from that background who came here [to the United States] for educational purposes to get various professional background to go back just stayed. And then of course you had the nearly twenty years, more than fifteen years of civil upheaval, the civil war that allowed thousands of people to vote with their feet and many of them on resettlement. Other people came here [to the United States] and gained political asylum. This is how we have the huge exodus that led to brain drain in Liberia.[5]

Trends in the regularisation of status of Liberians in the United States also mirror the conflict–peace cycles. Table 5.2 depicts how many Liberians were newly registered as permanent residents, naturalised US citizens, refugees, or asylum seekers over a fifty-year period. The figures for permanent residents were captured as early as 1970 to 1979 as this timeframe accounted for an initial spike in newly registered Liberians in the United States. The 1970s were indicative of increased

---

[5] Interview in Washington on 2 November 2012.

Table 5.2 *Newly registered Liberian-born US permanent residents/ citizens/refugees/asylees from 1960 to 2012*

Category/ years	Permanent residents	US citizens	Refugees	Asylees
1960–1969	841	N/A	N/A	N/A
1970–1979	2,391	N/A	N/A	N/A
1980–1989	6,420	N/A	N/A	N/A
1990–1999	13,587	N/A	N/A	N/A
2000	1,570	1,022	2,620	782
2002	2,869	1,047	560	746
2004	2,757	1,218	7,140	399
2006	6,887	2,193	2,402	113
2008	7,193	2,468	992	91
2010	4,837	3,360	244	61
2012	4,109	4,332	69	35

Sources: United States Department of Homeland Security, 2009, 2013

emigration as a result of brewing conflict in Liberia following the death of President Tubman in 1971.

As Table 5.2 illustrates, Liberian-born newly registered US permanent residents more than doubled in the 1990–1999 period when Liberia was its most unstable. Similarly, the number of Liberian-born newly registered US refugees spiked in 2004, one year after Liberia's second armed conflict ended, before steadily declining. Not surprisingly, Liberian-born newly registered US asylum grantees steadily declined from 2002 onwards as Liberia became more stable. Whereas the number of newly registered US permanent residents fluctuated from 2000 to 2012, the number of newly registered US citizens steadily increased. The US Department of Homeland Security official statistics on newly registered US citizens reinforce the findings of my study, in which eight of the twelve Liberian-born Washington-based residents who naturalised opted to do so in the 2000s although the vast majority of them were eligible for US citizenship long before this time. As will be discussed later in this chapter, respondents adamantly held onto their legal Liberian citizenship either opting for naturalisation long after the second armed conflict ended or dismissing naturalisation altogether.

Just as assumptions about naturalisation trends for Liberians abroad influenced the introduction of the 2008 dual citizenship bill, so too did post-war migration data, albeit scanty. According to United Nations (UN) figures, the number of Liberian refugees decreased since the cessation of armed conflict in 2003. The UNHCR (2007), for instance, estimates that there were up to 160,000 refugees still outside of Liberia as of February 2006 with numbers declining to just over 75,000 in 2008. It is unclear, however, how many Liberians currently live outside the country with the statistics on return migration to Liberia equally as inconclusive. Although policymaking and academic research have been infused by the recognised importance of Liberians abroad, the lack of reliable statistical data on Liberia's diasporas has proven to be a huge impediment in justifying policy prescriptions such as dual citizenship.

Regardless of the dearth of reliable data, however, it is clear that processes of immigration and emigration invariably influenced endorsement and rejection of the proposed bill. For instance, the migration patterns of Liberian-born informants speaking in unofficial capacities for this book are a particularly stark illustration of how mobility has become a mainstay in contemporary Liberian demography. As Table 5.3 demonstrates, of the 163 Liberian-born unofficial respondents, 84 per cent had travelled outside the territorial confines of the nation-state at some point in their lives. Though 16 per cent, principally homeland Liberians, had never left the country, all interviewees admitted to having at least one relative abroad primarily as a consequence of armed conflict. I did not capture the migratory patterns of foreign-born Liberians because I wanted to establish a baseline of first-time migration for *jus soli* nationals. Although I do not make any claims that percentages captured in the table are representative of Liberians worldwide, I suspect that they likely mirror Liberians' first-time migration patterns in general which certainly influenced the 2008 proposed dual citizenship legislation.

From the numbers tabulated in Table 5.3, it is clear that the highest spike in first-time migration amongst Liberian-born unofficial respondents occurred during the first armed conflict which brought Charles Taylor to power in 1997. Unsurprisingly, first-time migration also increased from the 1980 coup to the onset of the first insurgency by Taylor in 1989. Of the twenty-eight London-based Liberian-born

Table 5.3 *First-time migration patterns of 163 unofficial Liberian-born respondents*

Field site/ migration patterns	Left Liberia before 1980	Left Liberia between 1980 and 1989	Left Liberia between 1990 and 1997	Left Liberia between 1998 and 2003	Left Liberia after 2003	Never left Liberia
London (28)	1	10	14	2	1	N/A
Washington (24)	1	9	10	3	1	N/A
Freetown (15)	N/A	2	7	2	4	N/A
Accra (30)	N/A	3	19	7	1	N/A
Monrovia (66)	1	6	25	6	2	26
Total absolute number/	3/	30/	75/	20/	9/	26/
Percentage of total	2	18	46	12	6	16

I deliberately refrained from explicitly asking the twenty-one government officials and heads of regional diaspora organisations about their migration patterns as I realised early on that this information was not necessary for my analysis.

respondents, twelve had spent some time in Côte d'Ivoire, Gambia, Guinea, Nigeria, or Sierra Leone before inhabiting the United Kingdom, proving that West Africa served as a transit point before settlement in Europe. Of the twenty-four Washington-based Liberian-born respondents, only four had transited for some time in another African country – namely Ghana, Guinea, Nigeria, or Zimbabwe – before settling in the United States. Of the fifteen Freetown-based Liberian-born respondents, only three had passed through Côte d'Ivoire, Ghana, Guinea, or Nigeria before initially residing in Sierra Leone; the other twelve travelled directly to Freetown. This is predictable since Liberia and Sierra Leone share a common border. Of the thirty Accra-based Liberian-born respondents, five had spent some time in the United States or Europe before settling in Ghana while five transited in Guinea, Nigeria, Sierra Leone, or Togo before relocating to Ghana. The remaining twenty travelled to Ghana directly from Liberia. Of the twenty-four homeland Liberians who had lived temporarily abroad many had migrated for short stints to the West African subregion before returning to Liberia. Quite often their migratory patterns were circular in nature with emigration peaking during times of conflict and return migration increasing during times of relative peace.

In the section that follows, I explore how difficult adjustments embedded in the migration experiences of Liberians abroad influenced the introduction of dual citizenship legislation in 2008.

You Na Foreigner!

For migrants who travel to and inhabit another country the challenges can be innumerable – language barriers; lack of access to basic social services, rights, and privileges; prolonged status regularisation processes; social and cultural alienation, amongst others. One of the motivations underpinning the 2008 dual citizenship bill was recognition that migration can be a torturous process – for the highly-skilled and prosperous as well as for the low-skilled and poor – and that upholding citizenship ties to Liberia could somehow assuage the pain of separation from the homeland. A common thread throughout my interviews with informants was their varied encounters with discrimination across spatial landscapes regardless of socio-economic positioning abroad. For instance, a forty-three-year-old female respondent who transited through Côte d'Ivoire for two years before arriving in London in 2007 talked about how she was confronted with racism for the first time in the United Kingdom:

I first realised when I came to this country [the United Kingdom] that I was coloured whereas when you are in Liberia you don't see yourself as being coloured. ... And in terms of working in a local government or in a predominately white office, growth and career progression is far slower than in a multi-cultural employment environment. I mean, they do say that it's equality and everything but it's [racism's] really institutionalised. ... You can try to work your butt off and they have a very subtle way of keeping you where they want to keep you.[6]

Whereas this respondent's skin colour enabled her to blend easily in Liberia, a predominantly black country, her racial positioning in the United Kingdom catapulted her into a strange realm of otherness despite being a naturalised British citizen. Similarly, a fifty-seven-year-old medical doctor who migrated to the United Kingdom to continue his education in 1988 admitted that regardless of his highly specialised skills and knowledge, he has to constantly defend his British citizenship in both social and professional interfaces marked by covert and overt forms of institutional racism:

Well, sometimes in some communities they don't accept you as, especially some of the very conservative areas, they don't accept you as a citizen. And people will always ask you, 'Where do you come from?' ... I had gone to a conference and someone asked me, 'Where do you come from?' And I said, 'I'm from Dorset'. And they said, 'No, I mean, where do you come from?', and I said, 'I'm from Dorset'. ... And trying to keep calm when people challenge you time and time again about where you're from ... as a non-white [person] and also as someone who trained outside of the UK [United Kingdom], you find that you have to be twice as good as the indigenous [white British] person to get half way where they are. And besides that, you find that there are a lot of barriers that are in place to prevent you from getting any higher than the British person. ... Oh, for example, when I started my [medical] training they had a two-tiered system. Even though we all did the same training, we [foreigners] were classed as visiting registrars and those who were UK citizens were classed as career registrars. ... Automatically there was a post available for them whereas the visiting registrars didn't have a post to go to. So, unless you were extremely lucky, you weren't going to get

---

[6] [DL5] Interview in London on 10 June 2012.

a consulting post and you, the idea was that you would go back to wherever you came from.[7]

Whereas Liberians in the United Kingdom may assimilate into black British anonymity, thereby facing the same sets of challenges as their Caribbean and African brethren, their counterparts in the United States often have two choices: become African American or profess and display one's Liberianness conspicuously. The alternatives have varying consequences. On one hand, Liberians who assimilate as African Americans face discrimination borne by centuries of slavery and structural racism in the United States. On the other hand, those who maintain strong cultural ties to Liberia and are educated often serve as model immigrants and exceptions to a presumed African American malaise. Minimally tolerated by white American society but not wholly accepted, these Liberians often encounter strong anti-immigrant scapegoating, particularly from other racial minorities. For example, one fifty-nine-year-old Washington-based female medical practitioner who migrated to the United States in the early 1980s to pursue a master's degree, revealed how she was interrogated by an African American patient who asked her: 'Why is it that you foreigners come into this country and you get our good jobs? And our people there, our brothers and sisters, and children, they can't even, they can't hardly get a good job?'[8] Although this respondent admitted feeling deeply troubled by constantly having to prove herself as a naturalised US citizen, she seemed to accept discrimination as an inevitable consequence of immigrant life in America.

In Accra, Julia Richards, head of the United Liberian Association in Ghana (ULAG), also took on a somewhat defeatist stance by accepting anti-immigrant backlash as inescapable:

The difficulty is being a Liberian. ... Some [Ghanaians] do accept you but sometimes because of the behaviour of some [Liberians], yeah, people don't take you kindly or they don't accept you easily. And to be accepted you have to go to school here [in Ghana], you have to stay long here, be able to speak the dialect ... I think it's like that because everybody, like you and I ... everybody tries to protect his or her own, you understand? ... So, you have to know where to stop and where not to stop. As the saying goes, where one man's freedom begins ... another man's freedom ends.[9]

[7] [DL30] Interview in London on 23 June 2012.
[8] [DL56] Interview in Washington on 26 October 2012.
[9] Interview in Accra on 18 May 2013.

While Richards and others feel cowed by xenophobic sentiments, other respondents are less deflated. The forty-eight-year-old Freetown-based businessman and consultant profiled in Chapter 1 scoffed at the tendency of native-born Sierra Leoneans to discriminate against him and others investing in the post-war country:

There are people here . . . they are die-hard Sierra Leoneans and they're quick to put it in your face, 'You're a foreigner! You think you na come now here, you do this? You na foreigner!' . . . So, it makes you feel hurt, [you] say, 'But I'm here, I'm doing all of this. And still, they don't appreciate [it] and at the end of the day, they say you're a foreigner'. You know? So, using that word [foreigner], as an African, I think it's not appropriate because it kills your desire.[10]

Although the Liberian immigrants I interviewed in the so-called Global South and North face similar challenges varying in degree and scale, the discrimination borne by migration to West Africa is particularly debilitating, especially for poor and semi-educated migrants in Freetown and Accra. For example, Liberia's then ambassador to Sierra Leone, Thomas Brima, revealed in 2013 that despite his country's prominent position in the Mano River Union (MRU) and ECOWAS Liberian migrants were often banned from developing livelihood strategies such as farming and criminalised unnecessarily in Sierra Leone.[11]

Though the challenges for Liberians in Sierra Leone cannot be negated, Freetown-based respondents in this study encounter fewer obstacles to assimilation than their Accra-based counterparts. During my interviews in Accra, there was a clear recognition that Ghanaians could be exceedingly xenophobic with a strong sense of patriotic fervour, which stands in stark contrast to the apparent lack of patriotism in Liberia. As indicated in the introduction of this book, Liberia did not undergo a nationalist movement and the lack of a strong national identity could be attributed to century-long exclusionary citizenship. Liberians' continued tenuous positioning in Ghana calls into question that country's claims of being a haven for Africans and people of African descent. Unlike South Africa, which has exhibited periodic attacks against migrants of colour, the West Africa hub is truthfully only hospitable to black and brown people who can contribute concretely, that is, financially, to its political economy of belonging. For

---

[10] [DL79] Interview in Freetown on 19 April 2013.
[11] Interview in Freetown on 18 April 2013.

Accra-based Liberian respondents, particularly locally integrated former refugees, the challenges of migration are embedded in structural
and societal forces of containment. As suggested by a forty-two-year-
old female resident of the Buduburam Refugee Camp since 2000, the
threat of physical violence represents one of the mechanisms of control
because 'Liberians have been killed here [in Buduburam] and nothing
came out of it because they [the assailants] were Ghanaians'.[12] This
respondent was undoubtedly referring to the spate of violence against
Liberians at Buduburam in the 2010s, during which the Liberian
government had to intervene despite the embassy's reluctance to
involve itself in refugee matters.

Alienation is another form of containment that renders Liberians
inert and unable to voice their grievances, according to this fifty-six-
year-old female respondent who had lived in Ghana as a refugee since
fleeing Liberia's first armed conflict in 1992:

> I don't know what to say, they [Ghanaians], they don't really love strangers,
> only few, only the educated ones ... I don't care how long you have been with
> them ... they always want to let you know that you are not from here. ...
> They, I don't know, discriminate ... they love it a lot. ... So it's difficult, even
> to sell in the market. The accent, our [Liberians'] accent is different so if they
> are selling something to their people for [a] certain price, if you're a Liberian,
> go and ask, by the time you ask and they hear you, the accent, forget it. Your
> price will go up, your prices will go up. And [in] certain places they don't even
> allow you to talk, in their buses you have to be careful even if they do
> something and you want to defend yourself as a human being and not as
> a Liberian, oh, they will lash [out] at you.[13]

Tales of arbitrary, discriminatory treatment at the hands of Ghanaians
were commonplace amongst respondents in Accra, especially since the
Liberian embassy exhibited a hands-off approach concerning refugees.
A resident of Buduburam Refugee Camp since 2004, one fifty-three-
year-old university instructor explained how he was taunted when
a bus attendant insisted that he pay more than the fare Ghanaians
were paying on a routine ride from his job to the Camp:

> After I got down, before I got down, they said, 'Refugee!' I said, 'I'm not
> a refugee, I don't hold that status any longer'. And I showed them my ID card.

---

[12] [DL87] Interview in Accra on 11 May 2013.
[13] [DL89] Interview in Accra on 11 May 2013.

'I teach at the university here. I'm moulding the minds of people. So, I am not just any other person'.[14]

Apart from the challenges of social alienation, some Liberians in Accra also lamented the limited opportunities to attend school and develop professionally. A former refugee who fled Liberia's second armed conflict in 2001, one twenty-eight-year-old female respondent admitted that the high foreign student fees outside of the Camp setting had deterred her from pursuing university education and motivated her desire to return to Liberia.[15] Other Liberians in Accra, like this male respondent who relocated to Ghana in 1990, complain that their professional growth has been stunted because of national laws barring foreigners from taking certain jobs:

Ghanaians are friendly but there are a few who still harbour some form of xenophobic, you know, behaviour towards foreigners. . . . I mean, even the idea of going into business is a very big issue now in Ghana. The foreigner [is] restricted and the amount of money you need to start a business, I mean, is so much if you are a foreigner and then you are restricted to certain types of businesses. . . . And, I mean, it goes as far as even jobs, even jobs, you find that there are very few foreigners you find working and because the policy here is Ghanaians first. So, if there's a vacancy they look and see whether there's no Ghanaian to fill up that vacancy before a foreigner is given the option. And even if you open a company, I mean, by law you are entitled to employ a certain amount [number] of Ghanaians.[16]

Restrictions on employment and education opportunities represent the most salient forms of containment by host states like Ghana which embolden immigrants to yearn for their putative homeland. A twenty-seven-year-old male respondent in Accra since 2003 admitted that what fortifies him amidst the injustices of life in Ghana is his desire to repatriate:

I work with a contracting company and sometimes [I am] intimidated at [my] job because I'm not a Ghanaian, neither a naturalised Ghanaian . . . my salary is determined by whatever they think they can pay me and somehow I'm still not deterred. [I] can just accept it like that because I know I [will] one day return home [to Liberia].[17]

---

[14] [DL99] Interview in Accra on 18 May 2013.
[15] [DL98] Interview in Accra on 18 May 2013.
[16] [DL104] Interview in Accra on 20 May 2013.
[17] [DL100] Interview in Accra on 18 May 2013.

Indeed, the vagaries of immigrant life and the challenging migration experiences of Liberian actors abroad in many ways facilitated the introduction of proposed dual citizenship legislation in 2008. In the sections that follow, I explore how migration simultaneously expanded and contracted the menu of legal citizenship options for Liberians abroad thereby influencing their perspectives on the merits and demerits of resident- or non-resident forms of Liberian citizenship.

A Complex Web of Citizenship Configurations

Liberian citizenship has become nuanced, multi-dimensional, and largely brokered by processes of migration as demonstrated in Table 5.4 capturing the varied citizenship statuses of actors interviewed unofficially for this book. While the first category was born in Liberia and retained *jus soli* Liberian citizenship, the second category was born in Liberia but naturalised in a foreign country and retained foreign citizenship by naturalisation. Whereas the third category of respondents was born in Liberia, but retained the foreign citizenship of at least one foreign citizen parent, the fourth category was born abroad to at least one Liberian citizen parent and retained *jus soli* foreign citizenship. The final category was born abroad to at least a Liberian citizen father and therefore retained *jus sanguinis* Liberian citizenship.

As indicated in the table, the majority of unofficial respondents were Liberian-born Liberian citizens (65 per cent) followed by Liberian-born naturalised foreign citizens (24 per cent). Although these statistics are far from representative, they do indicate to me that slightly higher numbers of Liberians could have maintained their legal Liberian citizenship than naturalised abroad, contrary to popular lore. Thus, one assumption underlying the introduction of proposed dual citizenship legislation in 2008 – that Liberians abroad had naturalised in record numbers – may have been more politically motivated than factual and based on sentiments rather than empirical evidence (Pailey, 2013a). Nevertheless, given the rapid changes in immigration regimes from the time I conducted interviews in 2012–2013 up until I submitted the final version of this book in late 2019 – including the pathway to residency and citizenship created for TPS and DED beneficiaries in the United States – I recognise that my hypothesis may no longer hold.

In Table 5.4, the third largest category of respondents (8 per cent) was Liberians born abroad who automatically obtained *jus soli*

Table 5.4 *Citizenship status of 181 unofficial respondents*

Field site/ citizenship status	Jus Soli Liberian citizen	Liberian-born, naturalised foreign citizen	Liberian-born, Jus Sanguinis foreign citizen	Jus Soli foreign citizen of Liberian parentage	Foreign-born, Jus Sanguinis Liberian citizen
London (30)	6	22	N/A	2	N/A
Washington (30)	11	12	1	6	N/A
Freetown (20)	12	3	N/A	3	2
Accra (30)	29	1	N/A	N/A	N/A
Monrovia (71)	59	6	1	4	1
Total absolute number/	117/	44/	2/	15/	3/
Percentage of total	65	24	1	8	2

I deliberately refrained from explicitly asking the twenty-one government officials and heads of regional diaspora organisations about their citizenship statuses as I realised early on that this would be a sensitive subject to broach for those speaking in their official capacities. Therefore, this information is not captured in my analysis.

foreign citizenships. Like Denise, who was profiled in the introduction of this chapter, the respondents born abroad before the onset of contemporary conflict in 1980 admitted that their parents had lived outside Liberia at the time of their births because of school or work opportunities. This is supported by demographic migration trends for Liberians pre-1980. Contrastingly, *jus soli* foreign citizen respondents born 1980 and after admitted that they were born abroad because of continued instability in Liberia. This is further supported by the spike in emigration after the coup that removed Tolbert. One of the most salient ways in which migration altered Liberian citizenship is that it created a hybrid category of simultaneous *jus soli* foreign citizens and *jus sanguinis* Liberian citizens like Denise. By virtue of the Aliens and Nationality Law, dual citizenship had been recognised for these conditional Liberian citizens at least until mid-December 2019 although they had to decide at the age of majority whether to maintain their foreign citizenship by birth or their Liberian citizenship by parentage.

Other categories of Liberian informants tended to further complicate what appeared to be clearly defined stipulations on citizenship in the 1973 Aliens and Nationality Law prior to 2020, such as *jus soli* Liberians who retained foreign citizenship by virtue of being born to at least one foreign citizen parent (1 per cent of the respondent pool) and *jus sanguinis* Liberians born abroad who retained legal Liberian citizenship by virtue of having at least a Liberian citizen father (2 per cent of the respondent pool). These two categories of Liberians were fewer in number in my study, although I suspect that worldwide migration and citizenship data may reveal that they represent a larger Liberian demographic. Liberian-born *jus sanguinis* foreign citizens and foreign-born *jus sanguinis* Liberian citizens in my respondent pool occupy a unique space within the Liberian citizenship continuum because they made citizenship status choices that were contrary to their birthplace citizenship. While the *jus soli* Liberians took on the foreign citizenship of their foreign-born parents by the age of majority, their *jus sanguinis* counterparts maintained the citizenship of their Liberian-born citizen fathers. For example, thirty-five-year-old Monrovia-based permanent returnee Beyan, who was profiled in Chapter 2, retained his *jus sanguinis* Liberian citizenship despite being entitled to Kenyan citizenship by birth and eligible for US citizenship by naturalisation:

I met some Kenyan people in the UN system here [in Liberia] and they were like, 'You were born in Kenya! You should apply for Kenyan citizenship; you are entitled!' I'm like, I haven't really taken the time to investigate that but seeing once again the dual citizenship faux pas, and I haven't really been inspired to go after it [Kenyan citizenship]. ... When I went into Kenya [in May 2009], the immigration officer at the airport, when I paid my ten [US] dollars for the airport visa, he said, 'But you were born in Kenya, how come you have a Liberian passport?!' 'My parents were just working here', [I said], so [he said] ... 'You have to get a Kenyan passport!'. ... Well, I knew at the time that Liberia did not honour dual citizenship and I always felt like I would be selling my soul by going to another nationality. But that's just me.[18]

Beyan's decision to choose Liberian citizenship from a menu of three legal identity options because of fears of 'selling his soul' mirrors the anti-assimilationist stances of Malkki's (1992) camp-based refugee informants. Other respondents used sedentarist metaphysical language – with references to earth, soil, ashes, blood – to describe their rejection of naturalisation, such as this seventy-four-year-old Washington-based US permanent resident who had spent over eighteen consecutive years abroad from the onset of Liberia's first armed conflict in 1989: 'I refuse to become an American citizen. ... I told my family I must be buried in Liberia or Liberia is where my ashes are supposed to be. ... So, Liberia is in my blood'.[19] The motivations for making divergent, personal choices about which citizenship to maintain are entangled in a complex web of sedentarist and nomadic metaphysics. It is also indicative of contestations about being Liberian officially or unofficially and about practising de jure or de facto Liberian citizenship.

While I argued in Chapter 2 that contemporary constructions of Liberian citizenship by respondents transcend the legal definition enshrined in the 1973 Aliens and Nationality Law and 1986 Constitution – moving from passive, identity-based citizenship to active, practice-based citizenship – it is now important to explore nuanced trends in the legal citizenship status of Liberians interviewed for this book. After all, the ways in which respondents altered or maintained their Liberian citizenship demonstrate their varied life-worlds, social locations, and the circumstances that influenced those

---

[18] [PR7] Interview in Monrovia on 25 June 2013.
[19] [DL48] Interview in Washington on 24 October 2012.

choices. As a case in point, the highest proportion of unofficial Liberian-born respondents (65 per cent) retained their legal Liberian citizenship with a disproportionate number represented by 'near' diasporas in Accra and Freetown and Monrovia-based homelanders. Of the fifty homeland Liberians, slightly over half (52 per cent) said they had never travelled outside of Liberia, and therefore may not have been eligible for foreign citizenship. Of the 110 unofficial diaspora respondents, slightly over 50 per cent retained their legal Liberian citizenship despite having lived abroad for long periods of time. In the 'wider' diaspora (the United Kingdom and the United States), London-based Liberians naturalised at a far greater rate than their Washington-based counterparts. In the 'near' diaspora (Ghana and Sierra Leone), however, the number of naturalised Liberians in Accra and Freetown was negligible. As mentioned in previous chapters, this demographic trend in my respondent pool could be attributed to the fact that while Sierra Leonean and Liberian identity and citizenship are mutually inclusive, 60 per cent of the Liberian-born Liberian citizens in Accra were refugees and therefore ineligible for foreign citizenship before the UNHCR's revocation of refugee status for Liberians worldwide in 2012. Of the fifty 'near' diasporas in Accra and Freetown, slightly less than half (48 per cent) were refugees who would not have been eligible for foreign citizenship without formal resettlement proceedings.

Nevertheless, the record numbers of Liberians who apply annually for the Diversity Visa (DV) Immigration Programme[20] to travel to the United States or who still yearn for resettlement in Australia and Europe despite the cessation of automatic refugee status for Liberians abroad prove that ineligibility does not necessarily evidence diminished desire to naturalise, particularly in the so-called Global North. Similarly, eligibility does not necessarily evidence a strong compulsion to naturalise. Like me, many respondents profiled for this book held onto their legal Liberian citizenship despite being eligible to naturalise

---

[20] According to the United States Department of State website, the Diversity Visa (DV) Immigration Programme enables '"diversity immigrants" from countries with historically low rates of immigration to the United States' to apply for a limited number of visas available annually. These visas enable recipients to eventually become eligible for US permanent residency and citizenship. Source: https://travel.state.gov/content/travel/en/us-visas/immigrate/diversity-visa-program-entry.html.

abroad. Furthermore, for those who naturalised, the decision was often slow, measured, and calculated. In the sections that follow, I explore how respondents' decisions to naturalise or not were largely contingent upon their lived experiences of migration as well as influenced by (un) conscious alignment with nomadic and sedentarist metaphysical paradigms around rootlessness and rootedness, respectively.

Naturalisation as Betrayer and Betrayed

Pakistani writer Kamila Shamsie (2014) wrote in a 4 March 2014 *Guardian* essay that she was ambivalent about naturalising as a UK citizen even though naturalisation officially ended her panicked bouts of fear of deportation from a country that has become acutely anti-immigrant. In Shamsie's heart-felt piece naturalisation is described as a process of being both 'betrayer' and 'betrayed'. Though Shamsie was able to officially maintain her Pakistani citizenship, Liberians interviewed for this book who naturalised in the United Kingdom, the United States, New Zealand, and Sierra Leone felt more intensely 'betrayed' by a country that could not protect them during crises yet revoked their citizenship upon naturalisation abroad. Profiled in Chapter 2, forty-nine-year-old London-based Teta was brought by her foster mother to the United Kingdom in the mid-1970s and admitted to feeling compelled to naturalise in the mid-1990s because of protracted conflict in Liberia:

You know, being Liberian is more important to me than being British. . . . I think it's just, I'll put it down to nationalism, that sort of thing where you, you know, it's an identity. It's your identity you don't want to lose. If you don't have to you don't want to. But then now we [Liberians] find ourselves in a Catch 22 situation. We didn't want to [naturalise], we had to because of the war. And now we're being penalised for taking on British citizenship, and it was just about survival really, in a lot of ways. Whenever you went for a job [in the United Kingdom] or anything like that it was really difficult presenting your Liberian passport. When a war was going on in your country, a lot of people in England never really knew about Liberia. You say to them 'Liberia' and they're hearing 'Nigeria'. . . . So, it was really difficult in a lot of ways because you did not have a British citizenship. So, it was just a matter of you have to survive, you have to get on, you don't know when the war [in Liberia] is going to end. And even if the war ended . . . You had to make sure there was stability before you even start to think about going back home [to Liberia] or establishing yourself back home in any kind of way. So, for that reason, I think a lot of us [Liberians] decided, 'You know what? This war isn't going to end just now and we just need to carry on with our lives', so, we did.[21]

Respondents like Teta held onto their legal Liberian citizenship long after they were eligible to naturalise abroad because of deeply entrenched notions of rootedness and perhaps an abiding faith that they would one day participate fully again in Liberia's political economy of belonging. When hopes of an end to armed conflict were abandoned, they naturalised because of the political and economic entitlements in their countries of settlement. While these actors said they remained psychologically and/or financially invested in Liberia, still referring to the country as 'home', they admitted that the practical need to survive abroad trumped impractical, idealised notions of Liberian citizenship authenticity. Echoing these sentiments, a Monrovia-based homelander, who still carries a US Green (permanent residency) Card though he had not lived in America since 1998, defended the decision of his relatives who naturalised abroad and other Liberians who feel compelled to take on foreign citizenships:

As old as my parents were at the time, they took on American citizenship because it afforded certain benefits in the United States as old people. My dad passed away last year [in 2012], he was ninety-nine years old. You couldn't tell him that he wasn't a Liberian. He had held almost every [government] position in Liberia but he took on an American citizenship when he went in 1990 because at his age he got some benefits as compared to being a non-American. I have siblings who live here [in Liberia] permanently, and had green cards, and just said, 'Just for the hell of it, I'm going to get an American citizenship'.[22]

Nomadic metaphysical thinking, as espoused by the respondent previously quoted, maps onto transnational conceptions of citizenship thus influencing diasporic and non-diasporic Liberians alike. For many respondents, the immediate gratification of naturalisation outweighed the metaphysical guilt of revoking their legal Liberian citizenship status; I know that my mother certainly shared these sentiments when her naturalisation enabled me to secure a US Green Card in the early 2000s. While ease of travel did not appear to be a major motivator for

---

[21]   [DL6] Interview in London on 12 June 2012.
[22]   [HL18] Interview in Monrovia on 12 June 2013.

Washington-based respondents who naturalised, their London-based counterparts constantly referenced it as an impetus for taking on British citizenship. This is very likely because, as a global city, London represents a nucleus with very accessible European, African, North American, and Asian flight routes. One respondent, a thirty-six-year-old woman who migrated to the United Kingdom in 1986 to attend school, said that after obtaining the red British passport in 2000 she began to recognise the international system of citizenship tiers as theorised by Yuval-Davis (2000) in which passport holders from the so-called Global North are treated better than their so-called Global South counterparts, particularly Africans:

Just recently last year [in 2011], I went to Ghana by [Royal] Air Maroc. The flight was delayed and we had to be put up in a hotel for a couple nights. And it was interesting how they treated those who had a British passport and those who had African passports. ... And we [with British passports] were put in this hotel which was in the centre [of town] with all the amenities. ... And those who had like African passports who needed to, I don't know how they got [visas], whether they had to in the end, but they required a visa to get out [of the airport]. ... So, they had to wait and so they were really angry. They were put up in this hotel which was nearer to the airport. They were just handled differently and that was, you know, quite racist, actually.[23]

The respondent was alluding to alliances Morocco has made with the European Union (EU) to serve as a buffer for curbing sub-Saharan migration to Europe. Although many African countries – including Benin, Ethiopia, Ghana, Kenya, Namibia, Rwanda, and Seychelles – have since adopted visa-free or visa-on-arrival allowances for other continental passport holders, at the time of my completing this book in December 2019 Morocco still excluded Liberia from its short list of African nationals allowed to enter without visas. Also lamenting the severe limitations of travelling with a Liberian passport, a forty-seven-year-old London-based man, who had lived in the Soviet Union and United States previously, said: 'Our passports are not respected equally. ... A British passport holder can go anywhere in the world but a Liberian passport holder cannot go anywhere in the world'.[24] Unsurprisingly, the ease of travel is a recurring motivation for naturalisation, particularly for this thirty-year-old London-based man and

[23] [DL8] Interview in London on 13 June 2012.
[24] [DL27] Interview in London on 22 June 2012.

former US resident because 'travelling with my Liberian passport, I still can be randomly selected for searches at American airports. I'd still be denied entry into certain countries or denied visas'.[25] As someone who travels extensively with a Liberian passport solely, I can attest to the difficulty of navigating international visa regimes; I also sympathise with those who cannot stomach the arbitrarily racist and restrictive nature of citizenship tiers.

Besides ease of travel, one fifty-seven-year-old man in London, who migrated to the United Kingdom in 1989 to obtain a master's degree, listed a long menu of other benefits of naturalising in 1992, including opportunities for career advancement and reduced university fees, social security and retirement perks, investment incentives, and the opportunity to sponsor the migration of his Liberian-based relatives:

It [naturalising in the United Kingdom] was one of the ways out to help me promote my career. I was in the university as a researcher when my [Liberian] passport expired. They had to, they could not renew anything and so one of the suggestions my course tutor gave me was, ' … Try [and] get all your [naturalisation] papers together, that's the only way you can cross'. … Before you get a job here [in the United Kingdom], you have to either come from the Commonwealth, either you're a European or British. I didn't meet any of those [criteria] so only because of my stay in the university class, that was one of the things that picked me up. … My children are British, which means all the educational opportunities [are available to them]. … I've been able to take up employment that would have been ring fenced. … When I get old here [in the United Kingdom] they will give me [a] pension book. … When I retire, they will give me a book and a bus pass. … It [naturalising in the United Kingdom] gave me the opportunity to send for my two children [in Liberia]. … It gave me an opportunity to invest in this country [the United Kingdom]. It gave me an opportunity to identify with the reality which is I am in Britain and I have no other means of perhaps leaving Britain so quickly. So, I needed to become recognised through the paper [passport] and naturalisation. It was the best option.[26]

This respondent could not have anticipated during our interview in 2012 that years later Brexit would sever UK–EU ties with adverse implications for EU nationals in the United Kingdom, yet his point about the necessity of securing British citizenship in the midst of Liberia's lengthy turmoil has been reaffirmed by many others.

---

[25] [DL29] Interview in London on 22 June 2012.
[26] [DL18] Interview in London on 16 June 2012.

Narrowly focused on career progression, one sixty-three-year-old male Washington-based IT professional exemplifies what Aihwa Ong (1999) calls the 'flexible citizen' who accumulates Western citizenships to build economic, social, and political capital. His motivation for naturalising in 1986, one of the earliest recorded for this book, was purely strategic:

I naturalised in the United States, number one, for convenience, economic convenience ... Professional convenience ... Because in my profession as an IT specialist, all of my jobs are government related, all of my jobs, in fact, especially a sensitive job, all our jobs are sensitive so we got to have clearance. You see, right now I have top-secret clearance, SCI [sensitive compartmental information], and polygraph. That's what I got, the highest [clearance], and I work with the FBI [Federal Bureau of Investigation] right now. I do contract for the FBI. ... So, naturally you got to be a US citizen in order to work in some places with regards to my job. You see? That's one of the main reasons [I naturalised]. ... Yeah, to work with the federal government, companies that work for federal government, when they are hiring you, you got to be a US citizen.[27]

Besides professional advancement, political participation abroad, and the lack thereof in Liberia, motivated other Liberian actors to naturalise. These informants maintain that their crisis-induced inertia made it impossible for them to actually participate in Liberia's political economy of belonging, so naturalisation was the most appropriate alternative. Having travelled to America with her student parents in 1982, one thirty-nine-year-old female respondent based in Washington said that she finally naturalised in 2009 because she had never voted in a Liberian election and wanted to finally exercise her franchise after living in the United States for twenty-seven years:

I held on [to my legal Liberian citizenship], I really held on ... there were several things that served as impetus for my decision [to naturalise in the United States]. I think one had to do with my social capacity. I felt that, 'Ok, where am I a citizen of?' I couldn't really identify myself. Yeah, I'm Liberian by consanguinity. I'm born in Liberia but I can't vote there, then I can't vote here [in the United States], so where am I legitimised? ... I think it was best for me to vote, to become a US citizen. I had been here at that time for nearly thirty years and so my whole life is here.[28]

[27] [DL58] Interview in Washington on 27 October 2012.
[28] [DL49] Interview in Washington on 24 October 2012.

Whereas some respondents interviewed for my study, like the two described previously, admitted to naturalising for reasons both individualistic and strategic, others argued that they did it for the greater good of Liberia and for Liberians. Claiming that he needed the legitimacy of an American passport to remain politically engaged with TPS and DED advocacy on behalf of Liberians in the United States, one forty-nine-year-old Monrovia-based permanent returnee said he was driven by altruism to naturalise:

> I was deep into immigration advocacy at the time and I found myself walking the House of Congress talking for TPS and then also talking about peace [in Liberia]. We became very good friends with the Rhode Island Legislative Caucus. Every time we went to these places, I felt like I had a much smaller voice. I could not ask these guys to commit a lot more and, for me, I really wanted to make an impact, personally. So, I thought that going the next step up [by naturalising], I really didn't realise the depth of this. I didn't realise that tomorrow would come and you would come home [to Liberia] and you would be considered a stranger. If I could do it again, I would do it again. I feel that the [US] citizenship gave me access to something that helped this country [Liberia].[29]

For Freetown-based respondents, being politically active was not as much a compelling motivation for naturalisation as owning private property since, like in the case of Liberia, land ownership is one of the definitive rights of Sierra Leonean citizenship. For example, thirty-eight -year-old Freetown-based James, profiled in Chapter 2, said that he felt compelled to naturalise in 2012 because 'You need to at least be a citizen or else your property, it will not be authentic'.[30] While motivations for naturalising, like James's, are based on nomadic metaphysical understandings of rootlessness, as indicated in the section that follows sedentarist biases about rootedness galvanise some Liberians to staunchly oppose naturalisation and, by extension, dual citizenship.

No Matter How Long a Rock Stays in a River, It Can Never Turn to Catfish

While Liberian-born respondents who naturalised abroad did so because they felt 'betrayed' by Liberia, those who opted not to

[29] [PR3] Interview in Monrovia on 11 June 2013.
[30] [DL62] Interview in Freetown on 11 April 2013.

naturalise said they did not want to become a 'betrayer' of the country and its citizens, regardless of their limitations as immigrants. For example, using an African parable to describe his deep and abiding loyalty to Liberia, and motivations for not wanting to naturalise, even if eligible, one Accra-based fifty-eight-year-old former refugee, who had lived in Togo before relocating to Ghana in 2006, said:

No matter how long a rock stays in a river, it can never turn to catfish . . . it means that your nationality is just your nationality, unless you want to fool yourself. Even if you say you want to go naturalise in Great Britain, yeah, they will say African British. . . . If you turn to American, they will say African American. . . . So, it means, are you pure American? . . . No matter how long I stay outside [of Liberia], I'm still Liberian by birth, I'm still Liberian by nationalism.[31]

That Liberian migrants like the previous respondent prefer to retain their origin country citizenship is not peculiar; this reflects global trends (Alarian & Goodman, 2017: 140). Studies have shown that migration tends to be higher in volume when both origin and destination states allow dual citizenship (Alarian & Goodman, 2017: 135). Yet, migration rates are more likely to increase in cases where origin states permit dual citizenship and destination countries forbid it compared to when origin countries forbid it and destination countries permit it (Alarian & Goodman, 2017: 135). In essence, when origin (emigration) countries like Liberia forbid dual citizenship they have a significantly higher influence on global migration trends than when destination (immigration) countries like the United Kingdom outlaw it.

Liberians abroad whose views are explored further in this section prove that beliefs about single citizenship as a marker of rootedness are not confined to homelanders or the territorially rooted in Liberia. Moreover, these respondents fundamentally agreed that although they could not remain physically rooted in Liberia because of armed conflict, choosing to maintain Liberian citizenship in spite of migration signified their metaphysical rootedness. The perspectives of these actors – who indirectly adopted a sedentarist metaphysic in relation to citizenship and naturalisation – completely unsettle normative assumptions that migrants from the so-called Global South are utility maximising agents who clamour for citizenships from the so-called Global North.

---

[31] [DL101] Interview in Accra on 19 May 2013.

While some respondents discussed the philosophical tenets of retaining legal Liberian citizenship, others said that naturalisation simply was not necessary for immigrant life. A thirty-two-year-old London-based student, who migrated to the United Kingdom in 2010 after living in West Africa for sixteen years, said that he opted not to naturalise abroad because he was relatively comfortable after graduating from college and obtaining a good job in Nigeria. His admission that other Liberians may have naturalised out of necessity is an indication that the more settled abroad one is without foreign citizenship, the less inclined one will be to naturalise:

I had the opportunity to naturalise in Nigeria, actually. I lived in Nigeria for ten years and I think I felt like I didn't want to lose my [Liberian] identity, right? ... For other obvious reasons people will lose it simply because they feel that they need to get some benefits from the country [of settlement]. I do accept that. I do understand that. But I went to Nigeria with the intention of going to school. ... So, I was like, I don't think I need the [Nigerian] citizenship.[32]

Similarly comfortable in her position as a US permanent resident, one fifty-one-year-old Monrovia-based circular returnee said that naturalisation never appealed to her as a necessity even though she lived in the United States for twenty-two years on and off. Having emigrated after Liberia's 1980 coup, this woman also previously lived in four other African countries:

I still don't care to be a US citizen. ... I never really felt completely at home in America. Never, ever. And that's probably one of the reasons I kept finding my way back [to Liberia] one way or the other. It [the United States] never really felt like home for me. ... I was really hard pressed at one time [to naturalise], I wanted to do it 'cause all my family members were becoming US citizens and I remember one time having a discussion with my father and it was so funny. He came home that day with his [US] citizenship and I said, 'Ok, we have to be careful how we say certain things around you because you have defected'. But, I felt that all the certain privileges, I still was able to get student loans [in the United States]. ... They related to me as a black American. Yeah. So, I really didn't see what, how being a US citizen would have made a difference.[33]

[32] [DL12] Interview in London on 14 June 2012.
[33] [CR9] Interview in Monrovia on 27 June 2013.

Though other Liberians could not boast of relative comfort abroad described by the previous two respondents, many admitted that in spite of the dire challenges of immigration they still held onto their legal Liberian citizenship. While this fifty-six-year-old Washington-based man disclosed that he was on DED since migrating in 2002 and, therefore, ineligible to naturalise in the United States at the time of our interview a decade later, naturalisation had never occurred to him as a durable solution to his immigration limbo:

I was a full-grown man before I came to this country [the United States]. Maybe in the early [19]80s when I came here to do my grad degree, you know, I was young, frisky, and everything. Maybe had I been here at that time, you know, twenty-four, twenty-five, thereabouts, becoming an American citizen would be something of a celebration and what have you. But now, I'm just passing through, you know. I'm just passing through. I've invested much in Liberia in terms of human capital development and all that kind of a thing, not necessarily material things. My mind, you know, my soul . . . everything is out there in Liberia. That's what it is.[34]

It is this respondent's perspective that I turn to now to show that although conflict in Liberia may have presented few options beyond migration, settlement in a host country does not necessarily compel one to naturalise thereby revoking legal Liberian citizenship. Thus, backlash against the proposed dual citizenship legislation of 2008 was based on the fundamental interrogation of whether or not naturalisation is by necessity. One thirty-six-year-old female Monrovia-based permanent returnee, who had lived in Ghana previously as a refugee for eleven years, argued vehemently that naturalisation is a matter of choice for the rootless emigrant:

[Y]ou are free to decide whether you want to be a citizen or you don't want to be a citizen [of Liberia]. . . . I think it's a lame argument to say that because you wanted to leverage on the opportunities available [abroad], that's why you became a citizen [abroad] and now you want to enjoy the benefits of both countries. . . . It's [Liberian citizenship's] your birth right, the [Liberian] Constitution recognises your birth right, but it also recognises the fact that you have a will to decide to continue to maintain your birth right or to give it up.[35]

---

[34] [DL52] Interview in Washington on 25 October 2012.
[35] [PR5] Interview in Monrovia on 17 June 2013.

Other Monrovia-based respondents, however, adopted a more nuanced perspective about the choice/force binary. This fifty-three-year-old male homelander, who has extensive family ties to the United States and previously lived there for a decade, subscribes to the argument made by Van Hear, Brubaker, and Bessa (2009) that, where migration is concerned, some choices are more limited than others:

It [naturalisation] is by choice but that choice can be driven by necessity. So, yes, it's your choice to say, 'I pledge allegiance', but it is my choice to say, 'I want rice or I don't want rice'. But if I'm hungry, then really I don't have much of a choice in that matter. I will say, 'Please give me rice'.[36]

Though the line appears blurred between force and choice in motivations for naturalising where eligible – similar to the structure versus agency debate still raging in modern sociological theory – deciding not to naturalise when entitled was framed as a choice for respondents who attempted to validate their non-physical rootedness in Liberia. Fifty-five-year-old permanent UK resident Aisha, who was profiled in Chapter 2, said that although she faces challenges travelling with a Liberian passport her motivation for not naturalising is continued legitimacy in Liberia, especially at the port of entry where a Liberian carrying a foreign passport could be scrutinised more intently:

[W]hen I go home [to Liberia], nobody will tell me bullshit! No bullshit to that airport! ... I'm proud to be a Liberian. Despite everything we have been through, I think we are lovely people and I'm proud of it.[37]

While Liberians who adopted nomadic metaphysical thinking said they naturalised for strategic reasons, counterparts who espoused a sedentarist metaphysic said they rejected naturalisation to preserve political, economic, and social capital in Liberia thus legitimately participating in the political economy of belonging. Citing her patriotism and love of country, one forty-two-year-old London-based respondent who migrated to the United Kingdom in 1993 said that she retains her legal Liberian citizenship because she has political ambitions and assumed, correctly in 2012, that Liberian law prohibited non-citizens from holding elected office:

[36] [HL18] Interview in Monrovia on 12 June 2013.
[37] [DL9] Interview in London on 13 June 2012.

I love being a Liberian. And I was very doubtful of giving up my natural identity and to take on another one, when I was aware that if I were to change my nationality I wouldn't be able to participate in quite a few things in Liberia ... [like] working in certain public offices. I have ambition to some-day become a senator [in Liberia] and I know that will affect my rights so I've retained that [my legal Liberian citizenship]. ... I'm hopeful that, you know, at some point I will, I just wanted to be able to go home someday [to Liberia] ... and not be questioned about my obligations or my rights to being a Liberian.[38]

Although I did not ask her explicitly, I wonder if the respondent's conditional reason for maintaining her legal Liberian citizenship – that is, a desire to run for elected office – would have changed at all if the laws were altered at the time of our interview to accept would-be dual citizen public officials. Echoing her concerns, a forty-five-year-old Washington-based man who had previously lived in the Soviet Union, followed by Ghana, said that his political aspirations and loyalty to Liberia made him refrain from obtaining Ukrainian citizenship on the grounds that 'accepting foreign citizenship would have deprived Liberia of yet another potential intellectual skill'.[39] This respondent appears to have had a complex immigration history, claiming that the United States had refused him a Green Card because of his former residence in Soviet Russia.

Contrary to the examples explored thus far, the perks of maintaining one's legal Liberian citizenship while abroad are not only apparent for those who wanted to return to Liberia or maintain transnational lives. Whereas the advantages of settlement in the United States and United Kingdom may have been greater for Liberians who naturalised, the maintenance of one's legal Liberian citizenship in Ghana and Sierra Leone facilitated certain benefits from the UN for refugees. For instance, many Accra-based former refugees interviewed for this book admitted begrudgingly that, despite the challenges of refugee life, they had received access to free land at the Buduburam Refugee Camp on which to build their very own houses, scholarships to attend school, security, and protection from both UNHCR and the Ghanaian government, precisely because they were Liberian citizens. As a case in point, one university lecturer who had migrated to Ghana in 1990

---

[38] [DL10] Interview in London on 13 June 2012.
[39] [DL36] Interview in Washington on 20 October 2012.

admitted that, amongst other benefits, his high-level academic pursuits were due in large part to support from UNHCR:

My training for undergrad and master's was sponsored by the UN. . . . And a number of Liberians went to school here on UN scholarships. Then others had skills training for those who could not get the pre-tertiary [qualifications] and then even some had secondary education, so there've been a number of benefits. There was feeding before, during the emergency period they were rationing food and . . . What else? . . . They provided some medicare.[40]

Although maintaining one's origin country citizenship in refugee contexts presents some advantages, as the previously mentioned respondent demonstrates, it has been proven that naturalisation in much of Africa is exceedingly difficult for most people due to restrictive informal and formal bureaucratic procedures (Manby, 2016, 2018). This general rule has only been challenged by programmes instituted after the cessation of refugee status by UNHCR, or those facilitating naturalisation for select refugee populations such as the 162,156 Burundians who were officially granted Tanzanian citizenship in October 2014 after living in conflict-induced exile since 1972 (UNHCR, 2014).[41] In essence, it could be argued that Liberians' decisions to naturalise abroad or not may have been permitted/prevented as much by accessibility/inaccessibility as by sentiments of rootlessness/rootedness. Given heightened debates pitting rootlessness against rootedness, however, I have argued in this section that while some Liberians' motivations for naturalising abroad impacted the introduction of dual citizenship legislation proposed in 2008, others' motivations for not naturalising challenged the bill's relevance.

Conclusion

Just as she did as a child, in her adulthood Denise swung on a pendulum between Liberia and the United States until she finally settled permanently in Monrovia in her middle age. Hers is a story that typifies the

---

[40] [DL104] Interview in Accra on 20 May 2013.

[41] Although Tanzania's historic decision was the largest-ever mass naturalisation of refugees, the state had previously granted citizenship to 32,000 Rwandan refugees in 1982 and in February 2014 it naturalised 3,000 Somali Bantu refugees who had escaped Somalia in 1991 after President Siad Barre was deposed.

migration experiences of some Liberians explored in this chapter whose movements complicate the choice/force dichotomy. I have demonstrated that historical and contemporary migration to and from Liberia changed the country's citizenship norms, thereby generating roots for some and routes for others. In 1847, Liberia was a country of relative immigration yet citizenship norms were biased against those considered 'rooted' – primarily the sixteen ethnic groups already occupying the territory were formally excluded from the institution of citizenship. In 2019, however, while Liberia exemplified a country of relative emigration citizenship norms were biased against those deemed 'rootless' – essentially *jus soli* Liberians who naturalised abroad and *jus sanguinis* Liberians who maintained their birthplace citizenship remained excluded from formal Liberian citizenship.

This chapter moved beyond the rhetoric of politicians and policymakers to underscore that ordinary Liberians' contemporary notions of rootedness and rootlessness represent a continuum of sedentarist and nomadic metaphysical thinking thereby simultaneously challenging and strengthening claims for dual citizenship. While motivations for not naturalising abroad – largely based on sedentarist metaphysics – have defied core assumptions about the necessity of dual citizenship for Liberia, motivations for naturalising – largely based on nomadic metaphysics – have galvanised proponents of such a policy prescription and development intervention. Akin to Malkki's urban-based informants, the respondents I interviewed for this book who opted for naturalisation abroad viewed protracted armed conflict as inhibiting their ability to fully opt into Liberia's political economy of belonging. Like Malkki's camp-based informants, however, the Liberians I consulted who refused naturalisation believed that their legal citizenship purity/authenticity gave them more legitimacy in the political economy of belonging to Liberia. Opting in and out of naturalisation may have been prompted by more practical considerations in the hostland, however, such as accessibility/inaccessibility, including prohibitive costs and cumbersome procedures. Similarly, citizenship status choices may have been influenced significantly by Liberia's links with countries of diasporic settlement. For example, Liberian – American bonds are clearly stronger than Liberian – British ties because of historical and contemporary bilateral relations; as such, respondents in the United Kingdom may have naturalised at a faster pace than their counterparts in the United States because of concerns about the precariousness of their long-term immigration statuses. As Liberians become increasingly eligible for naturalisation abroad, such as the former TPS and DED beneficiaries who now have this option at their disposal, it remains to be seen whether claims for and against dual citizenship will actually transform.

In Chapter 6, I discuss how post-war recovery under the Sirleaf administration sparked heated debates about what kind of development Liberia should pursue and whether or not diasporas and dual citizenship would help or hinder reconstruction.

6 | *The Dichotomy of Diasporic Developmentalism*

Introduction

In 1985, soon to be warlord-turned-president Charles Taylor 'mysteriously'[1] escaped from a drab cell of the Plymouth Massachusetts Correctional Facility in the United States as a fugitive on the run. For sixteen months, he had awaited extradition to Liberia for allegedly stealing US$922,382 from the country's General Services Agency (GSA), a procurement arm of government he managed before absconding to his adopted home. In the early 1970s, the ambitious young Taylor had travelled across the Atlantic to attend Chamberlayne Junior College in Boston although he subsequently enrolled at Bentley College to study economics. A consummate politician, he became involved in both the Liberian Community Association in Massachusetts and the Union of Liberian Associations in the Americas (ULAA), the latter being a conduit for challenging True Whig Party (TWP) hegemony.

Travelling up and down the US East Coast for rallies and demonstrations, Taylor gained visibility and credibility as a critical voice for change in Liberia. Subsequently elected head of the Boston branch of ULAA, he and other stalwarts of the organisation were invited by President William R Tolbert Jr in early 1980 to help institute reforms for which they had advocated in the United States. Yet, Taylor declined until a more lucrative offer came from Samuel Kanyon Doe to run the GSA in 1983. Rumoured to have acquired US permanent residency and citizenship while abroad, Taylor – with his aborted extradition, jailbreak from Plymouth, and subsequent warmongering – would come to

---

[1] Taylor hinted in testimony during his trial for the Special Court for Sierra Leone that he had been aided and abetted by the Central Intelligence Agency (CIA) in his jailbreak because of the American government's desire to depose Doe.

symbolise Liberia's powerlessness to stop transnationals from pilfering meagre state resources and 'plunging the country into chaos'.[2]

   Almost three decades later, another indictment and looming extradition, this time involving a Liberian-born US citizen army pilot, Ellen Corkrum, resurrected Taylor's case. Appointed managing director of the Liberia Airport Authority (LAA) in 2011, Corkrum was accused in 2012 of 'economic sabotage, criminal facilitation, conspiracy to defraud the government, and making unauthorised transfers of funds from government accounts' (Pewee, 2019). After fleeing to the United States, she and her Liberian-born US citizen partner, Melvin Johnson – the first black judge to serve in Lithonia, Georgia – released unauthorised tapes they had recorded implicating other government officials in a bid to curry favour and sympathy from Liberians at home and abroad (Kanneh, 2014). Nevertheless, the government of Liberia requested their arrest in September 2013, prompting President Ellen Johnson Sirleaf (2014: 24) to publicly lament her faith in Corkrum's ability to lead aviation reforms. Although the accusations against Corkrum and Johnson were egregious – that is, violation of procurement laws by single-sourcing a consulting firm owned by Corkrum's friend for repairs at Roberts International Airport (RIA) that were never completed; contracting and paying Johnson for a security system that he was incapable of designing; transferring into their private accounts funds intended to purchase electronic equipment for RIA's clients – they were never extradited for their alleged malfeasance (Kanneh, 2014). Indeed, Sirleaf's sometimes misguided trust in returnees like Corkrum cast transnational actors as post-war saboteurs thus creating further backlash against the 2008 proposed dual citizenship bill. In a particularly embarrassing reversal years later, the Liberian government was forced in December 2019 to drop all charges against Corkrum because of its failure to officially serve the defendant an indictment or bring her to Liberia for judgement (Pewee, 2019); nevertheless, amidst public furore about Corkrum's voluntary return in January 2020, President George Oppong Weah's solicitor-general was forced to re-open the case by referring the matter to the Liberia Anti-Corruption Commission (LACC) for further investigation.

   In this chapter, I argue that Sirleaf's two terms in office cemented the need to balance citizenship rights with responsibilities while

---

[2] [HL29] Interview in Monrovia on 18 June 2013.

heightening debates about who could and should participate in post-war reconstruction. I employ what I term the dichotomy of diasporic developmentalism to demonstrate that post-war interventions by Liberians abroad and their returnee counterparts simultaneously enhanced and eroded the political economy of belonging to Liberia hence eliciting both endorsement and rejection of dual citizenship. The chapter is organised into three sections: First, I provide an overview of the literature on war to peace transitions and explore debates about Liberia's reconstruction trajectory. Second, I catalogue achievements and challenges in implementing the country's first major post-war development agenda, the *Lift Liberia* Poverty Reduction Strategy (PRS), and examine how it impacted citizenship construction and practice. And lastly, I assess how Sirleaf's diasporic ethos or *diaspocracy* – manifested in copious high-level political appointments of transnationals – simultaneously helped and hindered recovery thereby influencing claims for and against dual citizenship.

'Post-conflict' Makeover Fantasies and War to Peace Alternatives

In this book, I refrain from using the apolitical term 'post-conflict' to describe Liberia because, as indicated in Chapters 3 and 4, it does not sufficiently capture post-war clashes over dual citizenship, land, income, and transitional justice. I am aware that 'post-war' may suffer from the same analytical limitations as 'post-conflict', but what I appreciate about the former is that it captures what it says, whereas the latter does not account for how physical violence is a symptom and enduring consequence of structural violence. Although 'post-conflict reconstruction' is often used in policy and academic literature to describe countries recovering from physical violence, nations like Liberia are rarely devoid of structural violence. Accordingly, I believe that a country recuperating from war can never truly be 'post'-conflict. In fact, one of the fallacies generated by the 'post-conflict make-over fantasy' is that post-war polities are *tabula rasa* with histories of inequality that can somehow be sanitised with technical, bureaucratic reforms dictated by multilateral agencies such as the International Monetary Fund (IMF), the World Bank, and the United Nations (UN) (Cramer, 2006: 245, 255).

Just as 'post-conflict reconstruction' is a contested category of inquiry, war to peace transitions represent an array of intersecting processes that involve a number of competing priorities of governments, local constituents, and donors. Similar to the four-pillar priorities of *Lift Liberia* – namely, (a) peace and security, (b) economic revitalisation, (c) governance and the rule of law, (d) infrastructure and basic social services – 'post-conflict reconstruction' is premised on four war to peace principles largely derived and driven by donors: (1) security sector reform (restructuring the army and other security institutions); (2) political reconstruction (reorganising legal and electoral systems); (3) economic reconstruction (realigning macro-economic policies, budget and tax structures, banking and commercial codes, expenditures and revenue); and (4) social reconstruction (demobilising and integrating ex-combatants, repatriating refugees, restoring basic services, reigniting social cohesion, identity formation and consolidation) (Ottaway, 2003; del Castillo, 2008; Sesay et al., 2009: 7; Paris & Sisk, 2010). Although these deliverables are peddled as cure-all measures for stabilising states and improving government–citizen and citizen–citizen relations, in actuality they have produced unintended consequences for the political economy of belonging to Liberia.

Akin to post–Second World War reconstruction in Europe, there is often an 'externalisation of post-war efforts' wherein outsiders control 'the designing, financing, and implementation of reconstruction programmes', and this has become a particular affliction of countries emerging from war in Africa and further afield (Sesay et al., 2009: 8). According to Kieh (2012b: xix), Sirleaf's regime in particular 'haphazardly . . . embarked upon the implementation of the neoliberal project, as evidenced by efforts to, among others, liberalise the political institutions, reform the security sector, and recommit Liberia to the peripheral capitalist path to development'. In fact, Liberia's adoption of one-size-fits-all policies and programmes prompted former public works minister Samuel Kofi Woods to complain to me in 2013 about our country's externalisation of post-war development:

My frustration with most of these things is that it's [post-war recovery's] captured externally and imposed locally. And when you have these kinds of things happen, when we have to pander to the international demands and the dictates of the international community as to what model we should adopt, what will be good for our country, implementation becomes difficult. We need to develop our national drive, our domestic approaches to be able to address the problems of Liberia, not what happened somewhere else, or not what becomes the most romantic approach to development. And that's part of my frustration. So, nothing that is borrowed without appropriate understanding can be applied consistently in this country [Liberia]. And I don't think we have been able to do it. We want to be a darling of external people, probably some of us – not only the institution or the country – but as individuals, we also want to be a darling of those out there, hoping that our future can be embedded in their institutions, of the IMF, the World Bank, and so forth. So, we pander to them without under-standing that we need to do more for our own country.[3]

Despite Woods's contention, then Minister of Foreign Affairs Augustine Ngafuan, who was actively involved in the Heavily Indebted Poor Countries (HIPC) relief process as minister of finance, insisted that Liberia demonstrated more agency at the interface with donors than some care to admit by strategically accepting post-war conditionalities that were 'good for the Liberian people':

Well, because [of] the conditionalities, we agreed upon it. We called them triggers. One was to maintain macro-economic stability. That was good for the Liberian people, not just an IMF issue. We agreed to institute audits of five key government ministries and agencies, HIPC audits, including [the] Ministry of Finance, Education, Health, and that was good for the Liberian people that those entities were audited. We agreed to the establishment, and making functional, [of] an Anti-Corruption Commission. That was good for the Liberian people. We agreed to clean up . . . to regularise the Education Ministry payroll. That was good for the Liberian people. We agreed to pass an Investment Code that would take away discretion and that was good for the Liberian people. Of all the triggers agreed, those were triggers that were advancing the interest of Liberians. . . . No, it was not top-down. It was negotiated. We proffered most of these things and we had a common understanding with our partners – the World Bank, the IMF, and others – in the HIPC process. They say these are the conditionalities because they sprang from the exigent realities of Liberia. Yes, in other situations the neoliberalist critiques apply, but for us, to a large extent, we ensured that those triggers agreed upon were triggers that were in the interest of Liberia.[4]

As demonstrated by Ngafuan and Woods, even within the executive branch of government there was contestation about whether Liberia's post-war recovery under Sirleaf was externally imposed or domesti-cally driven, whether it strengthened or weakened government–citizen relations, and whether it advanced or challenged the political economy

[3] Interview in Monrovia on 25 June 2013.
[4] Interview in Monrovia on 11 June 2013.

of belonging. This is unsurprising. Central to discourses around war to peace transitions is the capacity of governments to negotiate the competing priorities of the state itself, local constituents, donors, and international actors. A simultaneous pursuit of state- and nation-building objectives in post-war contexts like Liberia is the only means of reconciling these tensions.

The Dilemmas of State- and Nation-building

President Sirleaf's administration focused entirely too much on state-building at the expense of nation-building and this adversely impacted the stalemate on dual citizenship. One of the problems with state-building as a war to peace agenda is its myopic focus on strengthening government institutions with the core assumption that no positive institutional practices existed before the 'post-conflict moment' – a fallacy of terra nullius as articulated by Cliffe and Manning (2008: 165). In this analysis, policymakers conflate the 'state idea' – our imaginations of what the state *should be* – with the 'empirical state' – how the state *actually* functions in practice (Abrams, 1988). This usually occurs at the expense of legitimising national cohesion and has the propensity to undercut government authority and damage government–citizen relations. Fundamental to Liberia's post-war recovery success or failure, therefore, is re-defining the tenets of both citizenship and the political economy of belonging while recognising nation-building and state-building as vital parallel processes.

Scholars and policymakers who examine and implement reconstruction projects, respectively, emphasise state-building, while often ignoring its analytical twin, nation-building. Whereas state-building focuses on public institutions such as laws, courts, and legislatures, nation-building refers to the 'strengthening of a national population's collective identity, including its sense of national distinctiveness and unity' or the 'orderly exercise of a nation-wide, public authority' (Bendix, 1996: 22). Nation-building has three central elements that define it as a success: 'a unifying, persuasive ideology, integration of society and a functional state apparatus' (Hippler, 2005: 7). This is a framework worth adopting in measuring post-war achievements in Africa and elsewhere because of its emphasis not only on mending government–citizen ties but also on repairing citizen–citizen relations. For example, Robinson's (2007) preoccupation with the social contract between governments and citizens illuminates how Liberians who naturalised abroad have evoked their state- and nation-building practices to justify the enactment of dual citizenship within the context of post-war recovery.

A number of features defining state- and nation-building position the two as binaries. While nation-building is 'people centric' and internally driven, requiring national agency, ownership, and resources, state-building is 'institution centric' and externally driven, often soliciting international resources and involving cookie-cutter social engineering (Pailey, 2011; Pailey, 2017a). Although both state- and nation-building have their advantages and disadvantages, the two processes cannot be transformational if pursued in isolation or fully operational without an interrogation of the meaning of citizenship. Moreover, both state- and nation-building are essential for consolidating the political economy of belonging. While the former is supposed to improve a government's capacity to provide privileges and protections, the latter ideally augments a citizen's ability to fulfil duties and obligations thus resulting in socio-economic transformation. Yet, the Liberian government has been repeatedly urged by donors to prioritise macro-economic policies such as liberalisation, privatisation, and deregulation, which actually hollow out the state and lead to an erosion of government–citizen relations. Whereas the focus of post-war recovery during Sirleaf's administration was building institutional structures at the expense of solidifying a cohesive national identity, debates about dual citizenship forced policymakers to see state- and nation-building as mutually constitutive. Claims for dual citizenship begged the question central to state- and nation-building processes: how does the government incorporate non-resident nationals in its recovery efforts without invalidating the needs and contributions of resident citizens? I explore this question in detail later in the chapter when I discuss how Liberian transnationals have simultaneously helped and hindered post-war development.

In the section that follows, I provide an overview of some of Liberia's post-war recovery successes and failures under Sirleaf with an emphasis on how they impacted citizenship construction and practice.

From Lifting Liberia to Lifting Liberians

From the cessation of armed conflict in August 2003 to the first transfer of presidential power after seventy-four years in January 2018, Liberia pursued a formulaic war to peace transition, moving from humanitarian relief to recovery and development. Though it is beyond the scope of this book to provide a comprehensive overview of reconstruction to date – especially since the Liberian government and its donors have already produced voluminous reports to that end – I have targeted particular efforts to support my argument that the demands of post-war development created incentives and opportunities for Liberian diasporas and their returnee counterparts to practise active citizenship which influenced both endorsement and rejection of dual citizenship.

Liberia's recovery was buttressed by a series of externally determined and financed agendas that simultaneously enhanced and undermined the principles of citizenship – from the Results-Focused Transitional Framework (RFTF) (2003–2005) of the National Transitional Government of Liberia (NTGL) to the 150-Day Action Plan (2006), Interim Poverty Reduction Strategy (2006–2008), *Lift Liberia* Poverty Reduction Strategy (2008–2011), and Agenda for Transformation (AfT) (2012–2017) of the Sirleaf administration. I focus analysis in this chapter exclusively on *Lift Liberia*, not only because I was involved[5] in its implementation as an aide to President Sirleaf but also because it appears to have been monitored and evaluated more intensely than all other development plans to date. Its goal was to reduce poverty by 4 per cent, from 64 per cent in 2007 to 60 per cent in 2011, with the government of Liberia committing a fraction (US$500 million) of the total US$1.6 billion required for implementation (Government of Liberia, 2012b: 9). Although *Lift Liberia* was dubbed the 'Poverty Enhancement Strategy' by citizens across the country, a second Core Welfare Indicators Questionnaire (CWIQ) conducted in 2010 indicates that poverty had already been reduced by 8 percentage points – to 56 per cent – even before the three-year PRS ended (Government of Liberia, 2010c: 76; Government of Liberia, 2011b: 15). Similarly, government of Liberia reports show that PRS completion rates improved dramatically from 20 per cent in 2008–2009 to 80 per cent in 2009–2010 with an overall average of 59 per cent as indicated in Table 6.1 (Government of Liberia, 2011b: 7).

---

[5] From 2009 to 2011, I co-hosted a radio programme, *Lift Liberia*, which tracked the progress of the first PRS. It aired on UN radio and was simulcast on Liberia's state broadcaster ELBC.

Table 6.1 *Summary of* Lift Liberia *deliverables and final completion rates*

Pillars/deliverables/completion rates	Number of deliverables	Completion rate (in percentages)
(1) Peace and security	94	67
(2) Economic revitalisation	118	69
(3) Governance and the rule of law	52	41
(4) Infrastructure and basic services	187	57

Source: Government of Liberia, 2012b

Capacity constraints were often listed as the main reason for slow implementation in the initial stages of *Lift Liberia*. According to former Civil Service Agency (CSA) director-general and then ambassador-designate to France, C William Allen, in 2013, Liberia's ability to execute certain deliverables was largely hampered by a low-level domestic human resource base:

The challenges, the challenges, first of all, would be capacity. Frankly, both human capacity and institutional capacity and I guess those two would add up into a general deficit in societal capacity. I think clearly those would be the greatest challenges because one may have all the ideas but if you don't have the resources to implement those ideas then the challenges become enormous.[6]

These limitations facilitated emergency capacity building programmes such as the Transfer of Knowledge through Expatriate Nationals (TOKTEN), the Liberia Emergency Capacity Building Support (LECBS), and the Senior Executive Service (SES) discussed in Chapter 4 thereby carving out a niche for diaspora returnees, entrenching their influence and that of donors in the entire PRS process. In fact, Liberia seems to have a chequered history of external technical assistance, whether imposed, like a financial advisor employed by Firestone in the 1920s, or voluntarily sought, like the Liberian senior executives actively recruited from abroad by Sirleaf in the 2000s and 2010s. For example, in 1934 President Barclay hired a Polish national as his economic advisor; in that same year, Liberia's first Three-Year Development Plan was devised with six American specialists enlisted

[6] Interview in Monrovia on 4 June 2013.

although their contracts were terminated when the Plan expired in 1937 (Van der Kraaij, 1983: 300). These historical examples show that Liberia's heavy reliance on international 'experts' – be they foreign 'expatriates' or diaspora 'repatriates' – for the implementation of its development goals fundamentally undermined government's capacity to deliver with autonomy thus worsening in many ways government–domestic citizen relations.

As I exhibited earlier, Liberia's entire *Lift Liberia* PRS superstructure was primarily propelled by a neoliberal race to HIPC Completion Point. Under the peace and security pillar of *Lift Liberia*, foreign agents led, financed, and implemented most deliverables. For instance, the deployment of 15,000 United Nations Mission in Liberia (UNMIL) military personnel in 2003 represents 'one of the most expensive operations embarked upon by the UN since 1945' (Sesay et al., 2009: 50). Nevertheless, there was a small measure of local ownership in security sector reform, argued then defence minister Brownie Samukai, the only cabinet official to serve the entire duration of Sirleaf's two terms in office:

Yes, the US government provided funding [to the Armed Forces of Liberia (AFL)] and the funding was dictated by them. ... They determine who they bring, who the instructors will be. They determine when the instructor will be here, how long they gonna be here, the kind of car the instructor rides, where the instructor lives and everything else ... we were building the Army in 2006, they [the US government] provided funding of close to US$200 million for the training, they gave the contract away [to DynCorp], that's their money. ... The training module [of the AFL] is based on the TRADOC of the US, that is the training doctrine of the United States. We are making that training manual to become what you call interoperability [interoperable] with other African countries so that a Liberian can work here and also work in Ghana, Sierra Leone, and Nigeria, like we have Liberians in Mali, there is no problem at all. ... The weapons system that we used is not an American M16, it's an AK47, which is pretty much predominant around [Africa]. LARS [Lower Airspace Radar Services] that are also used, we can use those weapons. RPGs [Rocket Propelled Grenades], we can also use those weapons. Pretty much that is what we are presently using, so we can operate within Liberia, outside Liberia, with other African countries and among other countries around the world.[7]

Despite Samukai's assurances about his adoption of a regional approach to reform, Liberia's autonomy in its own security

---

[7] Interview in Monrovia on 12 July 2013.

restructuring was marginal at best. The US government disbanded and reorganised the AFL by contracting DynCorp, an American security firm, with minimal input from the government of Liberia (Kieh, 2012b: 239). Under DynCorp's tutelage, only 2,000 soldiers were trained from 2006 to 2009 although the Liberian government's initial target was 4,000 (Kieh, 2012b: 239). From its inception, the restructured AFL was led by a Nigerian command officer in charge, Major General Suraj Alao Abdurrahman, until February 2014 when a Liberian, Brigadier-General Daniel D Ziankhan,[8] took over the reigns as chief of staff. Under the supervision of UN Police (UNPOL), an estimated US$0.5 million was spent on training 3,500 members of the Liberia National Police (LNP) from 2004 to 2007 (Kieh, 2012b: 239). While the army and police were priorities, other security outfits such as the National Security Agency (NSA), the Bureau of Immigration and Naturalisation (BIN), and the Drug Enforcement Agency (DEA) were virtually neglected because of a lack of donor support (Kieh, 2012b: 239; Pailey & Jaye, 2016). Samukai justified the single-minded pursuit of streamlining the AFL at the expense of other important security institutions claiming that it served to rebuild confidence in the sector:

Arising out of the civil conflict, people lost confidence in the security sector. People lost confidence in those who were entrusted to protect them, and so it was not the question of training and retraining but it's how do you build that confidence back both domestically, both on the regional level, and also in the diaspora as well. So, those were the steps we began to take. And working with the US government, through their full support for the restructuring process, we set out to conduct an empirical vetting process on the order of merits upon which all new entrants into the AFL had to conform to so that actually helped to raise the credibility of the process. . . . And with the support of the UN as observers and civil society as well on the Joint Personnel Board, all successful recruits into the AFL had to meet those standards as well. So, if there is anything that we can say that we may have ever done here over the past seven years [from 2006 to 2013] it's to regain the confidence of the Liberian people into the military, into the security sector, so that they can once again begin to trust that [the] AFL, you know, is a force for good.[9]

[8] The full story of the Liberian AFL chief of staff's induction was covered in an Executive Mansion press release on 11 February 2014, Liberia's Armed Forces Day: www.emansion.gov.lr/2press.php?news_id=2892&related=7&pg=sp.
[9] Interview in Monrovia on 12 July 2013.

However, so-called faith in the AFL would be completely dented during the Ebola outbreak when on 20 August 2014 they fired live rounds in a quarantined poor community in Monrovia and a fifteen-year-old boy, Shaki Kamara, bled to death from bullet wounds after being refused treatment at the country's major referral hospital. Initially quick to deny any wrongdoing by the AFL, the Ministry of Defence eventually acknowledged its role in Kamara's demise and offered to compensate the family. Samukai's assertion that Liberians had new-found trust in security institutions was neither entirely true for civilians nor army personnel. When probed, he admitted to me that there were major gaps in improving the material circumstances of soldiers which led to defections:

We have trained them [AFL soldiers], we have equipped them, we're provid-ing for them the salaries. We need to make sure the condition in which they live and work is much better than what it is today ... Because the concentra-tion of the troops here in Monrovia at the Edward Binyah Kesselly Barracks, which is actually constructed for 800 persons, now has 2,000 persons initially. ... Then eventually we tried to have some of them relocated to the Coast Guard Base, to Camp Ware and then as well as Camp Tubman in Gbarnga [Bong County]. And then we encouraged them to bring their families, so you had 200 families, now you got probably about 2,000 families. ... And then we have over 500 kids that are going to school, so all of these challenges suggest to us that the condition under which they [the AFL soldiers] live and work has been and continues to be a challenge for us.[10]

Samukai's confession about the lack of complete satisfaction within the AFL was one indicator among many that Liberia's peace remained very tenuous in 2013 when our interview was conducted. Furthermore, increased instability in the Mano River subregion persisted and there were acute concerns about the capacity of Liberia's security personnel to withstand a complete drawdown of UNMIL after presidential and legislative elections in late 2017 (UN Panel of Experts on Liberia, 2013; Pailey & Jaye, 2016).

Just as peace and security were fragile because of domestic abdica-tion to external agenda-setting, so too was Liberia's post-war economic recovery challenged because of the dictates of outsiders, as mentioned previously. For example, the government welcomed in 2005 the Governance and Economic Management Assistance Programme

----

[10] Ibid.

(GEMAP) whereby foreign bureaucrats were hired to oversee revenue-generating agencies in order to ensure fiscal discipline and transparent management (UN Panel of Experts on Liberia, 2005: 8–9; Kieh, 2012b: 229). This was undoubtedly based on recommendations from a UN Panel of Experts on Liberia (2003: 8) report recommending the establishment of an 'independent economic commission of inquiry' to 'conduct systematic investigations of all revenue-producing entities wishing to be active in Liberia'. Yet, the systematic review of revenue generation neither mitigated corruption beyond GEMAP's mandate nor facilitated economic diversification beyond natural resource extraction (Government of Liberia, 2011a: 6). Despite the precariousness of Liberia's post-war development at the time, Samukai praised GEMAP for laying the foundation of economic growth:

I mean there was nothing here [in Liberia], there was no process, no procedure, no system. I mean people were calling Liberia [a] completely failed state. All of the institutions of governance were already gone. The issue of accountability was not there. Credibility was not there. Confidence was also gone, so you needed [donor] partners to help you to lay the basis to get yourself going. For example, we had the GEMAP people who were sitting in every aspect of government co-signing every document; three to four years later we felt that we were confident enough to handle things ourselves . . . and we got rid of them and we continue our own process today.[11]

Other important technical, state-building reforms under the economic revitalisation pillar were largely brokered by collaborations between the Liberian government and donors, with some positive results, such as debt cancellation of US$4.9 billion; audits conducted by the General Auditing Commission (GAC); the establishment of internal audit systems in all government agencies; and the enactment of public financial management legislation such as the Public Financial Management Law (Government of Liberia, 2011a). These measures, including budget transparency mechanisms instituted, were intended to improve government's capacity to deliver thereby increasing citizen oversight of public finances. According to Ngafuan, Liberia's adoption of an open budget process represented one of the hallmarks of post-war economic recovery during which Liberia's cash-based budget increased dramatically from US$85 million in the 2005–2006 fiscal year to US$649 million in the 2012–2013 fiscal year alone (Government of Liberia, 2011a):

[11] Ibid.

One of the milestones was to have this sacred, [the] sacredness around the budget taken off and to make it a public instrument and that budgets became instruments to be discussed on radio, journalists having copies, hatai shops[12] discussing it and then lively budget debate. It was all part of the transition. Now, it's good that after we [my administration] left, my successor [Amara Konneh] has maintained this path with [the] Open Budget Initiative. But one of the key milestones given the immediate past was, one, we opened the budget process ... at least people are not as detached from the budget process today as they were detached before the government of Ellen Johnson Sirleaf came in.[13]

Completely unprecedented in Liberia, budget transparency expanded the scope for citizens to participate in prioritising and financing development thereby augmenting their role in the political economy of belonging. Although the establishment of County Development Funds (CDFs) in 2008 was also expected to decentralise fiscal authority to Liberia's fifteen sub-political divisions, thus bolstering government–citizen relations, the process was severely hobbled by mismanagement and discord between executive branch county authorities and legislative caucuses, prompting the Ministry of Internal Affairs to suspend disbursements to the Funds in December 2013 pending review.[14]

Akin to the first two pillars of *Lift Liberia*, governance and the rule of law in Liberia progressed in the post-war period due to policies devised and institutions founded to restore government–citizen and citizen–citizen relations, such as the establishment of the LACC, the Public Procurement and Concessions Commission (PPCC), and the Liberia Extractive Industries Transparency Initiative (LEITI); the devolution of public authority through the passage of a Community Rights Law, endorsement of a National Decentralisation Policy, and formation of county-level service delivery branches; the creation of a Civil Service Reform Strategy which removed 'ghost names' from the payroll; and improvements in access to justice for all by deploying public defenders and trained magistrates throughout the country (Government of Liberia, 2011a: 4). Despite these achievements, then justice minister Christiana Tah disclosed to me in 2013 that government–citizen and

---

[12] Hatai shops are local tea shops in Liberia where people go to debate current events and political issues.
[13] Interview in Monrovia on 11 June 2013.
[14] Visit http://allafrica.com/stories/201312161205.html for more information about the CDFs suspension.

citizen–citizen interactions were still undermined by Liberia's failure to reconcile formal and informal justice mechanisms:

I think the formal justice system has always had a challenge with the informal justice system. But I think there was better control in the past because of the relative peace and stability that we had. But, I think, with the war and the dismantling of the formal justice system, people always have a need to turn to someone or something for resolutions. And when you're on the run, and the formal system is not working, and the informal system is all that is available, it seems like it became more significant, more important to people, and so more people utilised the informal justice system, it appears to me, from my own observation, during the war years. ... So, now, to come back and re-establish the rule of law, you have to confront this. So, what we did, we actually created a dialogue between actors in both the formal and informal [justice systems]. We thought this is not the kind of thing you fight over, but this is the kind of thing you discuss; you have a dialogue. So, in April in 2010, we had a national conference on enhancing access to justice by harmonising the informal and the formal systems. ... So, rather than looking at it as a contention between the two, we're dialoguing and working together to see how we can bring them [the two systems] together.[15]

Although harmonising formal and informal justice was crucial for strengthening the political economy of belonging, as illustrated in Chapter 4 Liberia's perfectly pitched post-war polices could not resolve challenges in citizenship governance, particularly land administration and tenure. The lack of transparency and accountability also confounded policymakers as a major impediment to reconstruction. These lingering issues explain why rule of law and governance (pillar 3) recorded the lowest overall completion rate of 41 per cent.

As the most capital-intensive pillar of *Lift Liberia*, infrastructure and basic services were the most sought after by Liberia's citizens yet bankrolled extensively by donors and multinationals (Government of Liberia, 2012b: 9). During the government's nation-wide consultations in 2008, Liberians ranked roads, health, and education as their top three development priorities (Government of Liberia, 2008a). The Sirleaf-led administration responded by financing most of these citizen demands with donor dollars thus compromising what could have boosted government–citizen relations more meaningfully. During the PRS process, Liberia reconstructed or rehabilitated 2,500 kilometres of

---

[15] Interview in Monrovia on 19 June 2013.

laterite and paved roads; increased electrical generation from 0 to 23 megawatts; renewed or constructed 48 kilometres of power transmission and distribution lines; and began implementation of the West Africa Power Pool cross-border electrification project (Government of Liberia, 2011a: 4). Admittedly, all infrastructure developments were not entirely motivated by donor directives and funding priorities. In order to build the capacity of Liberian entrepreneurs, the Ministry of Public Works insisted that for infrastructure projects undertaken by concessionnaires investing more than US$25,000, 20 per cent of the projects should be reserved for Liberian firms[16] hence facilitating their participation in the political economy of belonging and recuperating government–citizen relations. According to Woods, under his guidance Liberia began to also link private investments by concessionnaires to social assets in order to upgrade the country's infrastructure:

In some cases, we had MOUs [Memoranda of Understanding], or we had commitment. In other cases, we tied it to concessions … the Putu Mining Company, for instance, in the Southeast, in Grand Gedeh [County] area, as part of the concession, there is a commitment to build a road that connects Zwedru, we call Grand Gedeh [County], to Sinoe County. It's a paved road, it's no longer a laterite road. So, the quality of the road and access become very important. In the case of ArcelorMittal, from Ganta to Yekepa, for instance, that was not part of the concession agreement; it was a commitment made by Mr [Lakshmi] Mittal himself to the president [of Liberia, Ellen Johnson Sirleaf], that the road will be paved. … In the case of Bong Mines, the China Union, for instance, also did not have any commitment, but it was an MOU. Initially it was a laterite road, but I insisted personally that we are not going to accept laterite roads in this day and age. We're going to have an asphalt road. So, for me, beyond the commitment, the partnership with the World Bank to build major roads, infrastructure, as well as the Swedish government to build feeder roads, it was important to begin to tie this thing, because for years, Bong Mining Company was here, they didn't build a road to the concession areas. We had many concessions, LAMCO [Liberian American Swedish Mining Company] and other people like that. So, that shift now to tie this kind of private investment to these social investments became very critical to re-establish faith in the communities, and to make sure that something is left behind that will benefit ordinary people, especially infrastructure.[17]

---

[16] Interview in Monrovia on 25 June 2013.   [17] Ibid.

Besides erecting physical infrastructure, enhancing service delivery was also important for implementing *Lift Liberia*. Although there is contestation about quality, Liberia improved its provision of health and education services, the second and third priorities outlined during county consultations in 2008. During the three-year PRS, the number of health workers increased from 5,000 to 8,000; health facilities nearly doubled, from 354 to 550; 439 schools were constructed or renovated across the country, with school enrolment numbers mushrooming; teachers were trained with commensurate salary increments; and curricula were harmonised with the Economic Community of West African States (ECOWAS) (Government of Liberia, 2011a: 4). In her 2014 Annual Message to the Legislature, Sirleaf (2014: 27) touted advancements in education – from primary to vocational and tertiary – as her government's response to citizens' capacity constraints in Liberia's post-war milieu:

According to the 2010 Census, the system, as currently exists, consists of 2,849 schools – 2,103 of which are public, 343 private, 226 religious and mission schools, and 177 community schools. There are six community colleges existing or in pre-operational status – Grand Bassa, Bomi, Bong, Grand Gedeh, Lofa, and Nimba; nine four-year, degree-granting institutions, including the University of Liberia and Tubman University which are public; two vocational training institutes – Booker Washington Institute, which plans to move from high school to junior college; and the Monrovia Vocational Training Centre, which should move this year [in 2014] into new modern and well-equipped facilities.

Regardless of these accomplishments, however, Liberia's post-war development was infused with obsessions about quantity over quality, which ultimately undermined government–citizen relations. Sirleaf's preoccupation with rebuilding physical infrastructure – that is, roads, ports, bridges, and electricity – was often at the expense of developing human infrastructure manifested in first-rate education and health services. For example, when in August 2013 all 25,000 students who sat the entrance exam for the University of Liberia failed, Sirleaf dubbed the education system 'a mess' and followed this in 2016 with a widely unpopular pilot scheme to privatise 120 government primary schools. Similarly, the outbreak of Ebola in 2014–2016 and the crisis that ensued exposed public health as severely neglected. Moreover, although public infrastructure improved because it was a major priority of the Sirleaf administration, electricity in particular remained confined to pockets of Monrovia and its environs or to the southeastern region which received power from Côte d'Ivoire through the West Africa Power Pool.

The difficulties posed by the infrastructure and basic services pillar mirror challenges throughout the entire three-year *Lift Liberia* PRS (Government of Liberia, 2011a: 5). It was assumed that these hurdles would be overcome in the five-year Agenda for Transformation (AfT), Liberia's second PRS from 2012 to 2017. Primarily an economic policy, the AfT came out of consultations within 154 Liberian districts in 2011 as the first step in a long-term *Liberia Rising 2030* vision to achieve the ambitious goals of wealth creation, inclusive growth, and middle-income status by 2030 (Government of Liberia, 2010b; Government of Liberia, 2011a: ix–x, xvi). Although the AfT was marketed as a grass-roots level, home-grown strategy of socio-economic transformation, the process of its consolidation was principally steered by foreign financiers. Moreover, according to the Liberian government its implementation would rely heavily on support from outsiders to cover estimated costs of US$3.2 billion, double that of *Lift Liberia* (Government of Liberia, 2011a: xvi, 152). The AfT's four pillars[18] – that is, peace, security and rule of law; economic transformation; governance and public institutions; and human development – represented replicas of the five-tiered, peace- and state-building goals of the New Deal for Engagement in Fragile States – that is, legitimate politics; security; justice; economic foundations; and revenue and services – a framework providing financial support to countries affected by conflict which was validated in November 2011 at the Fourth High-Level Forum on Aid Effectiveness (Government of Liberia, 2011a: 176). According to Woods, the AfT was a ploy to appease donors and an invalidation of what Liberian citizens initially advocated for in 2008 during nation-wide consultations:

People need simple things that we make complex. And throughout the county consultations [in 2008], it was very clear what they [Liberians] wanted. We made it quite difficult. From the time Toga [Gayewea] McIntosh was at

---

[18] The four pillars were supported by eight cross-cutting issues, namely, gender equality, child protection, disability, youth empowerment, environment, HIV/AIDS, human rights, labour and employment (Government of Liberia, 2011a: 125).

[Ministry of] Planning [from 2006 to 2008], the people were very clear, roads, health, education, they were very clear. . . . Why are we redefining it? Why are we not focusing on it since those consultations? Simple things they [Liberians] wanted. And if we'd focused on those things by now, we'd be far gone. Why are we reshaping it? Why are we making it complex, into *Liberia Rising*? . . . You know, I always said to people that [President William R] Tolbert [Jr] made it so simple. For me, the poverty alleviation plan was simple: from mat to mattress. Tell me, who in Liberia couldn't identify with what it meant, from mat to mattress? You know? *Liberia Rising*, this other one, Agenda for what? Transformation? Waste of time with that! You know? Who are we satisfying here? We need to have a language that the guy in the village will identify with. That's the language we need![19]

Yet, unlike previous recovery plans which focused almost exclusively on state-building – 'lifting Liberia', the government, through institutional capacity – AfT was expressly anchored on the tenets of nation-building – 'lifting Liberians', the citizens, through national cohesion, human development, and reconciliation (Government of Liberia, 2011a: 38–39). It is beyond the scope of this chapter to assess whether AfT fundamentally enriched government–citizen and citizen–citizen relations thereby making good on its promises. Regardless of its successes or failures, however, the strategy was doomed to remain an extension of the donor-driven aims of the Paris Declaration, the Accra Agenda for Action, and the New Deal for Engagement in Fragile States (Government of Liberia, 2011a: xvi, 176). As of December 2019, it looked very likely that President Weah's lofty, five-year Pro-poor Agenda for Prosperity and Development (PAPD) (2018–2023) would suffer a similar fate.

In this section, I have argued that Liberia's reconstruction agenda under President Sirleaf was mainly propelled by external actors with minimal agency asserted by the Liberian government. Therefore, it adversely impacted the political economy of belonging in two fundamental ways. First, it placed donors 'above' the state and subjected Liberia to conditionalities that undermined its sovereignty. Second, it weakened government–citizen relations by making Liberia more accountable to donors than to citizens. I discuss further how post-war recovery contributions by diaspora recruits in particular were

---

[19] Interview in Monrovia on 25 June 2013.

disputed, as donors' had been, during Sirleaf's presidency thereby influencing the trajectory of dual citizenship advocacy.

Post-war Transitions, Citizenship, and Sirleaf's *Diaspocracy*

While some argue that war to peace transitions are primarily facilitated by foreign financiers exerting a neoliberal agenda devoid of context, other scholars insist that these processes have become increasingly collaborative, due in large part to local actors pushing their own goals. Because there is often a binary of 'international' versus 'local' aspirations, rarely does the general literature on post-war recovery factor in diasporas who are neither entirely 'international' nor 'local' in their orientations yet fall somewhere in between. As Chapter 1 demonstrates, there are multiple ways diasporas insert themselves into post-war development processes – as political elites, entrepreneurs, government agents, humanitarians, and reconstruction spoilers – with some countries systematically proposing policy measures such as dual citizenship to attract and sustain transnational engagement. Just as Foner (1989) asserted that blacks were central to reconstruction after the Civil War in the post-bellum United States, I argue that diasporas are pivotal to recovery in Liberia and further afield. While they may be a silver lining, they are far from a silver bullet, however (Pailey, 2017b). Akin to Liberia, returnees in particular have served as conduits for post-war state-building in countries as diverse as Afghanistan, Iraq, Rwanda, Sierra Leone, and Somalia, with often contested claims to nation-building.

Liberia is a particularly important case study on the role of trans-nationals in war to peace transitions because of its observed dialectic of contestation-migration-exile-return. During her many trips abroad, President Sirleaf held meetings with diasporas from Accra, Ghana, to Freetown, Sierra Leone; from Washington, DC, to Minneapolis, Minnesota, United States; from Oslo, Norway, to London, United Kingdom, imploring Liberians in these population centres to re-engage with the country. Furthermore, a *Liberia Rising 2030* Steering Committee appointed in February 2012 consulted not only citizens in the fifteen homeland sub-political divisions but also those in West Africa, Europe, and North America. This was a clear indication that nationals abroad, considered the sixteenth county, represented a third post-war reconstruction sphere sandwiched between 'local' and 'international' domains. Given the Sirleaf administration's mandate of reaching middle-income status by 2030, a renewal of discussions about the role of diasporas in post-war recovery heightened considerations of the 2008 proposed dual citizenship bill. In 2012, the president established a Constitution Review Committee to examine the country's citizenship laws, among other provisions,[20] and during her Annual Message to the Legislature in January 2014, she (2014: 31) explicitly endorsed dual citizenship as a worthwhile, development-oriented policy prescription:

Honourable ladies and gentlemen: A great human capital resource for the development of this country lies in the Liberian diaspora. We trust that as you move forward during this session, and in your deliberations, you will give adequate consideration to the recognition of citizens' rights for those persons born as Liberians, and those born of Liberian parentage who wish to contribute fully to the development of this country as citizens. The grant[ing] of [legal] Liberian citizenship would enable us to draw on the wealth of financial, technical, and other resources available to that category of persons that could be deployed nationally.

Indeed, Sirleaf was so inextricably entangled with Liberia's sixteenth county that her administration could be labelled a *diaspocracy*, a term I coined to describe the dominance of repatriate nationals in homeland government policy and practice. Apart from Sirleaf, other African presidential *diaspocrats* include Rwanda's Paul Kagame whose predominantly Tutsi insurgency turned ruling party, the Rwandan Patriotic Front, was instrumental in ending a genocide in 1994; as well as Somalia's Mohamed Abdullahi Mohamed (affectionately known as 'Farmaajo'), who once served as prime minister and held dual Somali–American citizenship before renouncing the latter ahead of 2020 elections. While Kagame's nearly three-decade administration could be considered a 'near' *diaspocracy* because refugees who became political elites returned from within the subregion (i.e., Burundi, Congo, Uganda), Mohamed's shorter-term as head of state would be emblematic of a 'wider' *diaspocracy* because many high-ranking officials previously resided in Europe or North America. Like Mohamed, Sirleaf would qualify generally as a 'wider' *diaspocrat* because a significant number of her high-level political appointees were

---

[20] Visit www.emansion.gov.lr/2press.php?news_id=2351&related=20&pg=sp& sub=41for a press release about the establishment of the Committee.

recruited from outside West Africa, derived primarily from the networks she established while previously working with the World Bank and UN, amongst other international agencies.

It is worth noting here that during Sirleaf's two terms in office, the primary custodians of post-war recovery were diaspora recruits who hoisted up Liberia's externally financed reconstruction agendas, whether they were qualified to do so or not, with mixed results. As mentioned previously, Minister of National Defence Brownie Samukai managed the restructuring of Liberia's security sector under the auspices of the UN and the United States. Finance ministers Antoinette Sayeh led the country's preparation for HIPC and the development of *Lift Liberia* while Amara Konneh advanced the goals of the AfT, although he had no prior experience in economics or financial management. In fact, all of Liberia's major revenue generating semi-autonomous agencies, referred to locally as the country's 'cash cows', were headed at one time or another by Liberian returnees appointed during Sirleaf's first and/ or second terms in office – namely, the Liberia Airport Authority (led by Ellen Corkrum); the Liberia Petroleum and Refining Company (led by T Nelson Williams and the now late Harry Greaves); the National Port Authority (led by Matilda Parker); the Liberia Maritime Authority (led by Binyah Kesselly); and the Forestry Development Authority (led by Harrison Karnwea).

On the international affairs front, Olubanke King-Akerele and Toga Gayewea McIntosh at different times managed multilateral and bilateral economic and political arrangements as ministers of foreign affairs thus transforming Liberia from a 'pariah nation' to a donor darling. Previously a sociology professor at Morgan State University in Maryland, United States, Christiana Tah fronted rule of law reforms as justice minister; her predecessor, now retired associate justice of the Supreme Court, Philip Banks, also spent considerable amounts of time abroad. Returnee engineer Antoinette Weeks oversaw the rehabilitation of infrastructure at the Ministry of Public Works for a short stint after homelander Samuel Kofi Woods resigned in 2013, while her not-so-immediate predecessor Luseni Dunzo had been dismissed for alleged financial impropriety before being appointed the president's advisor in 2009.[21] During Sirleaf's second term,

---

[21] Dunzo was reappointed advisor in one of many cabinet reshuffles during Sirleaf's twelve-year tenure: www.emansion.gov.lr/2press.php? news_id=1144&related=7&pg=sp.

strategic ministries such as Public Works, Education, and Commerce and Industry were led briefly by 'relatively inexperienced and underqualified' male returnees (Pailey & Williams, 2017). While de facto dual citizenship may have been a general practice amongst Liberian transnationals prior to 2020, as demonstrated earlier in this book, rumours abound that many political appointees carried foreign passports despite the Aliens and Nationality Law's then explicit revocation of legal Liberian citizenship upon naturalisation abroad. Although cabinet reshuffles were common-place during Sirleaf's two successive administrations, one thing remained constant: a conspicuous presence of senior-level bureaucrats who once resided abroad as diasporas. Proponents of previously mentioned emer-gency capacity building programmes, which topped-up returnees' salaries, flaunted their success in improving bureaucratic processes and profession-alising the civil service. However, as previously indicated in Chapter 4, more careful analysis points to amplified hostilities in the public sector fuelled by stark disparities between Liberian returnees and their homeland counterparts.

A review of post-war reconstruction confirms that the return of dias-poras to their origin countries can lead to the emergence of a new political elite which can give rise to socio-economic friction (Chesterman, Ignatieff & Thakur, 2004). I observed this first-hand as an aide to Sirleaf at the Liberian Ministry of State for Presidential Affairs (MoS). An unpublished case study[22] that I spearheaded about the ministry after leaving revealed that although returnees significantly contributed to knowledge transfer and public sector productivity, their considerable power and influence may have been unwarranted. For example, at the time of interviews in late 2013, nearly all high-ranking MoS staff were returnees enlisted by the president – namely, Minister of State for Presidential Affairs (the now late Edward B McClain Jr); Minister of State without Portfolio (Conmany Wesseh); Legal Advisor to the President (Seward M Cooper); Deputy Minister for Administration (Elva Richardson); Director/Head of Public Affairs (Shirley Brownell); National Security Advisor (H Boima Fahnbulleh); Director-General of the Cabinet (Momo Rogers); Comptroller (Harry Sando); Head of the Programme Delivery Unit

---

[22] This was part of a larger International Development Research Centre (IDRC)-funded project entitled 'Diasporas as Neglected Agents of Change', with Haiti, Liberia, and Sri Lanka serving as case studies. Research assistant Mahmud Johnson conducted and transcribed the interviews for my analysis.

(W Gyude Moore); Deputy Chief of Protocol (Eleanor Cooper); and Assistant Chief of Staff for Human Resources (Loris Shannon).

President Sirleaf's apparent returnee hero worship made some home-landers feel that their own professional aptitudes were negated and invalidated thus resulting in low levels of motivation and output. Some returnees came across as pompous and contemptuous of those who had remained in the country during armed conflicts thereby stoking ten-sions. And while returnees were assumed to be better equipped to achieve development dividends, this was not always the case. Ultimately, the sharp schism between returnees and homelanders within the MoS epitomises what James Boyce (2010: 102) calls a 'dual public sector system' where an 'internal sector' funded and managed by government competes with an 'external sector' funded and managed by donors. This dual public sector is counter-productive for sustainable post-war recovery because: (1) it fails to build the government's own fiscal capacity; (2) it crowds out the 'external public sector' by recruiting diaspora professionals whom the government cannot afford; (3) it poses coordination problems for an 'external public sector' that is managed by competing agencies with their own priorities; and (4) there are no mechanisms that make gov-ernments and donors accountable to local citizens.

Indeed, Sirleaf's brand of *diasporacy* undermined the legitimacy of homeland citizen contributions to post-war recovery and severely polarised discourses on dual citizenship. This was corroborated by then senator Wotorson, chief sponsor of the 2008 bill:

What didn't help [the passage of dual citizenship] much was that when Ellen [Johnson Sirleaf] got in power most of the people that were coming [to work for government] were from the diaspora and which was not to the liking of those that were here at home [in Liberia]. And their jobs were being given to only diasporans, diasporans were preferred, and that didn't work too well and the results have not been too good.[23]

As Sirleaf's *diaspocracy* demonstrates, diasporas can often transform into the vectors of externally imposed reconstruction processes because of their transnationalism thus adversely impacting citizenship con-struction and practice in general and government–citizen relations in particular. According to Woods, Liberia's returnee bureaucrats

---

[23] Interview in Monrovia on 6 March 2013.

advanced a foreign agenda rather than adopting home-grown solutions to post-war development:

I think most of the time we perpetuate the international aspirations. . . . They [the donors] set the conditionalities; they have what appear to be the resources. Most of us are trained and educated outside, come home with a sense of that aspiration. . . . So, we pander to it even more. More and more, we get detached from the local realities, and that's the challenge – especially for those of us who are the educated elites – we go to school abroad and come back . . . none of us, in many ways – 90 per cent of the time – look at the local aspirations. We seek legitimacy internationally rather than locally. We're proud of our friendships, we're proud of the photo ops that legitimises us at international conferences without even understanding what they mean. . . . How many of us go in rural Liberia, take pictures with ordinary people, and get that publicised? How many of us celebrate the national efforts in Lofa or in River Gee [counties]?[24]

Furthermore, returnees tended to be out of touch with domestic realities and were not fully equipped to lead recovery efforts, continued Woods:

One of the challenges will be the difficulty of articulating or ensuring that the real views from people on the ground are translated in the national agenda. Because there's a gap in real communication with the majority of those who are in the decision-making positions of government. [The] majority have been out for long, came in, and so there's that gap. . . . But connecting with the people is a whole different process; it's a whole different conviction and passion that is built out of an experience on the ground, throughout the war. . . . I think that lack of coordination, that lack of a consistent, organised, national framework to drive policy creates a level of disorder, inflates ego, and personalises what often should be a national venture or collective vision.[25]

Although Woods remained convinced that Liberian returnees had been co-opted by external agents, diasporas have the propensity to both reinforce and challenge copy-and-paste reconstruction planning. Transnationals develop hybrid identities that conflate the values of homelands with those acquired or enhanced by hostlands, yet this does not always yield positive results (Brinkerhoff, 2007: 187). Informal contracts entered into between national elites, such as returnees, and international actors, such as donors, actually lead to the enforcement of weak states because their interests in creating a facade

[24] Interview in Monrovia on 25 June 2013.   [25] Ibid.

of change often leave fractured government–citizen relations unchanged (Barnett & Zurcher, 2010: 23–52). As argued by some actors interviewed for this book, for example, dual citizenship would inadvertently reinforce elite power structures that fuelled Liberia's armed conflicts in the first place by privileging returnees over those who are domestically rooted. This argument is particularly prolific amongst homelanders who claim that dual citizenship has the propensity to replicate pre-war fissures in social relations.

Hereafter, I transition from a limited discussion of returnees to examine how the post-war recovery participation of transnational Liberians in general represents a dichotomy of diasporic developmentalism that has influenced claims for and against dual citizenship.

How Diasporas Simultaneously Helped and Hindered Post-war Development

Empirical and anecdotal evidence show that Liberians abroad have been actively engaged with their homeland before, during, and after the inception of armed conflict in 1989, with both positive and negative outcomes. Although many homeland actors interviewed for this book negated transnationals' post-war contributions to the political economy of belonging, some, like this fifty-three-year-old man, fully acknowledged their positive involvement as citizens 'by heart':

> Well, some of them [diasporas and returnees] come with certain skill sets that are desperately needed, especially in those sectors – health, education, the private sector – not necessarily governmental. . . . I think sometimes they just try to change the attitudes of Liberians that haven't had that exposure.[26]

A fifty-four-year-old male homelander echoed these sentiments, arguing that Liberians from abroad advance post-war recovery with their time and talent:

> They [diasporas/returnees] have helped in trying to advocate for change, helped to express their desire. They have come with technical expertise to be able to contribute towards the rebuilding of our broken nation. So, in that respect, they have helped [post-war development].[27]

[26] [HL18] Interview in Monrovia on 12 June 2013.
[27] [HL22] Interview in Monrovia on 14 June 2013.

According to C William Allen, a returnee who was initially recruited as minister of information during the tenure of the National Transitional Government of Liberia (NTGL) from 2003 to 2005, diasporas and their returnee counterparts gave their time, talent, and treasure before the introduction of proposed dual citizenship in 2008 and continued to do so in spite of the bill's postponement:

During the war, and even now, there was a huge percentage of remittances from Liberians in the diaspora to their relatives and friends here [in Liberia]. ... We're talking about tens of millions of [US] dollars. There were families here [in Liberia] who survived almost wholly and solely on remittances. When they [homeland Liberians] were cashing in the Western Union remittances, they [homelanders] didn't say ... 'those people sending me money are not Liberians'. They were happy to receive it. So, why [reject dual citizenship] now? And those people who were sending those remittances are adding something to the GDP [gross domestic product] of Liberia. If you look along the Robertsfield [International Airport] Highway and towards Virginia and Brewerville [on the outskirts of Monrovia], you see a lot of construction going on there, and a sizeable number of these constructions are homes I know personally are being done by Liberians in the diaspora. That's contributing to the development of Liberia. There are businesses in Ganta [Nimba County] and Gbarnga [Bong County] and other places that are owned by Liberians in the diaspora through their relatives here. It is because they are making the money in the diaspora that they are able to send that kind of money here to contribute to the development of Liberia. There's also quite a bit of intellectual capital I think that Liberians in the diaspora bring to the table. When you talk about the reversal of the brain drain, that's what it is, you know. Liberians in the diaspora are bringing their talent here. Liberians in the diaspora are conducting research that can better inform the governance process in Liberia. They are acquiring skills, knowledge, and abilities that they would eventually bring home either permanently or sporadically. Liberians in the diaspora had a very key role of advocacy in calling international attention to the atrocities of the war. I mean, I attended demonstrations at the UN headquarters in the late [19]80s and early [19]90s where prominent Liberians were present. They didn't just remain silent when these things were going on. Many Liberians in the diaspora have been there to receive their relatives who went [abroad] as refugees, you know. I think Liberians in the diaspora have also been vocal and eloquent critics of public policy on the ground and to some extent have led to positive changes in those policies as a result of what they've said. I'm sure there are others but the key point I think is that no matter how hard we try, we as a nation cannot disconnect ourselves from Liberians in the diaspora.[28]

As evidenced by Allen's anecdotal menu of humanitarian and recovery efforts by diasporas, the list of *Lift Liberia* deliverables implemented by returnee political appointees mentioned earlier in this chapter, as well as the catalogue of transnational citizenship practices captured in Chapter 2, it is clear that Liberians abroad and their returnee counterparts have acted as development enablers regardless of their legal citizenship status. Yet, their disputed role in remittance transfers in particular mirrors contestations around their citizenship and development claims.

Remittances and Capital Flight as Two Sides of the Same Coin

It is important to note at the outset that remittances recorded in Table 6.2 capture World Bank data which is lower than Central Bank of Liberia (CBL) data referenced later. Despite the incompatibility of data, however, remittances were undeniably important during Sirleaf's twelve-year tenure. They eclipsed aid disbursals thus having a direct impact on how the Liberian government related to Liberians abroad and their domestically rooted counterparts. In this chapter and throughout the book, I deliberately refrain from documenting aid figures because they are strategic rather than altruistic and conceal more than they reveal; in particular, large amounts get depleted on administrative overhead in donor countries and on bankrolling exorbitantly paid foreign 'expatriates', essentially what Kapoor (2008: 81) calls 'fraudulent kindliness'. Remittances, on the other hand, prove to be more instructive.

Evidence shows that post-war remittances to Liberia have impacted citizenship and the political economy of belonging in contradictory ways. While the remitter abroad practises active Liberian citizenship by transferring money to build a home in Liberia, sponsor children in school, or invest in a business – as Liberian diasporas interviewed for this book admitted doing – the receiver in Liberia is constrained in her/his ability to fulfil citizenship obligations because of limited economic opportunities and the government's inability to provide basic social services. Thus, the receiver becomes more obligated to the remitter than

---

[28] Interview in Monrovia on 4 June 2013.

Table 6.2 *World Bank remittances data for Liberia
(2004–2017)*

Year/remittance flows	Inflows (millions in USD)
2004	58
2005	32
2006	79
2007	62
2008	58
2009	25
2010	294
2011	523
2012	547
2013	413
2014	512
2015	654
2016	580
2017	403

Sources: World Bank, 2011, 2014, 2018

to the government in the same way that government is more account-able to donors for aid. Because the remitter also fills gaps in poverty alleviation at the household level that the government cannot, the government comes to be equally beholden to the remitter thus placing the remitter 'above' the state. Ngafuan confirmed to me in 2013 that remittances staved off domestic citizen demands on Sirleaf's govern-ment thereby easing pressure on public spending:

There are a lot of Liberians who almost every month remit through Western Union keeping their people [relatives in Liberia] to survive, whether it's in the urban areas like Monrovia and others, whether it's in Zwedru [Grand Gedeh County]. Some poor families [in Liberia] live as a result of the work of a brother or sister somewhere in the diaspora and then there is this flow [of remittances] that is coming, it has helped us [the government] because it has helped to keep the country stable, because all those expectations would have been directed to government.[29]

---

[29] Interview in Monrovia on 11 June 2013.

As evidenced by Ngafuan's admission, remittances have invariably transformed African migrants from 'traitors' to 'development partners' in the eyes of their homeland governments while inserting them in domestic debates about socio-economic change and citizenship construction (Iheduru, 2011: 181). Moreover, it is often presumed that dual citizens have a higher propensity to send remittances for investment purposes and partner with foreign financiers in their countries of origin (Siaplay, 2014: 8). Using aggregate panel data collected from 1972 to 2009 in 133 mostly Global South states, including 45 in Africa,[30] Leblang (2017: 77, 83, 95–96) suggests that nationals abroad are 10 per cent more likely to send remittances and 3 per cent more likely to return to countries that authorise dual citizenship. However, the study is not entirely convincing since other causal factors could impact emigrant transfers and returns. Echoing claims made by Whitaker (2011), Iheduru (2011: 182) contends further that recent policies adopted by African governments to extend dual citizenship and voting rights to nationals abroad are less about enhancing homeland development and embracing egalitarian forms of citizenship and more about co-optation and strategically harnessing emigrant resources to compensate for weak government fiscal capacities in the midst of donor fatigue. While lowering tariffs on exports of raw materials and extending tax holidays to multinationals were attempts by the Sirleaf administration to sustain foreign investor interest, the introduction of proposed dual citizenship legislation in 2008 was intended to placate diasporas in a similar fashion. In Liberia, a core group of legislative and executive branch officials acknowledged the important role transnationals have played in remitting to their families during the slow pace of post-war development and sought to provide incentives for continued remittance flows.

However, remittances very likely enabled Sirleaf's government to abdicate its duties within the political economy of belonging, stifled

---

[30] The list includes Algeria, Angola, Benin, Botswana, Burkina Faso, Burundi, Cameroon, Central African Republic, Chad, Comoros, Congo Republic, Côte d'Ivoire, Djibouti, Egypt, Equatorial Guinea, Ethiopia, Gabon, Gambia, Ghana, Guinea, Guinea Bissau, Kenya, Lesotho, Liberia, Libya, Madagascar, Malawi, Mali, Mauritius, Morocco, Mozambique, Namibia, Niger, Nigeria, Rwanda, Senegal, Sierra Leone, South Africa, Swaziland, Tanzania, Togo, Tunisia, Uganda, Zambia, and Zimbabwe.

domestic citizen agency, and created a syndrome of dependency in Liberia, said this forty-three-year-old male homelander:

Our remittances have also fuelled the need for the blatant corruption that we have and created an ambience for the government to neglect its primary responsibilities to its people. So, for example, by sending money we have also reduced the chances for people's political consciousness, you know, to hold their government and their duty bearers accountable. .... So, you have families here [in Liberia], people who are fit, who can do things for themselves, but they are sitting every month waiting for the 50, or 100, or 200 [US] dollars to come.[31]

The apparent discord between the homeland respondent and then minister Ngafuan about remittances was not only prevalent in my interviews; it is also reflected in the academic literature. Critics and supporters of remittance-generated development agree that migrant transfers represent a significant share of external financing and capital for low-income countries, particularly post-war nations like Liberia (Kapur, 2003; Pieke, Van Hear & Lindley, 2007). Yet, debate is widespread about their actual impact on socio-economic transformation. While remittances help to augment private consumption and alleviate transient poverty, their impacts on structural poverty and long-term sustainable development are less quantifiable (Kapur, 2003: 355–356). Because the majority of migrants are not drawn from the most destitute households in an origin country, the effects of remittances on the poorest of the poor will remain limited (Kapur, 2003: 346). Furthermore, remittances alone are not the panacea to homeland development and nation-states like Liberia must adopt measures to ensure fiscal responsibility, such as improving their overall investment climate, in order to avoid becoming heavily reliant on migrant transfers (World Bank, 2006: xvi).

Nevertheless, when governments cease to function as in times of war, remittances often fill an important void. Echoing the position of many respondents interviewed for this book, a twenty-three-year-old Monrovia-based female homelander stated that remittances during periods of armed conflict in Liberia and immediately afterwards meant the difference between survival and demise for many:

After the war, most people started from zero so they were actually depending on foreign aid [remittances] as a source of livelihood. So, people [abroad]

---

[31] [HL3] Interview in Monrovia on 5 June 2013.

sending in money, it helped to stir up the economic activity around here [in Liberia] since there were no jobs, no companies, and no elected government at that time. Basically, almost more than half of the population [in Liberia] was living on aid [remittances].[32]

There is dissent, however, about the actual impact of remittances during Liberia's post-war period. Dismissing them altogether as inconsequential, a fifty-four-year-old male homelander argued that remittances have not fundamentally tipped the scales in favour of meaningful development because they are used primarily for household consumption:

Remittance is not enough because remittances are to family members. So, when they [Liberian diasporas] say, 'Oh, we are sending plenty money home', yeah, to whom are you sending it? If you are sending money to your blood relative [in Liberia], that is not a contribution because with or without the government, you will not allow your relative to die.[33]

Similarly, one sixty-five-year-old female permanent returnee in Monrovia argued that remittances to Liberia pale in comparison to those sent to other parts of West Africa, particularly Ghana, and are not invested sufficiently in infrastructure or the private sector:

What you see in Accra, not to mention Kumasi, Cape Coast, are Ghanaians in the United States of America working in the hospitals, the janitors, the teachers, the professors, they are the ones who remit money to build their homes, to start their businesses [in the homeland]. We got Liberians in the United States of America. How many of them remit money [to Liberia]? They might remit allowances to family members which goes into the pot or keeps them well, but how many Liberians have sat down in America to send home money regularly to say, 'Build me a house', or even, 'I want to start a business', and have been here [in Liberia] to check?[34]

This respondent's view is validated by World Bank data showing that annual migrant transfers to Ghana exceeded that of Liberia from 2004 to 2009, although Liberia surpassed Ghana in 2010 and 2011 (World Bank, 2011, 2014). Those who question the impact of remittances on Liberia's reconstruction, like the previous homeland and permanent returnee respondents, often discredit dual citizenship as a policy

---

[32] [HL37] Interview in Monrovia on 21 June 2013.
[33] [HL22] Interview in Monrovia on 14 June 2013.
[34] [PR6] Interview in Monrovia on 24 June 2013.

imperative because they fundamentally believe diasporas do not contribute substantially to socio-economic change. I address these somewhat faulty assumptions by recording throughout this and other chapters the significant contributions Liberians abroad have made to micro-, meso-, and macro-level post-war recovery.

While remittances remain contested, there is a parallel discourse on capital flight that interrogates how migrant transfers realistically affect homeland development. Relatively augmented, the Central Bank of Liberia (CBL) figures for remittances in Table 6.3 are different from the World Bank's in Table 6.2 because the CBL captures all inflows and outflows received and sent by embassies, service providers, the UN, non-governmental organisations (NGOs), and individuals through banks and private firms in Liberia (Government of Liberia, 2008b: 28). Exceptionally useful here is the CBL data on total remittance outflows and inflows, as respondents for this study who contested the development impact of remittances often counter-referenced capital flight as detrimental to Liberia's reconstruction.

Table 6.3 *Central Bank of Liberia remittances data (2005–2017)*

Year/ remittance flows	Total inflows (millions in USD)	Workers' personal inflows (millions in USD)	Total outflows (millions in USD)	Workers' personal outflows (millions in USD)
2005	630	N/A	598	N/A
2006	685	N/A	622	N/A
2007	753	N/A	710	N/A
2008	959	N/A	923	N/A
2009	760	185	787	135
2010	981	260	995	234
2011	1,261	488	1,362	231
2012	1,287	509	1,160	369
2013	N/A	375	N/A	324
2014	N/A	473	N/A	299
2015	N/A	615	N/A	293
2016	N/A	550	N/A	305
2017	N/A	569	N/A	445

Sources: Government of Liberia, 2008b, 2013b, 2014, 2015, 2016, 2017

As Table 6.3 shows, while total transfers entering Liberia were generally the same as those leaving the country on a yearly basis from 2005 to
2012, in particular workers' personal remittance inflows surpassed outflows from 2009 to 2017. This complicates capital flight claims. For
example, a recurring motif in my interviews with homeland Liberians,
capital flight was often invoked as justification for blocking the passage of
dual citizenship since returnees allegedly transfer money out of Liberia to
maintain transnational lives almost at the speed at which diaspora remittances enter the post-war economy. According to one forty-three-year-old
homeland man, dual citizenship would thus facilitate excessive capital
flight:

> You see Ghanaians, Nigerians, Sierra Leoneans who have dual citizenship,
> but they have only used the second country for expediency. They all come
> back home and invest. Liberia is the reverse. So, by even allowing them
> [diasporas], giving them approval now [for dual citizenship], you're going
> to have a huge capital flight. You're going to legitimise what is already
> happening.[35]

Speaking hypothetically yet referencing actual cases of returnee public
sector officials, this thirty-year-old homeland man also talked about
how capital flight strips the Liberian economy of essential foreign
exchange:

> If I'm working as a minister and my family lives abroad, my wife and
> everything [are] there, and I only come [to Liberia] to work, if, for any
> reason, I happen to earn maybe 20,000 to 25,000 [US] dollars, I'll ship it
> abroad. Cash will flow there [abroad] and the economy [in Liberia] will not
> boom. The economy will not boom. You ship the money to your family
> [abroad] because your family needs to survive, and the money that you['re]
> shipping abroad, that money will be circulated within the economy of that
> particular country.[36]

These concerns were corroborated by returnees interviewed for this
book who, when queried about receiving remittances from relatives
abroad, often scoffed in response, saying, 'I'm the remitter!' As Table
6.3 demonstrates, however, whereas respondents who expressed concerns about the scale of total foreign exchange leaving the country were
right to raise alarm about capital flight, they erred in using personal

---

[35] [HL3] Interview in Monrovia on 5 June 2013.
[36] [HL37] Interview in Monrovia on 12 June 2013.

workers' remittances as evidence since CBL data indicates inflows exceeded outflows between 2009 and 2017. It is evident from my analysis of remittances that while they have hoisted up citizens who otherwise would not be able to withstand the excruciatingly slow pace of post-war development, they have also eroded government–citizen relations by relieving the Liberian government of its responsibility to citizens and obligating homelanders to benefactors – that is, diaspora remitters – who operate 'above' the state.

The 'Janus-face' of Diasporas/Returnees

Although dual citizenship proponents often characterise diasporas and returnees as *the* antidote to post-war recovery, the previous discussion on remittances and capital flight proves this is simply not the case. According to a forty-five-year-old Washington-based male respondent, returnees in Sirleaf's government in particular were not fundamentally committed to advancing Liberia's post-war development or its political economy of belonging and this was evidenced by their maintenance of the status quo:

Right now, we all know 90 to 95 per cent of Ellen's [Johnson Sirleaf's] cabinet hold one form of foreign status ... Either they are residents or they are citizens [abroad], but if you look at their output you have scepticism as to the effectiveness of [proposed] dual citizenship [legislation]. ... They are not promoting the country's [Liberia's] interest. They are not promoting development. They are not wanting to be creative in their output for the country [Liberia]. They are contented with where the country [Liberia] is, literally, so to speak. If you give them dual citizenship just like that, in effect, what you are telling them, the ball-field is open for everybody to play.[37]

Despite public relations campaigns to the contrary and the forecasts of transformation, many of Sirleaf's development milestones were riddled with controversies. In addition to the lack of administrative, financial, and technical capacity, rampant corruption was also listed as a major impediment to sustainable growth with development (Government of Liberia, 2011a). Returnees were at the centre of these debates, often perceived by the government and international donors as the solution to capacity deficiencies while simultaneously viewed by homeland Liberians as the incubators of corruption with impunity. According

[37] [DL36] Interview in Washington on 20 October 2012.

to Ngafuan, some returnees undermined the positive contributions of transnational actors by succumbing to corruption:

[I]f you track the number of persons, whether public official or so, that have been engaged in fraud, persons that come from the diaspora take a disproportionate portion. So, it makes the locals [in Liberia] to get more and more [afraid] ... that, well, these people [returnees] come to loot; that they come with all their sophisticated degrees and at the end of the day they come and loot our funds. So, that hasn't helped the diaspora [or dual citizenship] cause, especially people from the diaspora recruited in the [Liberian] public service engaging in fraudulent activities to the extent that they disgrace and make it more difficult for acceptability for Liberians that come from the diaspora.[38]

Although Liberia established a number of autonomous agencies responsible for curbing public sector graft – the GAC (established in 2005); the LACC (established in 2008); the LEITI (established in 2009); and the PPCC (established in 2010) – corruption persisted under Sirleaf thus debunking assumptions about women's inherent incorruptibility. While Sirleaf (2006) promised Liberian citizens in her January 2006 inaugural address that corruption would be 'public enemy number one', many of her diaspora recruits, like Corkrum, were subsequently implicated in some of the most high-profile graft cases. For example, in 2010 Global Witness (2010, 2011: 9) investigated allegations that a UK citizen had been dubiously awarded 400,000 hectares of Liberia's forest to harvest carbon credits. In response, President Sirleaf instituted a special presidential committee headed by respected lawyer and homeland civil society activist Negbalee Warner to probe the allegations. Based on the committee's report, the president, among other actions, referred former PPCC executive director Peggy Varfley Meres (a diaspora recruit) and former Internal Affairs minister, Ambulai Johnson (Sirleaf's cousin, also a diaspora recruit) to the Ministry of Justice for further investigation and possible prosecution, as well as publicly admonished then Planning and Economic Affairs minister Amara Konneh (a diaspora recruit previously mentioned) for not following regulations on the issuance of a concession contract covering Liberia's forests (UN Panel of Experts on Liberia, 2010: 69). Neither Varfley Meres nor Johnson was ever pursued in court and the reprimand of Konneh was considered a slap

---

[38] Interview in Monrovia on 11 June 2013.

on the wrist. Moreover, the case eroded government–citizen relations and exposed Sirleaf as especially weak in tackling corruption involving returnees.

Other cases followed in succession, calling into question returnees' genuine commitment to post-war development, practice-based citizenship, and the political economy of belonging. For example, Albert Bropleh, former commissioner of the Liberia Telecommunications Authority (LTA), was declared guilty of economic sabotage in 2012 for defrauding the government of close to US$20,000 and mismanaging nearly US$300,000 (Government of Liberia, 2011c: 10; Government of Liberia, 2012c: 11). In 2012, the LACC successfully prosecuted former police inspector-general Beatrice Munah-Sieh Brown for misappropriating US$198,000 in donor funds intended to purchase uniforms for the Emergency Response Unit (ERU) (Government of Liberia, 2011b: 21–22; Government of Liberia, 2012c: 14). And in 2013, Liberia's then auditor-general Robert Kilby and GSA director-general Pearine Davis-Parkinson were both dismissed by the president for alleged conflict of interest; the auditor-general's private company had been contracted by the GSA thus violating procurement laws (Sirleaf, 2013). Other returnee government agency heads either resigned or were discharged for alleged corruption with no formal legal action taken against them – namely, Chris Toe of the Ministry of Agriculture; Joseph Korto of the Ministry of Education; Eugene Shannon of the Ministry of Lands, Mines, and Energy; Richard Tolbert of the National Investment Commission; Harry Greaves of the Liberia Petroleum and Refining Company; and Matilda Parker of the National Port Authority.[39]

Sirleaf's *diaspocracy* was often dubbed a *kleptocracy*, prompting former auditor-general John Morlu, a diaspora recruit himself, to declare in 2007 that her administration was 'three times more corrupt'

---

[39] With the exception of my inclusion of Matilda Parker, this list was corroborated on 29 July 2014 in an e-mail exchange I had with Thomas Doe Nah, then head of the Centre for Transparency and Accountability in Liberia (CENTAL) who was subsequently appointed commissioner-general of the Liberia Revenue Authority (LRA) in 2018. In 2020, nearly three years after Sirleaf left office, her defence minister Brownie Samukai was convicted of misappropriating over US$1 million intended for the AFL and asked to restitute said funds, thus demonstrating the diffuse nature of returnee graft.

than the erstwhile NTGL[40] although he did not substantiate this claim with evidence. Indeed, post-war profiteering by some returnees fundamentally underpinned backlash against proposed dual citizenship legislation, inciting one thirty-year-old male homeland respondent to contend: 'I don't think they've [returnees have] helped. I believe they have created so much problems ... they don't come back to Liberia to help to rebuild. ... They came back to accumulate wealth for themselves'.[41] Reiterating contempt for the theft seemingly prevalent in Sirleaf's administration, a fifty-four-year-old male homelander quipped that returnees 'become loose like mad dogs' when they assume public office:

They have not set a very good example; they are very corrupt ... as soon as they come here and get into [a] government job, they get blind or greed takes over them. ... The [good] practices that they do in America [or elsewhere abroad], they will not transmit them here [in Liberia].[42]

According to this forty-five-year-old male homeland respondent, returnee government recruits often claimed to be Liberian citizens 'by heart' but they were neither equipped for the positions they occupied nor committed to post-war recovery, and this was indicative of the lack of merit-based appointments made by Sirleaf:

I think most of the people who were brought in [to Liberia] to do X, Y, Z, a lot of them have really failed the president. ... In fact, they are more corrupt than even people who are here [homelanders] and they bring a new dynamism to corruption in our country [Liberia]. They bring a new order of corruption in our country because, mind you, most of these people, they will not get the kind of job they are doing here in the [United] States [or elsewhere abroad].[43]

Explicitly referencing Charles Taylor's botched banishment in 1984 from the United States for alleged embezzlement in Liberia, a forty-seven-year-old homeland man quoted in the introduction of this chapter argued that transnationals who violate Liberian laws with impunity are far from citizens 'by heart':

---

[40]   Morlu's remarks were captured in many news reports, including this BBC story: http://news.bbc.co.uk/2/hi/africa/6225422.stm.
[41]   [HL17] Interview in Monrovia on 12 June 2013.
[42]   [HL22] Interview in Monrovia on 14 June 2013.
[43]   [HL12] Interview in Monrovia on 10 June 2013.

[M]ost often when people kind of steal public money [in Liberia] . . . the most likely country they go to is America where they live freely and we can't have them come back, in the case of Taylor, for trial, in the case of several public officials now who Auditing Commission, I mean, GAC, audited and they found that they were liable. In as much as they're not guilty yet, but they [have] gone back to live in America. With allegations now, and it's going to take us [a] long time, you know, to kind of have them to come back [to Liberia], and under what law are we bringing them back? I'm asking. Under the Doe government, for corruption charges, the government asked for [Charles] Taylor to come back [to Liberia]. The US government refused because they were not pleased with the judicial system [in Liberia]. . . . And then, later on we saw the aftermath, how he [Taylor] came back [to Liberia] and what happened to the country, a terrible event that we don't want to talk about. . . . They [the US government] said he [Taylor] would have been executed [in Liberia], this, that. Instead of one man being executed, we had 300,000 lives in the country [Liberia] destroyed simply because he had some paper [Green Card/US passport] to stay in America without being troubled. . . . So, Liberians who take citizenship of the United States or Europe . . . come and take public funds and run.[44]

Taylor's late twentieth-century incomplete repatriation to Liberia was repeatedly evoked by respondents as an earlier manifestation of the twenty-first-century alleged theft at the LAA by Corkrum. In a strange twist of irony, Jewel Howard Taylor – Charles Taylor's ex-wife, co-sponsor of the 2008 dual citizenship bill, and vice president as of 2018 – referenced the Corkrum case to explain why she developed reservations about dual citizenship in 2013:

Half of the people in [the Liberian] government are US citizens. Really! And what's happening now, when you catch them for corruption they all leave. The woman at the airport [Ellen Corkrum] . . . is a critical component of what I'm talking about. She got in the big helluva trouble; she just got in the plane and went back [to the United States].[45]

I marvel at the contradictions in Taylor's declaration, not only at her explicit condemnation of Corkrum's alleged deceit but also at the implicit denial of her ex-husband's warlord racketeering. Like Taylor and the previous homeland respondent, however, many Liberians interviewed for this book alluded to Ellen Corkrum and/or Charles

---

[44] [HL29] Interview in Monrovia on 18 June 2013.
[45] Interview in Monrovia on 6 March 2013.

Taylor in their analysis of the potential pitfalls of enacting dual citizenship, prompting me to label these two tactile experiences of alleged transnational fraud the Taylor–Corkrum nexus. Nevertheless, then minister Tah cautioned that high-profile cases of corruption involving returnees were not exemplary of all repatriates but rather indicative of Liberia's endemic system of impunity which also implicates homelanders:

I'm trying to convince people that everybody is not Ellen [Corkrum]. ... I mean, they were already looking for some reason to reject people [returnees] who come from outside [of Liberia]. ... It makes whatever else they already felt, this now makes it easy. They know in their minds that it's not true, and she [Corkrum] doesn't represent the diaspora. But if you're already looking for a way to reject a group of people she makes it easy. And that's what hurts me about what she did.[46]

Contrary to contemporary discourses about the lack of accountability in Liberia, Sirleaf's *diaspocracy* was certainly not the genesis of corruption. Akin to white settler colonial polities such as Australia, Canada, South Africa, and the United States, Liberia was founded on principles of intrusion and exclusion, dispossession and theft (Pailey, 2013b). The bedrock of corruption was formed in the nineteenth century when American Colonisation Society (ACS) agents reportedly seized their first parcel of indigenous land from King Peter through the use of force. According to Clower et al. (1966: 10), corruption became further entrenched in the twentieth century during William VS Tubman's regime:

The governing authorities award loyalty and conformity with jobs, many of which are sinecures requiring only occasional attendance. To each level of government employment there is attached a special set of fringe benefits. The highest echelons and their kin obtain the most lucrative material prerogatives: purchases of shares of stock in iron ore concessions at bargain rates; purchases of tribal land along new roads; sales of phantom services (public relations, advertising) to foreign concessions; sales of real economic services to concessions (e.g., trucking), but at higher cost than the buyers would incur in providing their own services; acquiring compulsory labour for their rubber farms; the right to impose private levies in rice on tribal groups; the use of government vehicles and other equipment for private gain; extraordinarily

---

[46] Interview in Monrovia on 19 June 2013.

large expense accounts; free housing and trips abroad; and government scholarships for training and education abroad regardless of merit.

Following this trajectory, I have argued previously that twenty-first-century corruption in Liberia is 'enmeshed in daily human interaction ... a function of both poverty and greed' that involves not only government bureaucrats generally or diaspora recruits specifically but all of Liberian society (Pailey, 2013b). Given its historical antecedents, corruption has become central to debates about post-war recovery and to public discourse about dual citizenship. There is a recognition that building government institutions – state-building – is not a sufficient deterrent to curbing corruption; rather, a parallel process of nation-building must be anchored by active citizenship. Because contemporary constructions of Liberian citizenship are more practice-based, largely due to the demands of post-war recovery, those engaged in corruption can never truly be considered Liberians 'by heart' regardless of their legal citizenship or residence status. I have revealed herein that while some diasporas and returnees have lifted Liberia and Liberians, others have damaged government–citizen and citizen–citizen relations by engaging in corrupt forms of post-war profiteering. This has certainly stimulated claims for and against dual citizenship.

Conclusion

When Charles Taylor sat in Plymouth on the verge of deportation in 1984, little did he know that decades later he would come to personify the 'Janus-face' of Liberian diasporas. His apparent theft of homeland state resources in the twentieth century was reified by charges against Ellen Corkrum in the twenty-first century, with both serving as models of cosmopolitan citizenship gone awry. Liberia is exemplary of the dichotomy of diasporic developmentalism because transnationals have simultaneously advanced and undermined post-war recovery efforts thus polarising public discourse on non-resident forms of citizenship.

Cataloguing the myriad ways in which Liberians abroad and their returnee counterparts have impacted the transition from war to peace, I have proven that dual citizenship legislation was proposed with the intention of incentivising emigrants to contribute their time, talent, and treasure.[47] Yet, backlash against the 2008 bill escalated due in part to fraud allegations implicating some returnees. Although recovery requires the active participation of all Liberian transnationals in the political economy of belonging, the complicity of some in acts of corruption has severely hobbled socio-economic transformation. Moreover, post-war reconstruction as a political project has exposed the inherent tensions between external state-building agendas and internal nation-building aspirations which have produced conflicting outcomes for Liberian citizenship construction and practice. This chapter advanced my contention that one-size-fits-all approaches to post-war recovery are fundamentally flawed because context matters.

By way of conclusion, I assert hereafter that citizenship remains a peace-, state-, and nation-building development imperative for Liberia by contrasting government and non-government responses to the Ebola outbreak of 2014–2016.

---

[47] Interview in Monrovia on 4 June 2013.

Conclusion[*]

Liberian Citizenship and the War on Ebola

'We dodged bullets during the war, now Ebola is going to kill us?', my auntie Arinah C Pailey asked me in distress one evening in mid-July 2014, as we sat commiserating at my home in central Virginia on the outskirts of Monrovia (Pailey, 2014b). At the time, Ebola seemed like a looming threat to Liberia in the way that armed conflict had fifteen years earlier. By early August, the Liberian government had declared a 'state of emergency' and days later the World Health Organization (WHO) designated the Ebola outbreak in West Africa a public health emergency of international concern nearly five months after the first cases were reported to the agency. This was followed by a United Nations (UN) pronouncement in September that Ebola remained a threat to international peace and security prompting major airlines to suspend services to affected countries – most notably the Mano River Union (MRU) epicentres of Liberia, Sierra Leone, Guinea – and foreign investors to shut down operations. Yet, even before the highly infectious disease permeated Liberia's borders from neighbouring Guinea in March 2014, the country was already plagued by a crisis of citizenship as this book demonstrates.

In July 2014, before the Ebola outbreak reached a boiling point, a group of disaffected citizens clashed with riot police at the Mittal Steel concession area in Nimba County, north-central Liberia. They lamented that a much-touted iron ore mineral development agreement had not benefitted locals. The government branded the assailants thugs and unlawful, making appeals to the parent company ArcelorMittal even before launching a formal investigation into citizens' grievances.

[*] This concluding chapter is derived in part from the following four sources: (1) Pailey (2014b); (2) Pailey (2016); (3) Pailey (2017a); and (4) Pailey (2019).

221

This was the beginning of the bubbling cauldron. Ebola simply tipped the pot over and contributed to a succession of further crises. Lacking proper training and protective gear, more than one hundred Liberian healthcare workers, including doctors and nurses, succumbed to the disease one by one. Their colleagues refused to go to work fearing that they too would become infected. That the Liberian government had not invested heavily in reviving a crumbling health system was not lost on those who battled the silent killer without a cure. Defying government directives, entire communities barricaded themselves in their homes rather than visiting the limited number of resource-strapped health facilities across the country.

On 17 August 2014, looters carrying clubs raided a makeshift Ebola holding area in the overcrowded West Point community of central Monrovia declaring that the disease was not real and that the government was using it as a ruse to shore up donor funding. They made away with bloodstained mattresses and other supplies. Of the twenty-nine confirmed and suspected Ebola patients who escaped, seventeen were found three days later and taken to a treatment centre. In an attempt to allay growing hysteria and anxiety, President Ellen Johnson Sirleaf announced on 19 August 2014 that effective the next day a national curfew would inhibit movement from 9 pm until 6 am and that the rights of citizens would be severely curtailed. Quarantines were executed without warning in two communities, Dolo's Town and West Point, with the Armed Forces of Liberia (AFL) deployed to uphold law and order. After Shaki Kamara, mentioned in Chapter 6, was shot in both legs by security forces in West Point, the sprawling mass of sardined packed shacks on the sandy beaches of the Atlantic Ocean, restrictions on movement were lifted ten days later amidst domestic and international censure about the army's use of lethal force during a scuffle with civilians. A proverbial war on Ebola had commenced as homeland citizens condemned the government for failing them in the most profound ways.

Throughout this book, I have asserted that the Liberian government has continuously abdicated its responsibility of shielding citizens from political and socio-economic upheaval. Ebola confirmed my conviction. The Sirleaf administration's woefully inadequate response to the outbreak underscored how strained relations between government and citizens could threaten peace-, state-, and nation-building aspirations. As bilateral and multilateral donors publicly announced their pledges, commitments, and dispersals – some of which were either late or did not materialise at all – Ebola relief was misguidedly framed early on as the sole domain of non-Liberian agents. This blind spot in attribution was particularly glaring because while the post-war government and its foreign financiers were slow to intervene in the initial stages of the outbreak, as a direct response to deeply embedded inequalities in primary care, non-government Liberian actors at home and abroad embodied active citizenship by engaging in public health measures that reshaped how we envisage public authority in conflict-affected states. Essentially, Ebola demonstrated that while a vertical state-building agenda at the behest of external actors could crack under pressure, horizontal nation-building measures employed by domestic and diasporic actors could bring Liberia back from the brink of implosion.

In this concluding chapter, I maintain that eradicating Ebola represented an interface wherein peace-, state-, and nation-building goals converged. First, it averted sporadic outbursts of violence. Second, it forced Liberian bureaucrats to amend policy decisions in order to address the practical needs of citizens in-country. And third, it spurred Liberians at home and abroad to complement each other's public health interventions. Whereas counterparts across Africa had waged nationalist struggles decades before against European colonialism, Liberian domestic and diasporic actors for the first time collaborated to battle a common enemy, Ebola, outside of themselves. Their relatively successful[1] struggles against an existential threat illuminated how Liberia's political economy of belonging could be made manifest. I demonstrate further that the 2020 referendum proposition based on Liberia's Dual Citizen and Nationality Act of 2019 would be moot without reconciling disputes over the meaning and practice of Liberian citizenship amongst actors of divergent social locations and life-worlds. I also contend that my conceptualisation of Liberian citizenship as identity (passive), practice (active), and a set of relations (interactive)

---

[1] When there appeared to be a plateau of the crisis on 27 March 2016, Guinea, Liberia, and Sierra Leone had the most intense and widespread transmissions out of a total 28,646 confirmed, probable, and suspected cases and 11,323 deaths across ten countries. Despite surpassing Guinea's and Sierra Leone's early on, Liberia's infection rates began to decline in November 2014 and the country was declared 'Ebola-free' for the first time on 9 May 2015. This was followed by three flare-ups and more than a year later, on 9 June 2016, the WHO pronounced Liberia 'Ebola-free' for the fourth and final time.

could be used as a model for theorising citizenship generally given its multilayered meanings. And last, but not least, I propose areas of future research, such as a comprehensive study of Liberia's 'Negro clause' and its impact on post-war socio-economic development.

The Love of Liberia United Us Here?

While the lack of a robust healthcare system to confront an infectious disease unearthed the volatile nature of Liberia's government–citizen relations, citizen–citizen relations were strengthened considerably. This proved that the love of Liberia above all else could unite Liberians of very different lived experiences and socio-economic statuses at the interface of Ebola relief. By converting 'private activities and resources into resources for the public realm' (Ekeh, 1975: 91) – public health service delivery, in this instance – Liberian domestic and diasporic actors embodied active citizenship at meso- and micro-levels previously assumed to be the exclusive domain of government and international institutions. Their interventions were a combination of individual and organisational activities using private and collective resources that supplemented government and donor endeavours.

Domestic-level anti-Ebola measures involved a broad spectrum of Liberian actors, including established medical personnel and those with minimal to no previous public health experience. For instance, while twenty-two-year-old student nurse Fatu Kekula single-handedly treated four family members at home when they fell sick with Ebola, Lorenzo Dorr of Tiyatien Health supported the government's county health teams in Rivercess and Grand Gedeh counties by training midwives, community leaders, and health committees in contact tracing, infection prevention and control. Likewise, microbiologist, immunologist, and public health expert Mosoka Fallah – who returned to Liberia from the United States in 2013 to both establish a university curriculum on public health and train rural healthcare providers – led community efforts across Monrovia to identify the sick, trace contacts of suspected Ebola patients, and remove dead bodies. Although international media zoomed in on mostly white foreigners, Liberian epidemiologists, lab technicians, doctors, and nurses like Fallah, Dorr, and Kekula remained on the frontlines of patient care despite fears of contagion, with many ultimately paying the highest price with their lives. Other domestic actors with non-public health experience rapidly converted private activities and resources to mount a rigorous collective response thus surpassing the excruciatingly slow dispersal of government funding and donor aid to tackle Ebola. For example, working in his personal capacity, Liberian lawmaker Saah Joseph in July 2014 began running an emergency ambulance service in Montserrado County, one of the most acutely affected regions in the country, picking up the severely ill from their homes and delivering them to hospitals, testing centres, and treatment units at a time when Liberia only had two government ambulances.

Whereas Liberian domestic actors became actively involved in direct service delivery, their diasporic counterparts used networks abroad to complement them. This transnational domain comprised diaspora organisations and individual remitters who provided an alternative stream of aid. Although evidence of this is largely anecdotal and under-reported, diaspora-led Ebola assistance mitigated already strained government–domestic citizen relations. For example, the Liberian American Community Organisation of Southern California (LACOSC) donated to the Liberian government's Incidence Management Team over US$100,000 worth of Ebola relief materials in a forty-foot shipping container, including surgical gowns, gloves, body bags, and two EKG machines in perfect condition. Similarly, the Union of Liberian Organisations in the United Kingdom (ULO-UK) established the UK Liberia Ebola Task Force in July 2014 and subsequently airlifted in October 2014 two consignments of assorted medical supplies valued at £9,500 to the ELWA II Hospital in Monrovia and Phebe Hospital, a major referral facility in Bong County. Food and other provisions were sent to clinics across Monrovia and its environs, the Liberia National Police (LNP), and border authorities. Liberians abroad with substantial financial resources contributed in cash and kind. For example, New York-based 2011 co-Nobel Peace Prize laureate Leymah Gbowee launched the Ebola Outreach Awareness Initiative in July 2014, providing grants worth US$78,000 to over one hundred Liberian-based non-government community organisations and rural community radio stations engaged in health promotion campaigning, contact tracing, and outreach. As indicated in Chapter 6, remittance figures for 2014–2016 reveal that the most significant support may likely have come from monetary transfers to families in Liberia whose livelihoods were threatened by sharp declines in economic activity due to international flight suspensions, bans on cross-border trade, informal market closures, limited banking activities, and reductions in agricultural productivity. Anecdotal evidence also illustrates how transnational citizenship practices during Ebola strengthened claims in favour of dual citizenship in a way that lobbying alone had not done previously.

Broadly speaking, Liberian diasporic and domestic actors became the public face of Ebola relief which prompted President Sirleaf to acknowledge that, 'filled with resilience, [they] took charge of the Ebola fight initially when everyone, including the government, did not know how and where to start from' (Executive Mansion, 2015). Their interventions generally involved direct service delivery without cumbersome bureaucracy or red tape and, therefore, were fast-tracked. They were based on already established formal and informal relationships and supported by local and diasporic funding, making them Liberian-owned. Indeed, the human agency of Liberians at home and abroad and the strategies they employed to respond to Ebola uncovered a great deal about the reconfiguration of Liberian citizenship norms across space and time. Therefore, citizenship remains an important framework for discussing future development-oriented policy prescriptions for Liberia and other crisis-affected countries.

Citizenship Still Matters for Development Policy and Practice in Post-war Liberia

In this book, I have argued that Liberia's political economy of belonging has evolved since the founding of the nation-state in 1847. Primarily shaped by historical and contemporary factors such as conflict, migration, and post-war recovery, Liberian citizenship has been constructed and reconstructed over space and time. Therefore, the deadlock on dual citizenship legislation from 2008 to 2018 served as a contemporary manifestation of those spatial and temporal reconfiguration processes. While conflict interfaces between indigenes and settlers in the nineteenth century produced a hegemonic form of citizenship 'from above', contestation and conciliation in the twentieth and twenty-first centuries facilitated more expansive forms of citizenship 'from below'. Similarly, migration redefined Liberian citizenship in that it created categories of Liberians who, as of mid-December 2019, defied the legal definition of citizen enshrined in the 1973 Aliens and Nationality Law and 1986 Constitution. Nevertheless, based on sedentarist and nomadic conceptions of stasis and mobility, there has been disagreement amongst Liberians at home and abroad about whether or not naturalisation by choice or force warrants dual citizenship enactment. The globalisation of ideas – including egalitarian ideals around human rights and a diffusion of dual citizenship in Africa – has simultaneously widened and contracted support for transnational forms of Liberian citizenship. Moreover, post-war recovery opportunities and challenges under President Sirleaf effectively carved out a niche for contributions by diasporas and returnees alike, thereby increasing lobbying for dual citizenship; however, high-profile cases of post-war profiteering by returnees undermined advocacy in this regard.

Development, (Dual) Citizenship and Its Discontents in Africa thus suggests that citizenship mattered in nineteenth- and twentieth-century Liberia in the same way that it carries significant policy and practical importance for development today. My monograph defines how Liberians across various spatial landscapes conceive of themselves, express their identity through practice, and engage with the homeland government and with each other. Furthermore, Liberian citizenship is inextricably tied to the trajectory of post-war reconstruction. As I sat on my perch in London feverishly finalising this book in late 2019 – when popular support was mounting for a Monrovia-based 'Weah Step Down' protest in objection to deepening deprivation and rising inequality – questions persisted (and will continue to) about whether or not amendments to Liberia's 1973 Aliens and Nationality Law and 1986 Constitution would actually advance peace-, state-, and nation-building processes. While some argue that dual citizenship could facilitate reconciliation and socio-economic change, others believe it would instead exacerbate unresolved hostilities thus reversing progress in recovery and compromising Liberia's political economy of belonging. For instance, I have established throughout this book why citizenship-derived conflicts over land, income, and transitional justice must be addressed in the short term to deter future outbreaks of violence in the *long durée*. In order to mend domestic and diasporic relations, thereby mitigating resistance to dual citizenship, radical changes in policy and practice would need to include, amongst others, full implementation of the Land Rights Act of 2018, establishment of a war and economic crimes court, as well as enforcement of a civil-service pay scale commensurate with professional experiences and academic qualifications.

As evidenced by the three post-war, conflict-generating issues described earlier and detailed in Chapter 4, it is clear that Liberian citizenship still signifies a site of clashing life-worlds and social locations. Therefore, dual citizenship should not be single-mindedly pursued in the absence of resolving discord on citizenship governance. Furthermore, the focus of policy should be reconciling the 1973 Aliens and Nationality Law and 1986 Constitution to reflect how Liberian citizenship is actually conceived and practised domestically and transnationally, as exemplified by the empirical evidence presented in this book. In the same way that Liberia's national symbols are under siege, dual citizenship must be subjected to public debates and national/transnational consultations culminating in a referendum, with passage requiring stringent enforcement in order to curb abuse. While some have claimed that de facto dual citizenship was instituted in late December 2019 when the Liberian Supreme Court ruled in favour of US-based lawyer Alvin Teage Jalloh who challenged the constitutionality of Sections 22.1 and 22.2 of the 1973 Aliens and Nationality Law, it remains to be seen whether endorsement of a referendum proposition associated with the 2019 Dual Citizen and Nationality Act would make dual citizenship a de jure reality. Because contestation around non-resident belonging is so emotionally charged, and especially given that opposition to it is strongest in Liberia, rushed enactment of dual citizenship without domestic approval would ultimately damage already fraught relations between the Liberian government and homeland citizens even as it tries to strengthen ties with would-be dual citizens.

The historical and contemporary crises of citizenship that culminated in the Ebola outbreak of 2014–2016 have underscored the need for government to fortify relations with citizens in Liberia – by, for example, curbing corruption, investing domestic revenue in basic social services, and protecting labour rights in the midst of capitalist reintegration – before it can focus on expanding citizenship transnationally. Therefore, legislation introduced in Liberia and other countries in the so-called Global South to embrace transnationals must balance extending rights with extracting responsibilities. In walking this policy tightrope, context must be queen and king. For example, I remain preoccupied with how Liberian policymakers could merge Senegal's pro-dual citizenship privileges including absentee voting and parliamentary representation for diasporas with Eritrea's anti-dual citizenship obligations including a 2 per cent 'diaspora tax' established by the National Assembly in 1994 to reconstruct and rehabilitate the country. Would Liberian transnationals approve of incremental privileges that ultimately result in dual citizenship, including the right to purchase rural land in exchange for agricultural production? Would they agree in the first instance to the establishment of an advisory Diaspora Assembly in the National Legislature, in lieu of voting in general elections or holding public office? These considerations have far reaching implications for the political economy of belonging and should not be set aside for the sake of expediency. In Africa especially, rules and regulations on identity and belonging change so rapidly in response to claims for and against dual citizenship that it has been both daunting and fascinating keeping track of new developments for this book. Therefore, my detailed examination of the contested relationship between development and dual citizenship in Liberia serves as an important case study for Cameroon, Democratic Republic of the Congo, Equatorial Guinea, Eritrea, Ethiopia, and Tanzania, which categorically prohibited dual citizenship, at least up until I finalised this book in December 2019.

In the section that follows, I offer a visual representation of citizenship that could be generally applied as a means of resolving disputes over what the term means in theory, policy, and practice.

Liberian Citizenship Triad a Model for Constructing Citizenship Generally

In the same way that Galtung (1996) formulated his conflict triangle, I conceptualise Liberian citizenship as a set of three axes which reconcile the competing definitions of citizenship in the scholarly and policy literature. As Figure C.1 illustrates, my understanding of Liberian citizenship as identity (passive), practice (active), and a set of relations (interactive) encompasses political, legal, and sociological constructions of citizenship, thereby representing a holistic realisation of the term. For instance, Liberian citizenship as identity is passive and fixed, largely anchored by legal status. As practice, Liberian citizenship represents a series of economic and political activities such as investing in real estate and voting in national elections. And as a set of relations, Liberian citizenship denotes how Liberians interact with each other as social actors and with their homeland government as political actors.

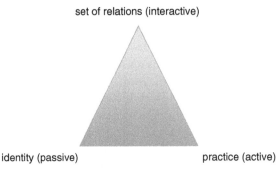

set of relations (interactive)

identity (passive)   practice (active)

Figure C.1 Liberian citizenship triad

Therefore, the Liberian citizenship triad is specific in that it provides concrete examples of how citizenship is defined in the literature and it could be applied in post-war emigrant-sending contexts or more broadly in others.

The model includes multiple levels of conceptualisation – moving from the individual to how the individual interfaces with her/his government and society. It reconciles contestations over whether citizenship should be solely residence-based because it does not include spatial categories of differentiation. Furthermore, my citizenship triad is informed by extensive empirical research about a country of immigration and emigration in which post-war reconfigurations of identities, practices, and relations between people have been enacted. It also transcends the often-siloed interpretations of citizenship, serves as a prototype for determining the changing features of countries' political economies of belonging across space and time, and provides an alternative to the overly theoretical and Eurocentric foundation of citizenship studies to date.

Moving citizenship from the abstract and Eurocentric to the concrete and Afrocentric, *Development, (Dual) Citizenship and Its Discontents in Africa* addresses glaring gaps in the citizenship literature by dissecting how citizenship is conceived and practised in a post-war African polity. Because the continent of Africa has seen some of the most violent citizenship clashes misguidedly portrayed as identity-based conflicts, it is essential to adopt a theoretical model of citizenship that takes this context into consideration. My citizenship triad does that and more. Employing the crisis of citizenship framework of analysis, as I have, is particularly instructive for post-genocide countries like Rwanda, post-war states like Sierra Leone and Angola, as well as protracted conflict situations in Central African Republic and South Sudan because it debunks overly simplistic, primordial paradigms often attributed to African crises. The crisis of citizenship concept would also be useful for non-African contexts including Sri Lanka, Northern Ireland, and Bosnia because it generally examines citizenship as identity, practice, and a set of relations between government and non-government actors in times of war and peace.

In the section that follows, I briefly mention areas of potential scholarly and policy inquiry coming out of this book.

Interrogating the 'Negro Clause' and Other Areas of Future Research

While countries like Chad, Equatorial Guinea, Malawi, and Mali at one time restricted citizenship to people of 'African descent', 'African origin', or 'African race', Liberia is one of two countries in Africa – Sierra Leone is the other – that still defines citizenship explicitly along racial lines and this represents one of the most intriguing and controversial elements of the country's 1973 Aliens and Nationality Law and 1986 Constitution. The 'Negro clause' demands full attention in its own right because of its theoretical and empirical distinctiveness as well as its political and socio-economic development implications following Liberia's fourteen years of intermittent armed conflict. Because Liberia hosts growing populations of Lebanese, Indian, and Chinese immigrants who dominate the commercial sector, it is important to understand how these and other non-black foreign nationals conceive and practise citizenship while being barred from formal recognition as Liberian citizens. That black people face major obstacles acquiring citizenship in Lebanon, India, and China adds a layer of complexity to the debate. As a distinct and otherwise little-known case study of a black African nation grappling with whether or not to permanently ban non-black 'others' from participating fully in the nation-state as political subjects, Liberia's maintenance of the 'Negro clause' could be considered an inversion of the rise in racialised, anti-migrant sentiments against black people worldwide – from a post-Brexit, stratified points-based system favouring 'highly-skilled' whites in the United

Kingdom to 'Muslim bans' in the United States. Although this book does not include a full evaluation of the 'Negro clause', I have already begun exploring it in a new project, *Africa's 'Negro' Republics*, which examines how slavery, colonialism, and neoliberalism in the nineteenth, twentieth, and twenty-first centuries, respectively, shaped the adoption and persistence of 'Negro' clauses in Liberia and Sierra Leone; how these race-based citizenship provisions in turn challenge white supremacy and assert black personhood; and what implications this has for contemporary Lebanese, Indian, and Chinese immigration, investment, trade, and aid.

Another sphere worth probing is an examination of citizenship governance in the midst of weak implementation in Liberia, in Africa, and across the globe. This would move beyond viewing citizenship as a set of procedural rules in written law to examine how it is actually regulated and experienced in practice. The lack of enforceable citizenship regimes was particularly stark in my Taylor–Corkrum nexus analysis in Chapter 6, although broader studies need to be conducted to assess how Liberia and other states administer citizenship laws at home and abroad, what gaps there are in application, and whether this influences how citizenship is conceived and practised domestically and transnationally. For example, concerns abound about the lack of reciprocal arrangements for Liberians who encounter barriers to naturalisation in other African countries when Africans of 'Negro descent' can naturalise in Liberia relatively easily. Polarised debates about dual citizenship to date have focused almost exclusively on *jus soli* and *jus sanguinis* Liberians, yet no real monitors existed at the time of my finalising this book in late December 2019 to assess whether naturalised Liberians actually had legitimate claims to Liberian citizenship or renounced their birthplace citizenships upon naturalisation. This all came to a head in March 2020 when President Weah appointed as National Elections Commission (NEC) chairman a Nigerian-born Liberian citizen whose naturalisation was called into question by members of the Legislature. In Liberia and across Africa, the enforceability of citizenship laws remains tenuous. As a case in point, it was clear from interviews conducted for this book that some Liberians practised de facto dual citizenship by carrying two passports – Liberian and one other – even though this was prohibited by law at the time. Given that Liberia's Law Reform Commission was established in 2009 followed by the Constitution Review Committee in 2012 to review and harmonise Liberia's general laws of application with the Constitution, and vice versa, it would be worth evaluating what recommendations these bodies have offered related to the enforcement of citizenship regulations. An investigation of Liberia's citizenship governance mechanisms is important because it has implications for how general citizenship entitlements – including private property ownership, voting, and running for elected office – would be managed and controlled with the possible passage of a 2020 referendum proposition based on the 2019 dual citizenship bill.

A third and final topic for analysis is the need to synthesise migration data for Africa generally and for Liberia more specifically. As my research shows, Africans' motivations for migrating are varied and nuanced; they range from extreme cases, such as the need to flee persecution, violence, and environmental disasters, to more mundane motivations, such as a desire to avoid boredom and professional stagnation. Evidence must be the bedrock of meaningful migration and development interventions. By gathering robust baseline data on African migrants, disaggregating them by gender, age, country of origin and citizenship, educational background, socio-economic status, and so on, researchers can help policymakers better address their needs. My study on Liberia's political economy of belonging, in particular, has proven that the dearth of reliable data on international migration flows to and from the country stifles empirically grounded policymaking related to diaspora engagement and dual citizenship. It could be argued that the lack of data did not impede the introduction of proposed dual citizenship legislation in 2008 or 2019. Yet, as of mid-December 2019, data in this regard had implications for the more recent bill's possible enforcement. For instance, one of the assumptions underpinning dual citizenship is that large numbers of Liberians have either naturalised abroad, or had *jus sanguinis* foreign-born offspring who want to qualify for legal Liberian citizenship after the age of majority. The absence of data to support this argument fundamentally weakens claims for enacting dual citizenship. Statistics on the sample size of Liberians, specifically, and Africans, generally, abroad are crucial for both instituting evidence-based policies that impact diasporas and conducting empirical research on this demographic.

Conclusion

Although Liberia celebrated ten years of uninterrupted peace in 2013, the Ebola outbreak of 2014–2016 classified tense relations between government and citizens as a peace-, state-, and nation-building conundrum. Furthermore, it underscored how Liberia had maintained a tenuous 'negative peace' – the absence of direct physical violence in the form of armed conflict – when it should be striving for a robust 'positive peace' – the absence of structural violence such as norms, rules, and regulations that fuel inequality and injustice (Galtung, 1996: 31–34, 221). I have demonstrated in this chapter that initially contentious government-citizen interactions transformed into collaborative anti-Ebola efforts that involved both domestic and diasporic Liberians. Ebola enabled Liberians at home and abroad for the first time to collectively rally around a common, external enemy, while employing public health measures that coupled identity with practice and rights with responsibilities. Their interventions made manifest the potential of Liberia's political economy of belonging to change interfaces of dissent and divergence into consent and convergence.

Despite the euphoria of Ebola eradication, however, as of December 2019 socio-economic cleavages and political tensions continued to challenge Liberia's citizenship architecture, with the 2008 contested dual citizenship bill replaced by an equally disputed one eleven years later. As I concluded this book in late 2019, Liberia's 1973 Aliens and Nationality Law still barred from citizenship *jus soli* Liberians who naturalised abroad, *jus sanguinis* Liberians who maintained the citizenship of their birth, as well as non-blacks. Moreover, for those who qualified as de jure citizens, citizenship was fundamentally differentiated and multilayered, based on structural forces that privileged some actors over others. Therefore, interrogating the meaning and practice of contemporary Liberian citizenship within the context of post-war development has been my attempt at bringing it closer to the aspirations of those who claim to be Liberians 'by heart', regardless of their legal citizenship status.

According to Falk (2000: 6), the struggle for citizenship is an unfinished one, and the Liberian case study is a stark example of that incomplete narrative. Given the nature of Liberian transnational citizenship pursuits, it is unlikely that diasporas will in the short- or long-term abandon the homeland. However, sustained demands by

Liberians abroad for de jure dual citizenship have intensified homeland citizen commands for meaningful socio-economic transformation. If achieved, the latter would definitively carve out a space for diasporas, some of whom identify as citizens 'by heart', to become transnational citizens 'by law'. While Liberia grapples with consolidating the features of its political economy of belonging, the country must also reconcile tensions between rootless and rooted conceptions of citizenship thereby flexing its muscles within a region, Africa, of expanding regimes of subjectivity.

Appendix I

A Proposed Act to Establish Dual Citizenship for Liberians by Birth and Background

The Liberian Constitution provides, at Article 22(a), that 'every person shall have the right to own property alone as well as in association with others; provided only Liberian citizens shall have the right to own real property within the Republic'. This sacred instrument provides also, at Article 27(a), that 'all persons who, on the coming into force of this Constitution, were lawfully citizens of Liberia shall continue to be Liberian citizens', and further, at Article 28, that 'any person at least one of whose parents was a Liberian at the time of the person's birth shall be a citizen of Liberia; provided that any such person shall upon reaching maturity renounce any other citizenship acquired by virtue of one parent being a citizen of another country'.

We, the drafters of this proposed Law, are of the belief that the intent of the framers of the provisions quoted above was to protect the Liberian heritage and the Liberian interest, and we most heartily subscribe to that intent. Consistent with that intent, we do not believe that the drafters of the Liberian Constitution contemplated at the time that our country would have degenerated into the unfortunate political turmoil, civil strife, and devastation that claimed the lives of over 250,000 of our citizens and caused hundreds of thousands of others to seek refuge and sanctuary in other lands, to preserve and safeguard their lives and security, guaranteed by the very Constitution, and thereby avoid the grave carnage taking place in their country.

It is further our sense that the drafters of the Constitution did not contemplate or intend that, as a consequence of the events surrounding our civil conflict, our people should endure the perpetual hardships of refugees and the attending economic destitutions; as at the time there was no foreseeable end to the carnage and the hardships of the war in

Liberia. Yet it was under these conditions and for these reasons that many of our fathers, mothers, brothers, sisters, and children, still loving their country, faced the ultimate dilemma and imperative of taking on the citizenship of the nations that offered them sanctuary, security, and livelihood for survival. In a number of cases, their actions were driven by the events of the necessity for life, preservation, and survival and/or the results of natural occurrences over which a majority of them had no control. Most of them could not fully enjoy the social and civic benefits of their host country, which included securing decent well-paying jobs commensurate with their educational background, or acquiring proper education, which is very expensive and often priced much higher for immigrants not having citizenship of the host countries.

Under the Aliens and Nationality Law of Liberia, their involuntary actions for life, security, safety, and survival deprived them of their Liberian citizenship and consequently the enjoyment of the attending benefits of such citizenship, including the right to ownership of real property. Many of these Liberians have earned very good education and have accumulated resources which they believe they owe a duty to their native land to share, impart, and invest, but have difficulty doing so because of the Liberian statutory prohibition. Additionally, these Liberians have not forgotten their country and they continue to positively impact the economy of Liberia by their remittances to the tune of over US$50 million a year to assist their kinship cope with the difficulties and experiences of livelihood in Liberia during and long after the war; and they continue these remittances up to the present. We are of the strong belief that as a result of the experiences of fourteen years of civil war in Liberia, the Liberian people are prepared to take a fresh look at the true intent of the framers of the Liberian Constitution, which is to preserve to Liberians the right to retain their citizenship, consistent with the preservation of the Liberian heritage referenced by the Constitution.

Against the background of the several requests and petitions we have received and continue to receive from citizens at home and abroad, we, the undersigned, hereby submit to the Liberian Legislature this proposal to grant DUAL CITIZENSHIP to Liberians who are citizens by birth, but who have acquired the citizenship of other lands under the conditions mentioned above are allowed to retain, reacquire, or preserve their Liberian citizenship, preserve their lives and security, and enable them to obtain economic and professional development which they are eager to transfer to their country of birth. The Republics of Ghana and Nigeria are thriving from the economic and social contributions from their willingness to grant citizenship to their fellow countrymen and women who had secured new nationality and/or citizenship in other countries. This proposal therefore is not only unique to Liberia.

While we do not subscribe to the continued and persistent creation of non-contributory laws, we are of the conviction that the below suggested proposition is so critical to the experiences we have had since the promulgation of that instrument, and we feel that the intent of the provisions of our Constitution deserve the reconsideration of the Liberian people. And so we most humbly appeal to the consciences of the Liberian people through their legislators to see reason for our submission consistent with current national realities. We are seeking the repeal of the Aliens and Nationality Law to provide dual citizenship for Liberians by birth who lost their citizenship due to the necessities of life and survival.

An Act to Amend Certain Sections of the Aliens and Nationality Law of Liberia

WHEREAS, Article 11(b) of the Liberian Constitution provides that 'All Persons, irrespective of ethnic background, race, sex, creed, place of origin or political opinion, are entitled to the fundamental rights and freedom of the individual, subject to such qualifications as provided for in our Constitution'; and

WHEREAS, Article 11(c) of the said Constitution guarantees that 'All Persons are equal before the Law and are therefore entitled to the equal protection of the Law'; and

WHEREAS, Article 28 of the Liberian Constitution provides that 'Any person, at least one of whose parents was a citizen at the time of the person's birth shall be a citizen of Liberia; provided that any such person shall upon reaching maturity renounce any other citizenship acquired by virtue of one's parent being a citizen of another country. *No citizen of Liberia shall be deprived of citizenship or nationality except as provided by law*; and no person shall be denied the right to change citizenship or nationality'; and

WHEREAS, Article 34(h) of the Constitution also gives the Legislature the authority to 'establish laws for citizenship, naturalisation and residence' not inconsistent with the Constitution; and

WHEREAS, believing that the intent of the quoted provision is to ensure that Liberians who are citizens of Liberia by virtue of the provisions of the Constitution are not deprived of their citizenship on account of events of necessity for life, preservation, and survival which are largely out of their control and/or which are the results of natural occurrences over which they have no control; and

WHEREAS, Article 13(a) of the Liberian Constitution also provides that 'All Persons lawfully within the Republic of Liberia shall have the right to move freely throughout Liberia, to reside in any part thereof and to leave therefrom, subject however to the safeguarding of Public Security'; and

WHEREAS the circumstances stated herein, i.e., the departure of our citizens to other lands for their safety and security, and their lives and the lives of their families and relations do not present any interference or imposition to the safeguarding of the Public Security to the nation; and

WHEREAS the Liberian Constitution, at Article 2, states 'This Constitution is the supreme and fundamental law of Liberia and its provisions shall have binding force and effect on all authorities and persons throughout the Republic', and further 'Any laws, treaties, statutes, decrees, customs and regulations found to be inconsistent with it shall, to the extent of the inconsistency, be void and of no effect ... '; and

WHEREAS, certain sections of the Aliens and Nationality Law of Liberia, enacted prior to the coming into effect of the new (1986) Liberian Constitution, stand in contrast to provisions and intent of the Liberian Constitution, referenced above, thus defeating the objective of the provisions of the Constitution and the equal protection of the Law; and

WHEREAS, it has become imperative to amend certain sections of the existing Aliens and Nationality Law of Liberia, consistent with current national realities and international best practices, to have them conform to the present Liberian Constitution, and as would grant to all Liberians the preservation of the right of citizenship guaranteed by the Constitution; and

WHEREAS, free movement of the individual and the creation of an environment free of intimidation and harassment are important conditions for long-term national and individual development, social progress, peace, unity, and security:

NOW, THEREFORE, THE Liberian Senate and the House of Representatives in legislature assembled hereby amend certain sections of the Aliens and Nationality Law of Liberia as follows:

Part III – Nationality and Naturalisation

Section 1: Chapter 20: Nationality at Birth, and specifically Section 20.1, citizen of Liberia at birth, which reads:

'The following shall be a citizen of Liberia at birth:
    A person who is a Negro, or of Negro descent, born in Liberia subject to the Jurisdiction thereof:

A person born outside Liberia whose father

 (i)   Was born a citizen of Liberia;
 (ii) Was a citizen of Liberia at the time of the birth of such child; and
 (iii) Had resided in Liberia prior to the birth of such child'.

Is hereby amended to read as follows:

The following shall be a citizen of Liberia at birth:
    A person who is Negro, or of Negro descent, born in Liberia and subject to the Jurisdiction thereof:

A person born outside Liberia whose father *or mother*

 (i)   Was born a citizen of Liberia;
 (ii) Was a citizen of Liberia at the time of birth of such child; and
 (iii) Had resided in Liberia prior to the birth of such child.

Section 2: CHAPTER 22: LOSS OF CITIZENSHIP, and specifically Section 22.1, Acts Causing Loss of Citizenship, which reads as follows:

'From and after the effective date of this title, a person who is a citizen of Liberia whether by birth or naturalisation shall lose his citizenship by:

(a) Obtaining naturalisation in a foreign state upon his own application; upon the application of a duly authorised agent, or through the naturalisation of a parent having legal custody of such person, provided citizenship shall not be lost by any person under this section as a result of naturalisation of a parent or parents while such person is under the age of twenty-one years, unless such person shall fail to enter Liberia to establish a permanent residence prior to his twenty-third birthday; or

(b) Taking an oath or making an affirmation or other formal declaration of allegiance to a foreign state or a political subdivision thereof; or

(c) Exercising a free choice to enter services in the armed forces for a foreign state unless, prior to such entry or services, such entry or services is specifically authorised by the president; or

(d) Voting in a political election in a foreign state or voting in an election or plebiscite to determine the sovereignty of a foreign state over foreign territory; or

(e) Making a formal renunciation of Liberian nationality in a court in Liberia or before a diplomatic or consular officer of Liberia in a foreign state in such form as may be prescribed by the Minister of Foreign Affairs of the Republic of Liberia'.

Is hereby amended to read as follows:

22 LOSS OF CITIZENSHIP

22.1 Acts Causing Loss of Citizenship

(a) From and after the effective date of this title, no person who is a citizen of Liberia at birth shall lose his/her citizenship for reasons of marriage to a citizen of a foreign state; naturalisation in a foreign state or naturalisation of a parent or parents in another state; entering or serving in the armed forces for a foreign state or voting in a political election in a foreign state;

(b) From and after the effective date of this title, Liberian Citizenship by Birth is hereby restored to all persons who were citizens by birth and who lost citizenship as a result of the conditions laid out in the previous Aliens and Nationality Law;

(c) A person who is a citizen of Liberia at birth but who makes a free choice of a formal renunciation of Liberian nationality before a court in Liberia or before a diplomatic or consular officer of Liberia in a foreign state, in such manner as may be prescribed by the **Minister of Foreign Affairs** of Liberia, and not growing out of circumstances over which he or she has no control or is not in control of, shall lose his/her citizenship;

(d) By the passage of this Act, the Republic of Liberia shall, within the limits prescribed herein and under the conditions stated hereinbefore, RECOGNISE **'Dual Citizenship'** in which a citizen of Liberia at birth may become a citizen of another state without losing **HIS/HER** Liberian citizenship; and

(e) This Law shall apply only to persons who are Liberian Citizens at Birth.

ANY LAW TO THE CONTRARY IS NOTWITHSTANDING

SUBMITTED TO THE SENATE AND HOUSE OF REPRESENTATIVES IN LEGISLATURE ASSEMBLED

SECOND SESSION OF THE FIFTY-SECOND LEGISLATURE OF THE REPUBLIC OF LIBERIA

SPONSORED BY: Cletus Segbe Wotorson
                     Senior Senator, Grand Kru County
CO-SPONSORED BY: Sumo G Kupee
                     Senior Senator, Lofa County
                     Jewel Howard Taylor
                     Senior Senator, Bong County
                     Abel Massalay
                     Senior Senator, Grand Cape Mount County

CAPITOL HILL, MONROVIA
MONTSERRADO COUNTY

Appendix II

Dual Citizen and Nationality Act of 2019

Article I

Any person, at least one of whose parents is a citizen of Liberia at the time of the person's birth, shall remain a citizen of Liberia. Any such persons shall upon reaching maturity continue to be a citizen of Liberia. Citizenship by birth shall remain a right and no citizen of Liberia shall be deprived of citizenship or nationality except as provided by law; and no person shall be denied the right to change citizenship or nationality. This Law is applicable to only citizens by birth and naturalised citizens of Negro descent of Liberia.

Article II

Dual citizen is a person with dual nationality. No person who is not a citizen by birth or a naturalised citizen of another country shall be eligible for dual citizenship of Liberia. Multiple citizenship shall not be allowed under the laws of Liberia.

Article III

Dual national is required to enter Liberia and leave Liberia using the Liberian passport. The Liberian passport provided to such citizen must be marked clearly by the word (dual) inscribed on the signature page of the passport. The passport will cost twice the price of the passport of the ordinary Liberian passport. Dual national must visit Liberia once every three years. Renewal of such passport must be followed by evidence of tax clearance.

Article IV

A citizen who acquires the citizenship of another country in addition to Liberian citizenship shall notify in writing about the acquisition of the additional citizenship to the Liberian immigration services stating clearly the status of applicant (birth, naturalised) and after processing shall be provided a certificate signed by the President.

IV(a)

Application for dual citizenship and nationality of Liberia by any national who is not qualified as a citizen of Liberia under the Constitution of Liberia shall be made to the Liberian immigration service for processing and thereafter issued a certificate signed by the President.

IV(b)

Without prejudice to Articles 30 & 52 of the Constitution of Liberia no dual citizen or national shall be qualified to hold the following positions:

1. President
2. Vice President
3. Speaker and Pro Temp of Liberian Senate
4. Chief Justice and Associate Justices of the Supreme Court
5. Ambassador or High Commissioner
6. Secretary to the Cabinet
7. Chief of Staff & Deputy of Armed Forces of Liberia
8. Commissioner General of Liberia Revenue Authority
9. Inspector General of Liberia National Police
10. Head of Prison Service
11. Cabinet Minister and Confirmation Nominee
12. Rank of Colonel or above in the Army or equivalent in any security and paramilitary services
13. Any other public legislative office as prescribed by the President as ad-hoc

Article V

A citizen of Liberia who is a citizen of another country shall be subject to and governed by the laws of Liberia while in Liberia as any other Liberian citizen.

Article VI

No citizen shall be qualified for election to the Senate or House of Representatives who is not a citizen by birth of both mother and father or a dual citizen or with dual nationality.

Article VII

Dual citizens by naturalisation cannot own above twenty-five acres of farm land except as a result of a concession from the Republic of Liberia and five acres of prime city property in one area. Naturalised dual citizens can own property as any other Liberian citizen except for the provision above.

Appendix III

Joint Resolution Leg-002/2019 Of At Least Two-Thirds Of The Total Membership Of The Liberian Senate And The Honourable House Of Representatives Of The Fifty-Fourth Legislature Of The Republic Of Liberia On Three Propositions To Amend Articles 28, 45, 47, 48, 49, 50, & 83(A) Of The 1986 Constitution Of The Republic Of Liberia

We, members of the Liberian Senate and House of Representatives, having met the requirements of the Constitution of Liberia, have resolved to propose and do hereby propose the amendment of the below described and mentioned Articles of the 1986 Constitution of Liberia for reasons set forth below each proposal, as follows:

PROPOSITION #1: To amend Article 28 of the Constitution to provide for the inalienability of the citizenship of natural born citizens of Liberia (Dual Citizenship)

Article 28 Reads
Any person, at least one of whose parents was a citizen of Liberia at the time of the person's birth, shall be a citizen of Liberia; provided that any such person shall upon reaching maturity renounce any other citizenship acquired by virtue of one parent being a citizen of another country. No citizen of the Republic shall be deprived citizenship or nationality except as provided for by law; and no person shall be denied the right to change citizenship or nationality.

Suggested Amendment to Article 28
Any person, at least one of whose parents was a citizen of Liberia at the time of the person's birth, shall be a natural born citizen of Liberia; a natural born citizen's right to citizenship of Liberia is inherent and

246

inalienable; no law shall be enacted or regulation promulgated which deprives a natural born citizen of the Republic of his/her citizenship right; and any law or regulation which alienates or deprives a natural born citizen of his/her Liberian citizenship right is null and void ab initio.

A natural born citizen of Liberia may hold another/additional citizenship but shall not qualify for elected national or public service positions and the following appointive positions:

1. Chief Justice and Associate Justices of the Supreme Court of Liberia;
2. Cabinet Ministers and Deputy Ministers;
3. All Heads of Autonomous Commissions, Agencies and Nonacademic/Research/Scientific Institutions;
4. Ambassadors Extraordinary and Plenipotentiaries; and
5. Chief of Staff and Deputy Chief of Staff of the Armed Forces of Liberia.

A Liberian with dual citizenship shall have certain rights, including the right to hold elected national or public service positions and all the appointive positions, if s/he relinquishes the other citizenship.

The Legislature shall enact laws on the process by which natural born citizens of Liberia who have obtained additional citizenship will maintain all of the rights pertaining to their Liberian citizenship.

Reason for Proposed Amendment

As a consequence of the civil war, hundreds of Liberians fled Liberia as refugees, assumed residency in other countries and obtained citizenship of other countries. Many obtained citizenship because that was the only way for them to get certain jobs or to enjoy certain opportunities, such as education. Most of these Liberians also had children and continue to have children who are automatically citizens of the countries of their birth.

Whatever the circumstances of these Liberians may be, one thing that is certain is that their loyalty to their motherland remains unquestionable; they continue to provide support to relatives and friends and to remain connected to their motherland through financial remittances. They continue to cling to the belief that they will be able to enjoy all the rights and privileges of Liberian citizenship, such as inheriting real property from their parents and being able to return to their motherland and be accepted and regarded as natural born citizens, not as foreigners. This amendment of the Constitution will enthuse all natural born Liberians to invest in Liberia and will give them hope of a permanent home in their motherland. To ensure that the loyalty of these Liberians will not be questioned, they are prohibited from holding certain positions in the Government of Liberia.

...

BY ORDER OF THE PRESIDENT
GBEHZOHNGAR M FINDLEY
MINISTER OF FOREIGN AFFAIRS

MINISTRY OF FOREIGN AFFAIRS
CAPITOL HILL, MONROVIA, LIBERIA
OCTOBER 8, 2019

References

Abrams, P. (1988). Notes on the difficulty of studying the state. *Journal of Historical Sociology*, 1(1), 58–89.

Adamson, F. B. (2002). Mobilising for the transformation of home: Politicised identities and transnational practices. In N. Al-Ali and K. Koser, eds., *New Approaches to Migration? Transnational Communities and the Transformation of Home*. London, UK: Routledge, pp. 155–168.

Adamson, F. B. and Demetriou, M. (2007). Remapping the boundaries of 'state' and 'identity': Incorporating diasporas into IR theorising. *European Journal of International Relations*, 13, 489–526.

Adejumobi, S. (2005). Identity, citizenship and conflict: The African experience. In W. Alade Fawole and C. Ukeje, eds., *The Crisis of the State and Regionalism in West Africa: Identity, Citizenship and Conflict*. Dakar, Senegal: Council for the Development of Social Science Research in Africa (CODESRIA), pp. 19–44.

African Union (AU). (2003). *Protocol to the African Charter on Human and Peoples' Rights on the Rights of Women in Africa*. Maputo, Mozambique: African Union.

Afrobarometer. (2012). *Afrobarometer Survey of Results: Round 5 Afrobarometer Survey in Liberia*. Accra, Ghana: Afrobarometer.

(2015). *Afrobarometer Survey of Results: Round 6 Afrobarometer Survey in Liberia*. Accra, Ghana: Afrobarometer.

(2018). *Afrobarometer Survey of Results: Round 7 Afrobarometer Survey in Liberia*. Accra, Ghana: Afrobarometer.

Afrofusion. (2012). 'Liberian documentary filmmakers talk to Afrofusion TV', Afrofusion, 13 March 2012, www.youtube.com/watch?v=A2B-b-nfCqk.

Alarian, H. M. and Goodman, S. W. (2017). Dual citizenship allowance and migration flow: An origin story. *Comparative Political Studies*, 50(1), 133–167.

American Bar Association (ABA). (2009). *Analysis of the Aliens and Nationality Law of the Republic of Liberia*. Washington, DC, USA: American Bar Association.

Anderson, B. (1992). *Long Distance Nationalism: World Capitalism and the Rise of Identity Politics*. Amsterdam, The Netherlands: Centre for South Asian Studies, University of Amsterdam.

Appadurai, A. (1995). The production of locality. In R. Fardon, ed., *Counterworks: Managing the Diversity of Knowledge*. London, UK: Routledge, pp. 204–225.

Arce, A. and Long, N. (2000). *Anthropology, Development and Modernities: Exploring Discourses, Counter-tendencies and Violence*. London, UK: Psychology Press.

Armstrong, J. A. (1976). Mobilised and proletarian diasporas. *The American Political Science Review*, 70(2), 393–408.

Banton, C. A. (2019). *More Auspicious Shores: Barbadian Migration to Liberia, Blackness and the Making of an African Republic*. Cambridge, UK and New York, NY, USA: Cambridge University Press.

Baranbantseva, E. and Sutherland, C. (2011). Diaspora and citizenship: Introduction. *Nationalism and Ethnic Politics*, 17(1), 1–13.

Barnett, M. and Zurcher, C. (2010). The peace-builder's contract: How external state-building reinforces weak statehood. In R. Paris and T. Sisk, eds., *Dilemmas of State-building: Confronting the Contradictions of Post-war Peace Operations*. London, UK: Routledge, pp. 23–52.

Barry, K. (2006). Home and away: The construction of citizenship in an emigration context. *New York University Public Law and Legal Theory Working Papers Review*, 81, 11–59.

Bendix, R. (1996). *Nation-building and Citizenship: Studies of Our Changing Social Order*. New Brunswick, NJ, USA: Transaction Publishers.

Bhabha, H. K. (1994). *The Location of Culture*. London, UK: Routledge.

Black, R., Crush, J., Peberdy, S., Ammasari, S., Hilker, L. M., Mouillesseaux, S., Pooley, C. and Rajkotia, R. (2006). Migration and development in Africa: An overview. In South African Migration Project (SAMP), *African Migration and Development Series No. 1*. Cape Town, South Africa: Idasa, pp. 1–8.

Blyden, E. W. (1884). *Sierra Leone and Liberia: Their Origin, Work, and Destiny*, lecture, Court Hall of Freetown, Sierra Leone, delivered 22 April 1884. London, UK: John Heywood.

Bøås, M. and Dunn, K. (2013). *Politics of Origin in Africa: Autochthony, Citizenship and Conflict*. London, UK: Zed Books.

Bosniak, L. (2000). Citizenship denationalised. *Indiana Journal of Global Legal Studies*, 7(2), 447–509.

Bourdieu, P. (1977). *Outline of a Theory of Practice*. Cambridge, UK: Cambridge University Press.

(1990). *The Logic of Practice*. Cambridge, UK: Polity Press.

Boyce, J. (2010). Fiscal capacity building in post-conflict countries. In M. Berdal and A. Wennmann, eds., *Ending Wars, Consolidating Peace: Economic Perspectives*. Abingdon, Oxon and New York, NY, USA: Routledge, pp. 101–120.

Brand, L. A. (2006). *Citizens Abroad: Emigration and the State in the Middle East and North Africa*. Cambridge, UK: Cambridge University Press.

Brinkerhoff, J. (2007). Contributions of digital diasporas to governance reconstruction in fragile states. In D. W. Brinkerhoff, ed., *Governance in Post-conflict Societies: Rebuilding Fragile States*. London, UK and New York, NY, USA: Routledge, pp. 185–204.

(2008). *Diasporas and Development: Exploring the Potential*. Boulder, CO, USA and London, UK: Lynne Rienner Publishers.

Brubaker, R. (2005). The 'diaspora' diaspora. *Ethnic and Racial Studies*, **28**(1), 1–19.

Burrowes, C. P. (2004). *Power and Press Freedom in Liberia, 1830–1970*. Trenton, NJ, USA: African World Press, Inc.

(2016a). *Black Christian Republicanism: The Writings of Hillary Teage (1805–1853), Founder of Liberia*. Bomi County, Liberia: Know Your Self Press.

(2016b). *Between the Kola Forest and the Salty Sea: A History of the Liberian People before 1800*. Bomi County, Liberia: Know Your Self Press.

Call, C. T. (2010). Liberia's war recurrence: Grievance over greed. *Civil Wars*, **12**(4), 347–369.

Castles, S. and Davidson, A. (2000). *Citizenship and Migration: Globalisation and the Politics of Belonging*. New York, NY, USA: Palgrave.

Chesterman, S., Ignatieff, M. and Thakur, R. (2004). *Making States Work: State Failure and the Crisis of Governance*. Tokyo, Japan, New York, NY, USA, and Paris, France: United Nations University Press.

Clegg, C. A., III. (2004). *The Price of Liberty: African Americans and the Making of Liberia*. Chapel Hill, NC, USA: University of North Carolina Press.

Cliffe, S. and Manning, N. (2008). Practical approaches to building state institutions. In C. T. Call and V. Wyeth, eds., *Building States to Build Peace*. Boulder, CO, USA: Lynne Rienner Publishers, pp. 163–186.

Clower, R., Dalton, G., Harwitz, M. and Walters, A. A. (1966). *Growth without Development*. Evanston, IL, USA: Northwestern University Press.

Collins, P. H. (1985). Learning from the outsider within: The sociological significance of black feminist thought. *Social Problems*, **33**(6), S14–S32.

Cramer, C. (2006). *Civil War Is Not a Stupid Thing*. London, UK: C. Hurst & Co.

Crenshaw, K. (1989). Demarginalising the intersection of race and sex: A black feminist critique of antidiscrimination doctrine, feminist theory and antiracist politics. *University of Chicago Legal Forum*, 1989(8), 139–167.

Cresswell, T. (2006). *On the Move: Mobility in the Modern Western World*. London, UK: Routledge.

Dagger, R. (2000). Metropolis, memory and citizenship. In E. F. Isin, ed., *Democracy, Citizenship and the Global City*. London, UK: Routledge, pp. 25–47.

Danforth, L. (1995). *The Macedonian Conflict: Ethnic Nationalism in a Transnational World*. Princeton, NJ, USA: Princeton University Press.

Dannreuther, R. (2007). *International Security: The Contemporary Agenda*. Cambridge, UK: Polity.

del Castillo, G. (2008). *Rebuilding War-torn States: The Challenge of Post-conflict Economic Reconstruction*. Oxford, UK: Oxford University Press.

de Montclos, M.-A. P. (2005). *Diasporas, Remittances and Africa South of the Sahara*. Pretoria, South Africa: Institute for Security Studies.

Desforges, L., Jones, R. and Woods, M. (2005). New geographies of citizenship. *Citizenship Studies*, 9(5), 439–451.

Dorman, S., Hammett, D. and Nugent, P. (2007). *Making Nations, Creating Strangers: States and Citizenship in Africa*. Leiden, The Netherlands: Brill.

Duffield, M. (2008). Global civil war: The non-insured, international containment and post-interventionary society. *Journal of Refugee Studies*, 21(2), 145–165.

Dunn, D. E. (1979). *The Foreign Policy of Liberia during the Tubman Era 1944–1971*. London, UK: Hutchinson Benham, Ltd.

(2009). *Liberia and the United States during the Cold War: Limits of Reciprocity*. New York, NY, USA: Palgrave MacMillan.

(2017). 'Presidential power transfer: From Joseph Jenkins Roberts to Ellen Johnson Sirleaf', *The Bush Chicken*, 17 September 2017.

Dunn, D. E., Beyan, A. J. and Burrowes, C. P. (2001). *Historical Dictionary of Liberia*, 2nd ed., Lanham, MD, USA and London, UK: The Scarecrow Press, Inc.

Easterly, W. (2006). *The White Man's Burden: Why the West's Efforts to Aid the Rest Have Done So Much Ill and So Little Good*. New York, NY, USA: Penguin Press.

Ekeh, P. P. (1975). Colonialism and the two publics in Africa: A theoretical statement. *Comparative Studies in Society and History*, 17(1), 91–112.

Everts, J., Lahr, M. and Watson, M. (2011). Practice matters: Geographical inquiry and theories of practice. *Erdkunde,* 65(4), 323–334.

Executive Mansion, Republic of Liberia. (2015). *President Sirleaf applauds community leaders and communities in their fight against Ebola* [Press release]. 19 March. Available at www.emansion.gov.lr/2press.php? news_id=3238&related=7&pg=sp

Falk, R. (2000). The decline of citizenship in an era of globalisation. *Citizenship Studies,* 4(1), 5–17.

Fierke, K. M. (2007). *Critical Approaches to International Security.* Cambridge, UK and Malden, MA, USA: Polity Press.

FitzGerald, D. S. (2000). *Negotiating Extra-territorial Citizenship: Mexican Migration and the Transnational Politics of Community.* Boulder, CO, USA: Lynne Rienner Publishers.

(2006). Rethinking emigrant citizenship. *New York University Law Review,* 81(90), 90–116.

(2012). Citizenship a la carte: Emigration and the strengthening of the sovereign state. In T. Lyons and P. Mandaville, eds., *Politics from Afar: Transnational Diasporas and Networks.* London, UK: Hurst Publishers, pp. 197–212.

Foner, E. (1989). *Reconstruction: America's Unfinished Revolution, 1863–77.* New York, NY, USA: Harper and Row.

Foucault, M. (1984). *L'usage du plaisir. L'histoire de la sexualite, Vol. II.* Paris, France: Gallimard.

Galipo, A. (2019). *Return Migration and Nation Building in Africa: Reframing the Somali Diaspora.* London, UK and New York, NY, USA: Routledge.

Galtung, J. (1969). Violence, peace, and peace research. *Journal of Peace Research,* 6(3), 167–191.

(1996). *Peace by Peaceful Means: Peace and Conflict, Development and Civilisation.* London, UK: Sage.

Gamlen, A. (2006). Diaspora engagement policies: What are they, and what kinds of states use them? Working Paper 32, Centre on Migration, Policy and Society (COMPAS), University of Oxford. Available at http s://www.compas.ox.ac.uk/wp-content/uploads/WP-2006-032-Gamlen_ Diaspora_Engagement_Policies.pdf

Gershoni, Y. (1985). *Black Colonialism: The Americo-Liberian Scramble for the Hinterland.* Boulder, CO, USA: Westview Press, Inc.

Geschiere, P. (2009). *The Perils of Belonging: Autochthony, Citizenship, and Exclusion in Africa and Europe.* Chicago, IL, USA: University of Chicago Press.

Giddens, A. (1979). *Central Problems in Social Theory: Action, Structure and Contradiction in Social Analysis.* London, UK: Macmillan.

(1984). *The Constitution of Society: Outline of the Theory of Structuration*. Cambridge, UK: Polity Press.

Glick Schiller, N. (2009). A global perspective on transnational migration: Theorising migration without methodological nationalism. Working Paper No. 67, Centre on Migration, Policy and Society (COMPAS), University of Oxford. Available at https://www.compas.ox.ac.uk/wp-content/uploads/WP-2009-067-Schiller_Methodological_Nationalism_Migration.pdf

Glick Schiller, N., Basch, L. and Blanc-Szanton, C. (1992). Transnationalism: A new analytic framework for understanding migration. *Annals of the New York Academy of Sciences*, 645, 1–24.

GLOBALCIT. (2017). *Global Database on Modes of Loss of Citizenship, version 1.0*. San Domenico di Fiesole, Italy: Global Citizenship Observatory, Robert Schuman Centre for Advanced Studies, European University Institute. Available at http://globalcit.eu/loss-of-citizenship

Global Witness. (2010). *Global Witness statement on alleged Liberian carbon corruption* [Press release]. 10 November. Available at www.global witness.org/en/archive/global-witness-statement-alleged-liberian-carbon-corruption/

(2011). *Forest Carbon, Cash & Crime: The Risk of Criminal Engagement in REDD+*. London, UK: Global Witness.

Global Witness and International Transport Workers Federation. (2001). *Taylor-made: The Pivotal Role of Liberia's Forests and Flag of Convenience in Regional Conflicts*. London, UK: Global Witness.

Government of Liberia. (1944). *William VS Tubman Inaugural Address*. Monrovia, Liberia: Government of the Republic of Liberia.

(1949). *Revised Laws and Administrative Regulations for Governing the Hinterland*. Monrovia, Liberia: Government of the Republic of Liberia.

(1973). *Aliens and Nationality Law of Liberia*. Monrovia, Liberia: Government of the Republic of Liberia.

(1986). *Constitution of the Republic of Liberia*. Monrovia, Liberia: Government of the Republic of Liberia.

(2008a). *Liberia Poverty Reduction Strategy*. Monrovia, Liberia: Government of the Republic of Liberia.

(2008b). *Central Bank of Liberia Annual Report 2008*. Monrovia, Liberia: Central Bank of Liberia.

(2008c). *A Proposed Act to Establish Dual Citizenship for Liberians by Birth and Background*. Monrovia, Liberia: Senate, Republic of Liberia.

(2009). *Republic of Liberia 2008 National Population and Housing Census Final Results*. Monrovia, Liberia: Liberia Institute for Statistics and Geo-Information Services (LISGIS).

(2010a). *Mid-term Independent Review of the Senior Executive Service Programme*. Monrovia, Liberia: Government of the Republic of Liberia.

(2010b). *Liberia Retrospective Analysis: Long-term Perspective Study (National Vision 2030)*. Monrovia, Liberia: Ministry of Planning and Economic Affairs and Governance Commission.

(2010c). *Core Welfare Indicators Questionnaire (CWIQ) Survey Abridged Report 2010*. Monrovia, Liberia: Liberia Institute of Statistics and Geo-Information Services (LISGIS).

(2011a). *Agenda for Transformation: Steps Toward Liberia Rising 2030*. Monrovia, Liberia: Government of the Republic of Liberia.

(2011b). *Republic of Liberia Lift Liberia Poverty Reduction Strategy: Second Annual Progress Report April 2009–March 2010*. Monrovia, Liberia: Government of the Republic of Liberia.

(2011c). *LACC 2011 Annual Report*. Monrovia, Liberia: Liberia Anti-Corruption Commission (LACC).

(2012a). *Rebuilding Public Leadership in Post-conflict Liberia: Case Studies from the Liberia Emergency Capacity Building Support (LECBS)*. Monrovia, Liberia: Civil Service Agency.

(2012b). *Republic of Liberia Lift Liberia Poverty Reduction Strategy: Final Report, A Results-Focused Assessment June 2008–December 2011*. Monrovia, Liberia: Government of the Republic of Liberia.

(2012c). *LACC 2012 Annual Report*. Monrovia, Liberia: Liberia Anti-Corruption Commission (LACC).

(2013a). *Land Rights Policy 2013*. Monrovia, Liberia: Land Commission.

(2013b). *Central Bank of Liberia Annual Report 2013*. Monrovia, Liberia: Central Bank of Liberia.

(2014). *Central Bank of Liberia Annual Report 2014*. Monrovia, Liberia: Central Bank of Liberia.

(2015). *Central Bank of Liberia Annual Report 2015*. Monrovia, Liberia: Central Bank of Liberia.

(2016). *Central Bank of Liberia Annual Report 2016*. Monrovia, Liberia: Central Bank of Liberia.

(2017). *Central Bank of Liberia Annual Report 2017*. Monrovia, Liberia: Central Bank of Liberia.

(2018). *An Act to Establish the Land Rights Law of 2018, Republic of Liberia*. Monrovia, Liberia: Government of the Republic of Liberia.

(2019a). *Dual Citizen and Nationality Act of 2019*. Monrovia, Liberia: Senate, Republic of Liberia.

(2019b). *Proposition #1: To Amend Article 28 of the Constitution to Provide for the Inalienability of the Citizenship of Natural Born Citizens of Liberia (Dual Citizenship)*. Monrovia, Liberia: Senate and House of Representatives, Republic of Liberia.

Government of Liberia and the European Commission. (2007). *Republic of Liberia–European Community: Country Strategy Paper and Indicative Programme for the Period 2008–2013.* Monrovia, Liberia: Government of the Republic of Liberia and the European Commission.

Guannu, J. S. (1983). *Liberian History up to 1847.* Smithtown, NY, USA: Exposition Press of Florida, Inc.

(1989). *A Short History of the First Liberian Republic.* Pompano Beach, FL, USA: Exposition Press of Florida, Inc.

Hazen, J. M. (2013).*What Rebels Want: Resources and Supply Networks in Wartime.* Ithaca, NY, USA: Cornell University Press.

Hippler, J. (2005). Violent conflicts, conflict prevention and nation-building —Terminology and political concepts. In J. Hippler, ed., *Nation-building: A Key Concept for Peaceful Conflict Transformation.* London, UK: Pluto Press, pp. 3–14.

Hoffman, J. (2004). *Citizenship beyond the State.* London, UK: Sage.

hooks, b. (1989). Choosing the margin as a space of radical openness. *The Journal of Cinema and Media,* **36,** 15–23.

Iheduru, O. C. (2011). African states, global migration, and transformations in citizenship politics. *Citizenship Studies,* **15**(2), 181–203.

Isin, E. F. (2000). Introduction: Democracy, citizenship and the city. In E. F. Isin, ed., *Democracy, Citizenship and the Global City.* London, UK: Routledge, pp. 1–21.

Isin, E. F. and Turner, B. S. (2007). Investigating citizenship: An agenda for Citizenship Studies. *Citizenship Studies,* **11**(1), 5–17.

Jacobson, D. (1996). *Rights across Borders: Immigration and the Decline of Citizenship.* Baltimore, MD, USA: Johns Hopkins University Press.

Jaye, T. (2003). *Issues of Sovereignty, Strategy, and Security in the Economic Community of West African States (ECOWAS) Intervention in the Liberian Civil War.* Lewiston, NY, USA: The Edwin Mellen Press.

Joppke, C. (1999). How immigration is changing citizenship: A comparative view. *Ethnic and Racial Studies,* **22**(4), 629–652.

(2005). *Selecting by Origin: Ethnic Migration in the Liberal State.* Cambridge, MA, USA: Harvard University Press.

Kanneh, J. (2014). 'Where is the indictment? Corkrum/fiancé ask government', *Frontpage Africa Newspaper,* 11 June 2014.

Kapoor, I. (2008). *The Postcolonial Politics of Development.* London, UK and New York, NY, USA: Routledge.

Kapur, D. (2003). Remittances: The new development mantra? In S. M. Maimbo and D. Ratha, eds., *Remittances: Development Impact and Future Prospects.* Washington, DC, USA: World Bank, pp. 331–360.

(2007). Janus-face of diasporas. In B. J. Merz, L. C. Chen and P. F. Geithner, eds., *Diasporas and Development*. Cambridge, MA, USA: Global Equity Initiative, Asia Centre, Harvard University, pp. 89–118.

Kashyap, S. C. (1997). *Citizens and the Constitution: Citizenship Values under the Constitution*. New Delhi, India: Publications Division, Ministry of Information and Broadcasting, Government of India.

Keller, E. J. (2014). *Identity, Citizenship, and Political Conflict in Africa*. Bloomington, IN, USA: Indiana University Press.

Kieh, G. K., Jr. (1992). *Dependency and the Foreign Policy of a Small Power: The Liberian Case*. San Francisco, CA, USA: Mellen Research University Press.

(2004). Irregular warfare and Liberia's first civil war. *Journal of International and Area Studies*, 11(1), 57–77.

(2009). The roots of the second Liberian civil war. *International Journal on World Peace*, 26(1), 7–30.

(2011). Peace agreements and the termination of civil wars: Lessons from Liberia. *African Journal on Conflict Resolution*, 11(3), 53–86.

(2012a). Neo-colonialism: American foreign policy and the first Liberian civil war. *Journal of Pan-African Studies*, 5(1), 164–184.

(2012b). *Liberia's State Failure, Collapse and Reconstruction*. Cherry Hill, NJ, USA: African Homestead Legacy Publishers, Inc.

Konneh, A. (1996a). *Religion, Commerce, and the Integration of the Mandingo in Liberia*. Lanham, MD, USA: University Press of America, Inc.

(1996b). Citizenship at the margins: Status, ambiguity, and the Mandingo of Liberia. *African Studies Review*, 39(2), 141–154.

(2002). Understanding the Liberian civil war. In G. K. Kieh Jr and I. Rousseau Mukenge, eds., *Zones of Conflict in Africa: Theories and Cases*. Westport, CT, USA: Praeger Publishers, pp. 73–89.

Koslowski, R. (2001). Demographic boundary maintenance in world politics: Of international norms on dual nationality. In M. Albert, D. Jacobson and Y. Lapid, eds., *Identities, Borders, Orders: Rethinking International Relations Theory*. Minneapolis, MN, USA: University of Minnesota Press, pp. 203–223.

Kuisma, M. (2008). Rights or privileges? The challenge of globalisation to the values of citizenship. *Citizenship Studies*, 12(6), 613–627.

Leblang, D. (2017). Harnessing the diaspora: Dual citizenship, migrant return and remittances. *Comparative Political Studies*, 50(1), 75–101.

258

Leitner, H. (2003). The political economy of international labour migration. In E. Sheppard and T. Barnes, eds., *A Comparison to Economic Geography*. Oxford, UK: Blackwell Publishing, pp. 450–467.

Levitt, J. I. (2005). *The Evolution of Deadly Conflict in Liberia: From 'Paternaltarianism' to State Collapse*. Durham, NC, USA: Carolina Academic Press.

Liberty, C. E. Z. (1977). *Growth of the Liberian State: An Analysis of Its Historiography*. PhD Thesis (later published in 2002 by New World African Press). Palo Alto, CA, USA: Stanford University.

Long, N. (1990). From paradigm lost to paradigm regained: The case for an actor-oriented sociology of development. *European Review of Latin American and Caribbean Studies*, **49**, pp. 3–24.

(1992). Introduction: Research practice and the social construction of knowledge. In N. Long and A. Long, eds., *Battlefields of Knowledge: The Interlocking of Theory and Practice in Social Research and Development*. London, UK: Routledge, pp. 3–15.

(2001). *Development Sociology: Actor Perspectives*. New York, NY, USA: Routledge.

Longman, T. (2017). *Memory and Justice in Post-genocide Rwanda*. Cambridge, UK and New York, NY, USA: Cambridge University Press.

Lund, C. (2006). Twilight institutions: An introduction. *Development and Change*, **37**(4), 673–684.

Lyons, T. and Mandaville, P. (2012). Politics from afar: Transnational diasporas and networks. In T. Lyons and P. Mandaville, eds., *Politics from Afar: Transnational Diasporas and Networks*. London, UK: Hurst Publishers, pp. 4–39.

Malkki, L. H. (1992). National geographic: The rooting of peoples and territories and the territorialisation of national identity among scholars and refugees. *Cultural Anthropology*, **7**(1), 24–44.

(1995). *Purity and Exile: Violence, Memory and National Cosmology among Hutu Refugees in Tanzania*. Chicago, IL, USA and London, UK: University of Chicago Press.

Mamdani, M. (1996). *Citizen and Subject: Contemporary Africa and the Legacy of Late Colonialism*. Princeton, NJ, USA: Princeton University Press.

Manby, B. (2009). *Struggles for Citizenship in Africa*. London, UK and New York, NY, USA: Zed Books.

(2010). *Citizenship Law in Africa: A Comparative Study*. New York, NY, USA and Johannesburg, South Africa: Open Society Foundations, AfriMap, and Open Society Justice Initiative.

(2016). *Citizenship Law in Africa: A Comparative Study*, 3rd ed., New York, NY, USA: Open Society Foundations.

(2018). *Citizenship in Africa: The Law of Belonging*. Oxford, UK: Hart Publishing.

(2020). Citizenship law as the foundation for political participation in Africa. In N. Cheeseman, ed., *Oxford Encyclopedia of African Politics*. New York, NY, USA: Oxford University Press, pp. 247–270.

Marshall, T. H. (1950). *Citizenship and Social Class and Other Essays*. London, UK: University Press.

Moran, M. H. (2006). *Liberia: The Violence of Democracy*. Philadelphia, PA, USA: University of Pennsylvania Press.

Nyamnjoh, F. B. (2006). *Insiders and Outsiders: Citizenship and Xenophobia in Contemporary Southern Africa*. London, UK: Zed Books.

O'Connell Davidson, J. (2013). Troubling freedom: Migration, debt, and modern slavery. *Migration Studies*, 1(2), 176–195.

Ong, A. (1999). *Flexible Citizenship: The Cultural Logics of Transnationality*. Durham, NC, USA and London, UK: Duke University Press.

Organisation of African Unity (OAU). (1981). *African Charter on Human and Peoples' Rights*. Nairobi, Kenya: Organisation of African Unity.

(1990). *African Charter on the Rights and Welfare of the Child*. Addis Ababa, Ethiopia: Organisation of African Unity.

Østergaard-Nielsen, E. K. (2001). The politics of migrants' transnational political practices. Working Paper No. 22, Transnational Communities Programme, University of Oxford. Available at http://www.transcomm.ox.ac.uk/working papers/WPTC-01-22 Ostergaard.doc.pdf

Ottaway, M. (2003). Rebuilding state institutions in collapsed states. In J. Milliken, ed., *State Failure, Collapse and Reconstruction*. Malden, MA, USA and Oxford, UK: Blackwell Publishers, pp. 245–266.

Pailey, R. N. (2007a). Slavery ain't dead, it's manufactured in Liberia's rubber. In P. Bond and F. Manji, eds., *From the Slave Trade to 'Free' Trade: How Trade Undermines Justice and Democracy in Africa*. Nairobi, Kenya and Oxford, UK: Fahamu, Networks for Social Justice, pp. 77–83.

(2007b). A diaspora returns: Liberia then and now. *Humanitas*, 9(1), 3–35.

(2011). Evaluating the dual citizenship/state-building/nation-building nexus in Liberia. *Liberian Studies Journal*, 36(1), 1–24.

(2013a). 'Why Liberia's proposed dual citizenship legislation should be based on evidence and not sentiments', African Arguments, 18 July 2013.

(2013b). 'Children in the fight against corruption', *International New York Times*, 17 July 2013.

(2014a). *SDI's 10-year Positive Peace Crusade*. Monrovia, Liberia: Sustainable Development Institute.

(2014b). 'Ebola has caused Liberia's cauldron of dissatisfaction to boil over', *The Guardian* (UK), 22 August 2014.

(2014c). *The Love of Liberty Divided Us Here? Factors Leading to the Introduction and Postponement in Passage of Liberia's Dual Citizenship Bill*. Unpublished PhD Thesis. London, UK: SOAS, University of London.

(2016). Birthplace, bloodline and beyond: How 'Liberian citizenship' is currently constructed in Liberia and abroad. *Citizenship Studies*, 20(67), 811–829.

(2017a). Liberia, Ebola and the pitfalls of state-building: Reimagining domestic and diasporic public authority. *African Affairs*, 116(465), 648–670.

(2017b). Silver lining, silver bullet or neither? Post-war opportunities and challenges for Liberian diasporas in development. In *Liberian Development Conference Anthology: Engendering Collective Action for Advancing Liberia's Development*. Monrovia, Liberia: United States Agency for International Development (USAID), Embassy of Sweden, and the University of Liberia, pp. 213–230.

(2017c). 'Legal invisibility was the best thing to happen to me', *Al Jazeera English*, 23 May 2017.

(2018). Between rootedness and rootlessness: How sedentarist and nomadic metaphysics simultaneously challenge and reinforce (dual) citizenship claims for Liberia. *Migration Studies*, 6(3), 400–419.

(2019). 'The struggles for Liberian citizenship', *Al Jazeera English*, 29 January 2019.

(2020). De-centring the 'white gaze' of development. *Development and Change*, 51(3), 729–745.

Pailey, R. N. and Jaye, T. (2016). 'The UN had to go, but is Liberia really prepared for peace?', openDemocracy, 12 July 2016.

Pailey, R. N. and Siakor, S. K. (2018). 'What Liberian president-elect George Weah must do', *Al Jazeera English*, 19 January 2018.

Pailey, R. N. and Williams, K. R. (2017). 'Is Liberia's Sirleaf really standing up for women?', *Al Jazeera English*, 31 August 2017.

Paris, R. and Sisk, T. (2010). *Dilemmas of State-building: Confronting the Contradictions of Post-war Peace Operations*. London, UK: Routledge.

Pewee, M. M. (2019). 'Court drops charges against controversial ex-airport authority boss Ellen Corkrum', *The Bush Chicken*, 11 December 2019.

Pieke, F., Van Hear, N. and Lindley, A. (2007). Beyond control? The mechanics and dynamics of 'informal' remittances between Europe and Africa. *Global Networks*, 7(3), 348–366.

Reckwitz, A. (2002). Toward a theory of social practices: A development in culturalist theorising. *European Journal of Sociology*, 5, 243–263.

Robinson, N. (2007). State-building and international politics: The emergence of a 'new' problem and agenda. In A. Hehir and N. Robinson, eds., *State-building: Theory and Practice*. London, UK: Routledge, pp. 17–44.

Rubenstein, K. and Adler, D. (2000). International citizenship: The future of nationality in a globalised world. *Indiana Journal of Global Legal Studies*, 7(2), 519–548.

SA3. (2007). *Study of Tanzania's Old Settlement Hosting the 1972 Refugees from Burundi*. Dar es Salaam, Tanzania: SA3.

Safran, W. (1991). Diasporas in modern societies: Myths of homeland and return. *Diaspora: A Journal of Transnational Studies*, 1(1), 83–99.

Sassen, S. (1991). *The Global City: New York, London, Tokyo*. Princeton, NJ, USA: Princeton University Press.

(2005). The repositioning of citizenship and alienage: Emergent subjects and spaces for politics. *Globalisations*, 2(1), 79–94.

Sawyer, A. (1987). *Effective Immediately: Dictatorship in Liberia, 1980–1986: A Personal Perspective*. Liberia Working Group Paper No. 5. Bremen, Germany: Liberia Working Group 1987.

(2005). *Beyond Plunder: Toward Democratic Governance in Liberia*. Boulder, CO, USA and London, UK: Lynne Rienner Publishers.

Schroven, A. (2016). Contested transnational spaces: Debating emigrants' citizenship and role in Guinean politics. In J. Knörr and C. Kohl, eds., *The Upper Guinea Coast in Global Perspective*. Oxford, UK and New York, NY, USA: Berghahn Books, pp. 77–94.

Schultz, A. and Luckmann, T. (1973). *The Structures of the Life-world*. Evanston, IL, USA: Northwestern University Press.

Sen, A. (1999). *Development as Freedom*. New York, NY, USA: Knopf.

Sesay, A., Ukeje, C., Gbla, O. and Ismail, O. (2009). *Post-war Regimes and State Reconstruction in Liberia and Sierra Leone*. Dakar, Senegal: Council for the Development of Social Science Research in Africa (CODESRIA).

Shafir, G. and Brysk, A. (2006). The globalisation of rights: From citizenship to human rights. *Citizenship Studies*, 10(3), 275–287.

Shain, Y. and Barth, A. (2003). Diasporas and international relations theory. *International Organisation*, 57, 449–479.

Shamsie, K. (2014). 'Kamila Shamsie on applying for British citizenship: "I never felt safe"', *The Guardian* (UK), 4 March 2014.

Sheffer, G. (1996). Wither the study of diasporas? Some theoretical, definitional, analytical and comparative considerations. In G. Prévélakis, ed., *Networks of Diasporas*. Paris, France: Nicosia, L'Harmattan, Kykem, pp. 37–46.

(2003). *Diaspora Politics: At Home Abroad*. Cambridge, UK: Cambridge University Press.

Siakor, S. K. and Knight, R. (2012). 'A Nobel laureate's problem at home', *New York Times*, 12 January 2012.

Siaplay, M. (2014). Do countries that recognise dual citizenship have healthier economies? Evidence from the Economic Community of West African States. *Migration and Development*, 3(2), 254–271.

Sirleaf, E. J. (2006). *Inaugural Address of HE Ellen Johnson Sirleaf, January 16, 2006*. Monrovia, Liberia: Executive Mansion, Republic of Liberia.

(2009). *This Child Will Be Great: Memoir of a Remarkable Life by Africa's First Woman President*. New York, NY, USA: HarperCollins Publishers.

(2013). *Statement by HE Ellen Johnson Sirleaf on Dismissal of GAC and GSA Heads, Investigation of Other GoL Officials*. Monrovia, Liberia: Executive Mansion, Republic of Liberia.

(2014). *Consolidating the Processes of Transformation: Annual Message to the Third Session of the Fifty-third National Legislature of the Republic of Liberia*. Monrovia, Liberia: Executive Mansion, Republic of Liberia.

Spiro, P. (1997). Dual nationality and the meaning of citizenship. *Emory Law Journal*, 46(4), 1412–1485.

(2012). Citizenship and diaspora: A state home for transnational politics? In T. Lyons and P. Mandaville, eds., *Politics from Afar: Transnational Diasporas and Networks*. London, UK: Hurst Publishers, pp. 213–228.

Tololyan, K. (1991). The nation-state and its others: In lieu of a preface. *Diaspora*, 1(1), 3–7.

(1996). Rethinking diaspora: Stateless power in the transnational moment. *Diaspora*, 5(1), 3–36.

Truth and Reconciliation Commission of Liberia (TRC). (2009a). *Volume I: Preliminary Findings and Determinations*. Monrovia, Liberia: Truth and Reconciliation Commission of Liberia.

(2009b). *Volume II: Consolidated Final Report*. Monrovia, Liberia: Truth and Reconciliation Commission of Liberia.

Tubman, W. V. S. (1944). *First Inaugural Address of President William VS Tubman*. Monrovia, Liberia: Executive Mansion, Republic of Liberia.

Turner, B. S. (2000). Cosmopolitan virtue: Loyalty and the city. In E. F. Isin, ed., *Democracy, Citizenship and the Global City*. London, UK: Routledge, pp. 129–147.

United Nations (UN). (1948). *Universal Declaration of Human Rights*. New York, NY, USA: United Nations.

(1961). *Convention on the Reduction of Statelessness*. New York, NY, USA: United Nations.

(1969). *International Convention on the Elimination of All Forms of Racial Discrimination*. New York, NY, USA: United Nations.

(1979). *Convention on the Elimination of All Forms of Discrimination against Women (CEDAW)*. New York, NY, USA: United Nations.

United Nations High Commissioner for Refugees (UNHCR). (2004). *2002 UNHCR Statistical Yearbook Liberia*. Geneva, Switzerland: United Nations High Commissioner for Refugees.

(2007). *2005 UNHCR Statistical Yearbook Liberia (400–401)*. Geneva, Switzerland: United Nations High Commissioner for Refugees.

(2014). *Tanzania begins granting citizenship to over 162,000 former Burundian refugees, ending more than 40 years of exile* [Press release]. 17 October. Available at www.unhcr.org/uk/news/briefing/2014/10/54 4100746/tanzania-begins-granting-citizenship-162000-former-burun dian-refugees-ending.html

United Nations (UN) Panel of Experts on Liberia. (2003). *Report of the Panel of Experts Appointed Pursuant to Paragraph 25 of Security Council Resolution 1478 (2003) Concerning Liberia*. New York, NY, USA: United Nations Security Council.

(2005). *Report of the Panel of Experts Appointed Pursuant to Paragraph 14e of Security Council Resolution 1607 (2005) Concerning Liberia*. New York, NY, USA: United Nations Security Council.

(2010). *Final Report of the Panel of Experts Submitted Pursuant to Paragraph 9 of Security Council Resolution 1903 (2009)*. New York, NY, USA: United Nations Security Council.

(2013). *Final Report of the Panel of Experts on Liberia Submitted Pursuant to Paragraph 5f of Security Council Resolution 2079 (2012)*. New York, NY, USA: United Nations Security Council.

United States Department of Homeland Security. (2009). *2008 Yearbook of Immigration Statistics*. Washington, DC, USA: United States Department of Homeland Security, Office of Immigration Statistics.

(2013). *2012 Yearbook of Immigration Statistics*. Washington, DC, USA: United States Department of Homeland Security, Office of Immigration Statistics.

Urry, J. (2000). Global flows and global citizenship. In E. F. Isin, ed., *Democracy, Citizenship and the Global City*. London, UK: Routledge, pp. 62–78.

Utas, M. (2005). The reintegration and re-marginalisation of youth in Liberia. In P. Richards, ed., *No Peace, No War*. Athens, OH, USA: Ohio University Press, pp. 137–154.

  (2009). Malignant organisms: Continuities of state-run violence in rural Liberia. In B. Kapferer and B. E. Bertelsen, eds., *Crisis of the State: War and Social Upheaval*. New York, NY, USA and Oxford, UK: Berghahn Books, pp. 265–285.

Van der Kraaij, F. P. M. (1983). *The Open Door Policy of Liberia: An Economic History of Modern Liberia*. Bremen, Germany: Im Selbstverlag des Museums.

Van Hear, N. (2009). The rise of refugee diasporas. *Current History*, **108** (717), 180–185.

Van Hear, N., Brubaker, R. and Bessa, T. (2009). Managing mobility for human development: The growing salience for mixed migration. Research Paper 2009/20, United Nations Development Programme Human Development Reports. Available at http://hdr.undp.org/sites/d efault/files/hdrp_2009_20.pdf

van Steenbergen, B. (1994). The condition of citizenship: An introduction. In B. van Steenbergen, ed., *The Condition of Citizenship*. London, UK: Sage, pp. 1–9.

Villarreal, M. (1992). The poverty of practice: Power, gender and intervention from an actor-oriented perspective. In N. Long and A. Long, eds., *Battlefields of Knowledge: The Interlocking of Theory and Practice in Social Research and Development*. London, UK: Routledge, pp. 247–267.

Vink, M., Schakel, A. H., Reichel, D., Luk, N. C. and de Groot, G.-R. (2019). The international diffusion of expatriate dual citizenship. *Migration Studies*, 7(3), 362–383.

Washington, I. (2011). *A Man from Another Land: How Finding My Roots Changed My Life*. New York, NY, USA: Centre Street.

Waugh, C. (2011). *Charles Taylor and Liberia: Ambition and Atrocity in Africa's Lone Star State*. New York, NY, USA and London, UK: Zed Books.

Weah, A. (2012). Hopes and uncertainties: Liberia's journey to end impunity. *International Journal of Transitional Justice*, 6(2), 331–343.

Weah, G. M. (2018). *Annual Message by His Excellency, the President George Manneh Weah, President of the Republic of Liberia, to the Fifty-fourth National Legislature*. Monrovia, Liberia. Executive Mansion, Republic of Liberia.

Whitaker, B. E. (2011). The politics of home: Dual citizenship and the African diaspora. *International Migration Review*, **45**(4), 755–783.

Williams, G. I. H. (2006). *Liberia: The Heart of Darkness*. Bloomington, IN, USA: Trafford Publishing.

World Bank. (2006). *Global Economic Prospects. Economic Implications of Remittances and Migration*. Washington, DC, USA: World Bank.

   (2011). *Migration and Remittances Factbook 2011*, 2nd ed., Washington, DC, USA: World Bank.

   (2014). *Remittances Data Inflows, as of April 2014*. Washington, DC, USA: World Bank.

   (2018). *Remittances Data Inflows, as of December 2018*. Washington, DC, USA: World Bank.

Yuval-Davis, N. (2000). Citizenship, territoriality and the gendered construction of difference. In E. F. Isin, ed., *Democracy, Citizenship and the Global City*. London, UK: Routledge, pp. 171–188.

Index

African Studies Series

9 781108 836548